A good browsing book.
Enjoy!

Pop & Mummy

SKYHOOKS

SKYHOOKS

RIDING THE CREST
OF THE INDUSTRIAL REVOLUTION

ALGO D. HENDERSON

LETTERS TO MY GRANDCHILDREN

Reverchon Press
Dallas, Texas

Copyright © 1981 by Algo D. Henderson.
All rights reserved. No portion of this text may be reproduced
except quotations for review purposes.

Library of Congress Catalog No: 81-53001
International Standard Book Number: 0-9601902-1-x

Typeset in Sabon type by Eileen Ostrow and printed at the
West Coast Print Center, Berkeley, Ca. 94703.
Published by Reverchon Press, Dallas, Texas.

Please address inquiries to Reverchon Press, 239 Glorietta
Blvd., Orinda, Ca. 94563. (415)254-6840.

The hidden complex realities of life
come alive in our legends told at
night during the winter months inside
the great tule winter lodge.

       Yakima tribal wisdom

BOOKS BY ALGO D. HENDERSON

Educating for Democracy—a symposium

Vitalizing Liberal Education

Antioch College, Its Design for Liberal Education
Coauthor: Dorothy Hall

Policies and Practices in Higher Education
La Educacion Superior en los Estados Unidos (Spanish edition)

The Role of the Governing Board

Higher Education in Tomorrow's World—a symposium

Training University Administrators
La Formation des Administrateurs d'université (French edition)
Assisted by: Joseph Adwere-Boahmah, Katharine Kunst

The Innovative Spirit

Admitting Black Students to Medical and Dental Schools
Coauthor: Natalie Gumas

Higher Education in America
Coauthor: Jean Glidden Henderson

Ms Goes to College
Coauthor: Jean Glidden Henderson

Skyhooks

Special thanks to:

Don McCormick, artist, who did the drawings

Jean Henderson and Joanne Henderson Pratt, who helped prepare the copy for publication

Philip C. Henderson, architect for the cover design

Alexandra Pratt, Carol Violé, and Wendy Welsh, who assisted with the design

Jerry Henderson, James Pratt, and all the grandchildren for ideas and inspiration

CONTENTS

I
Skyhooks and feutrons   Richard III and Richard M   11
Yale foresees the future   Butterfly catching
Meditation and Massage   Girls

II
Life without telephone   Farming in Kansas   Butchering a hog   29
Dirt and dirty work   Trapping skunks   Fishing in a corn field
The education Algo got   Careers

III
Inherited genes   67

IV
Making a Model T out of junk   Trout and wild raspberries   81
Creating Appegesamok Nodin
In London and Moscow as World War II began
Tea in the tea house of the First Shogun
Writing for UNESCO

V
Casting bronze in a barn   Experiential education   129
The philosophy of Antioch College
Transforming a provincial community   Creating Glen Helen
A beach development in Florida   Financial crises

VI
Birth of the TVA   167
Changing national and state policy in higher education
Planning the State University of New York
First Center for the Study of Higher Education
American Indian community development

VII

Surgery with Dad's razor   Sins, time, and space   203
On the doorstep of politics   Racism
Saving the world for democracy   When the banks crashed
Money and power chasing   Parasites in a conglomerate

VIII

Horsefeathers   Ode to a chamber pot   Llama ears and DNA   271
Using a bionic arm to capture a monster

Orinda, California
September 1, 1981

To my Grandchildren,

    My grandfathers looked funny in their long beards, and my grandmothers very severe with their parted hair tightly pulled back. I wish that I really knew them—what they were like, what they thought about things. Most people crave to know their ancestors.

    So here is my story.

    Writing about one's life may be "much ado about nothing." And as Dogberry announced: "When the age is on, the wit is out." Somehow it's hard to be witty when one describes how he shovelled manure from the cow barn. And what stirs my memories may make dull reading for others, especially you kids.

    However, I have endeavored also to picture the changes in American life during my period, which began in 1897. And interpret their meaning. Some of you are now in college, so you may be curious about what I say; but don't expect my sage remarks to equal those of Plato or Emerson.

    My, what an exciting, stimulating period it has been. We've literally been riding the crest of the Industrial Revolution.

    But now we have reached an era of transition. While making heart pacers, airplanes, microwave ovens, and war on our fellow men, we have been squandering our natural resources. They are going, going —and in some cases gone. And teaching our children that a green tomato turned red by chemicals is just as tasty and nourishing as a garden-ripened one is sheer nonsense. The more affluent people become, the fewer their satisfactions. They rush around, grabbing fast food on the run, while trying to make more money. As though money were the aim of living.

    Kids, I think we are in the midst of change, change from the exploitation of our resources, natural and human, plus military confrontations and disastrous wars, to a society in which fresh concepts and better values will prevail. At least I hope so.

With much love,

I

You teenagers are probably being swamped with new ideas and fresh problems. Well, here are ideas and a bit of advice from your grandfather.

December 19, 1975

Dear Ilya,

As we approach Christmas I want to tell you of a couple of new ideas I have just thought up.

I think better when I have music playing and just now Maria Callas is singing to me about the glories of Egypt in the days of the Pharaohs, and her trials and tribulations as a slave. Poor Aida didn't even know that there was a Christmas. It had not yet been created. For that matter, Hanukkah also was unknown since Antiochus Epiphanes did not desecrate the Temple of Jerusalem until 168 BC, long after Aida's time. So if there were feasts and celebrations, they were for some other reasons. But even the nomadic hunters celebrated a good hunt with a feast.

Did you ever hear of a feutron? Of course not. I had not yet conceived the term. I haven't even sent it to Webster.

A feutron is a unit of time that measures 1/100,000th of your life. It differs from our standard time units in that they are based on the calendar which stems from the rotation of the earth around the sun and its own rotation every 24 hours. Now I have figured that we need a unit of time that is not based on the sun and earth, but on man himself, his life. OK, man has a life. From the time he is born to the time he dies is exactly 100,000 feutrons. Now isn't that sensible?

An advantage is that it is highly individual. Each person has his own feutrons. Now do you know how many years, days, and hours you will live? No! But under my plan, you know you will live exactly 100,000 feutrons. Everyone has the same number of feutrons—100,000. That's all Methuselah had, so I will live as long as he did. So will you.

Peter is nine; but wouldn't he like to be older, say 2,000 feutrons? Ilya, when you become 39, don't worry about getting old—no one can possibly figure out how many feutrons you have lived.

Here I am, 78, but regardless of health or infirmities, I know I will live to be 100,000. So why worry about dying?

Jean says nobody will know when to celebrate a birthday. That's silly. Does the Queen of England celebrate her birthday on the right date? No, she picks a date to suit the weather. Under my concept of time you can have as many birthdays as you wish and whenever you wish.

My goodness, you can also have lots of Christmas parties, with presents, roast goose, and all that.

I have also perfected an invention. It is wonderful. It is a skyhook. I use it to help me get up in the morning. All I have to do is reach my arms up, grab the skyhook with both hands, and zippo I am up.

A skyhook also has another, very important use. You take hold of one, lift yourself high enough to see beyond your neighborhood, the local customs and habits, the ideas that prevail in your environment, and look about for interesting people, attractive vocations, and fresh ways of doing things; also speculate on the meaning of life and how to create a good life for yourself.

So, as a Christmas present, I am sending you these two new ideas. Cherish them. Share them with Sabrina and Alex, and Peter and Matthew.

GRANDFATHER

August 15, 1974

Dear Sabrina,

Recently at a University of Kansas dinner, given at the Presidio, something real nice happened. Jean and I were sitting across from the top FBI agent in charge of the Patty Hearst case, asking him why he had not caught the Harrises, because my research assistant, Natalie Gumas, had seen Emily in Berkeley, when, out of one ear I heard the Chancellor saying, "I want you to know an alumnus who is very distinguished, etc., etc., I want to introduce Algo Henderson. Algo, stand up."

It pays not to be asleep during a speech. Maybe KU thinks I am distinguished; they gave me the distinguished alumnus award—in 1949.

After working most of the day on a bibliography, I went out doors to work in the yard. My gorgeous bed of some fifty roses needed a bit of attention. But it was pretty hot out there, so I came in and read a chapter in *America*. If you have this book by Alistair Cooke—Carol gave it to me as a present—read it, since it tells well the story and has good pictures. One chapter is about the pioneers in Kansas, based on the decade just before the Donmyers got there. But Indians were still around when my mother was a child.

On our farm we had dozens of buffalo wallows and also prairie dog mounds. In the mad delight of many men shooting buffalo and drowning prairie dogs, we have almost caused their extinction. As to the wallows, I had never seen a buffalo in one. But in Africa, I did see an African buffalo lying and wiggling in the mud of a wallow. Surely this was not a way to keep clean. Perhaps a buffalo is attacked by lice, or ticks, or some other itchy, meany little thing and gets relief in a wallow instead of spraying itself with DDT or Malathion.

Well, there goes Richard Nixon escaping from the scene of his crimes against the American people, just as his partner, Agnew the Greek, did earlier. I have been trying to adapt Richard III to Richard Milhous by creating an appropriate poem. How's this:

A copter, a copter—my kingdom for a copter!

or

A helicopter! I must away
to San Clemente—'tis another day.

or

Mine enemies, they surround me,
To San Clemente I must flee.

or

A helicopter! Grant me one O Lord,
I must in haste make way for Ford.

The assassin of Lincoln jumped on a horse and sped away, just as Richard III wanted to do. Poor Richard M, when encircled, had to climb into a helicopter. It would have been so much more dramatic to have jumped on a horse and galloped furiously across the Arlington Bridge.

GRANDFATHER

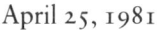

Dear Alex,

At Yale they foresee the future by peering into the past. Jean and I are at a Yale seminar on "The Future: Past and Present." Since you

are at Yale, I think I should report the proceedings to you.
In front of me is a podium on which there is a BIG "Y." I asked Tom Nevins, a Yale man, what that meant. In the army "Y" meant the YM. Perhaps others were equally fooled because just now they have put up a banner, "Yale."

At last they have the loud speaker working. In the future a computer chip will control everything, so no troubles or delays. Like our computerized Bart trains; that is, when they run.

The audience, in a good mood, just applauded the technician, who smilingly showed us that everything is now OK. We've been here exactly an hour. A Yale contrivance to get everyone talking with his neighbors. To recruit students for Yale. Our group of 16, all well past fifty, won't send many!

How come the speaker doesn't get up there and do his thing? Ah! He has slides; he not only has foreseen the future, but painted some slides to show what it will be like. My goodness, they are putting up *two* screens. But they have hidden the Yale banner. Well, back to the "Y."

A guy is now at the mike making notes. Do you suppose he is reviewing old class notes; or maybe making a last-minute preparation for his talk? He just stands there! Oh Dear, he is president of the Yale alumni, not the speaker.

Finally a speaker did come on, Professor Bryan Wolf, and gave a magnificent talk. Only it was an illustrated lecture on painting. Yale knows that the topic "Lecture on Painting" wouldn't go, so they bill the program as "the future and the past." Covers everything. Mighty smart thinking. It did arouse our curiosity about the future.

But Wolf was good. I learned a lot about painting criticism. He let his imagination roam over several canvasses and it was amazing the ideas he extracted. Things that were in the unconscious minds of the artists. So I timidly raised my hand and asked whether Orosco and Rivera consciously did what the classical painters did unconsciously. He said the Mexican muralists were "political." True. But they were using art in an effort to reform social attitudes and practices. I thought of an incident at Antioch College. We had authorized an artist to use a wall in our new gymnasium for a mural. The left and right panels portrayed strife among ethnic and religious groups, the center panel people with radiant faces in whom colors and types had been blended. The contrast between violence caused by hatreds and the assimilation achieved through cultural intercourse was apparent.

Well, two women from Springfield called upon me one day and demanded that the mural be removed. They said it was Communist propaganda. Political? Or, social idealism? The mural was left in place.

As he introduced Professor Wendell Bell, the chairman said that he had struggled with his topic. No wonder; his talk was mind-boggling. MY! He took off into space and I thought he would never get back to earth. Electronic revolution; telecommunication; extrasensory communciation; brain growth and transformation; under sea exploration; space exploration; lunar and asteroid mining; new products to be made in space; gene splicing. Gracious!!!

Once again I raised my hand and asked if he foresaw communication with intelligent beings in other solar systems. He answered that he didn't have time to go into that.

The best idea came not from Yale but from Stanford. Professor Robert Textor is developing a seminar called "ethnographic studies." This is designed to cause the students to consider values underlying the developments in the "computer revolution era"—that is, computerized life, nuclear energy, gene experimentation, and all that, can as easily destroy as to create. The problem is to guide activities so they will advance the welfare of man on earth. Ethnographic studies mean anticipating the kind of life men, men everywhere want, and directing the forces of change toward that goal.

So, man has been through the agricultural revolution, the printed-word revolution, the industrial revolution; and now with breathtaking blast we're off on the computer/space revolution.

Happy journey, Alex.

GRANDFATHER

June 6, 1980

Dear Matthew,

Are you getting excited about celebrating the fiftieth year at Appegesamok Nodin? I am. Of course I was there when it all started. Where were you?

I have discovered a neat way to catch butterflies. You string a cable across a gorge from one cliff to another. Then mount on it a swinging rig with pulley that will ride on the cable. Now get in the rig and go buzzing out over the canyon. Stop at intervals and wave a net around at the butterflies. When you have caught several, just come back. How do you get back? Well, the important thing is first to catch the butterflies. Worry about getting back when you need to get back.

Do you think this would work on the cliff at the second Titus Bluff? Shall we try it? Maybe we would catch more Monarchs. I am enclosing a picture from the Smithsonian Magazine that shows the scheme.

The man who designed this great idea also built himself a tree house 100 feet above the jungle in Costa Rica. But we don't have any trees that high. Maybe that tall stump on which the osprey built its nest would do. Or maybe we could hold it up with skyhooks—you know the kind I grab hold of when I lift myself out of bed in the morning.

Just think of all the 50th anniversaries we are having. First your father had his 50th birthday. Then Fels Research Institute at Antioch College, in which your father was among the first guinea pigs, and Glen Helen, the beautiful extended campus of the college, are also celebrating their 50th year. The years 1930 and 1931 must have been truly creative ones.

Here's another idea for camp this summer: How about celebrating the 500,000,000th birthday of the brachiopods in our little beach muscum?

GRANDFATHER

June 25, 1977

Dear Alex,

I recall that you know all about DNA. The discovery of the DNA molecule is so new that we have little realization of what its further development may be. Just a few days ago there was reported by researchers at the University of Michigan and the University of California medical schools—did you notice it—that they had been able to identify and remove from rats a DNA molecule that tells the rat to produce insulin; and then to implant the DNA in bacteria. So now this new strain of bacteria can produce insulin. Think what this means. Instead of relying on the relatively short supply of insulin that comes from cows, we now will be able to breed bacteria by the millions and readily produce all of the insulin that is needed. The insulin is important, but the technique developed by these researchers is terrifically important. Don't you think so?

Speaking of doctors, I have been reading the book *The Relaxation Response* by Herbert Benson, M.D., of the Harvard Medical School. Since my blood pressure zoomed a bit high recently, I have been trying to inform myself about treatments. Most doctors use chemicals—pills—and they are effective to some degree. But I attributed my rise in pressure to the tensions about going to China. So the question is, how does one relieve stress? Dr. Benson has done some research that shows that meditation can reduce the pressure.

So I am trying to learn to meditate. Since my purpose is to get better control over my bodily reactions to stress, I am using the meditation technique of focussing the mind successively on the various parts of the body. I start with my big toe and move upwards. I use 20 minute periods daily and this is just about the right length of time to go from toe to brain and part way back again. Dr. Benson finds that whether you use a mantra, or simply repeat the word, "one," makes no difference. Suzuki thinks you must use the zazen position—the one Buddha used—but my purpose is to relax the body, so I sit in a position that is entirely comfortable rather than one that strains the muscles.

My purpose at this point is not to purify myself, Buddha like, but rather to extend the control of my brain over my body.

This control seems quite feasible, doesn't it? For example, by practicing the piano, or the flute, it is possible to achieve a high degree of coordination between the mind and the fingers. Consider Serkin sitting at the piano making his fingers fly over the keys so fast one can hardly see them. The interesting thing is that he doesn't have to take time out to "think" about each note he plays next. But his mind does send a signal to the right finger at the right moment to get the desired result. Some people learn to wiggle their ears by practicing. We all learn how to control evacuating our urine, which is different from the way we performed as babies. When I was a small child and had to be changed Dad told me when Mom was cleaning me up and powdering my chafed behind, I would yell: "Don't put pepper in my frackley."

Control of urination is a funny business. As a young boy I wet my bed frequently. I recall with agony one terrible experience I had when I was in high school. Riding my pony home after school, it became so stormy that I stopped at the home of Uncle Billy which was about a third of the way, and asked to stay overnight. I had a bit of a sniffle, and my well meaning aunt insisted on my taking some quinine. That night, sleeping in my drawers I wet them in great style. Well, in the morning I borrowed a pair from my uncle. Then, not knowing what to do with my wet ones, I took them to the sitting room. The round bellied stove was red hot, warming up the house after an unusually cold night. So I chucked the underdrawers in the stove. Immediately the house began to smell to high heaven. Golly, what a smell! Aunt Hett came rushing in, and exclaimed: "What is that smell!" I was both bashful and terribly ashamed so I just grinned sheepishly. She said no more, but she certainly later discovered the wet bed. How terrible! Well, the moral is, never, NEVER, throw urine soaked drawers in a red hot stove.

Although I got over the habit, the bed wetting was still a problem on my mind until I was 17. Being on a trip to Kansas City, I went to see a psychologist about it. This psychologist told me that there is a valve at the bottom of the bladder, and that it needed to be closed properly. Then he laid me on a table, face down, and said: "When I strike your back the valve will close and then you will never have any more trouble with it." Whereupon he took a big wooden mallet and gave me a good strike right in the middle of the back. I have never had another bed wetting. I once mentioned this case to a medical doctor, and he said, "pulled the old psychology on you, didn't he?"

It's funny, isn't it, how you can control your urination by just focussing your mind on it. The trouble with an older man is that he usually develops a swollen prostate and that makes urination more difficult. One of the things I would like to accomplish through meditation is to learn how to relax the prostate gland. One can do it by sitting in a tub of hot water, so why not by mind control?

But my main objective is to relax the pressure from my heart. So part of the time I concentrate on the heart telling it I want it to be more relaxed. Well, we shall see. But Buddha said if you want to build a good dam, don't do it hastily. If you take plenty of time it will be a good dam.

The pace of American life is becoming so fast it must be adding all kinds of stress to our living. Also, our hurry prevents us from seeing, hearing, and doing so many enjoyable things. In the old days of touring, we took time to see all the interesting things along the way, and to chat with our camping neighbors in the evening. If we saw a wild flower along the road, we stopped to photograph it. Now that we travel by freeways, we have to tear along at furious speed, see little, and have lots of crashes. If we pause, we get a moving traffic ticket. So maybe we should relax, and meditate, whether or not we have any problems.

I am also having a massage once a week. I believe that a regular massage should keep the muscles in better trim and bring the blood to the surface. That should help keep the epidermis renewed. Older people ordinarily get very bad skin, covered with black spots and wrinkles. Sort of like when the fresh, green leaves of a rose bush get infested with the black spot. Only it doesn't help people to spray spots with fungicides. Their skin needs care through diet and massages. If you examine a piece of skin under a powerful microscope you will see that the skin is alive with cells that bounce around all over the place. If you get sunburned these cells all die, so then your skin looks dead. Skin cancer has become very common, an indication that people should take better care of their skin.

A good massager, interested in health, also knows how to reach the nerve centers in the body. It is sort of like acupuncture, but instead of sticking pins in the body to reach these centers, the massager presses in with his fingers. Incidentally, I am impressed by what all the people who have seen acupuncture in China say about it. This includes Jean who saw a thyroid operation in which acupuncture was used instead of an anesthetic.

I don't mean to be funny when I say that it reminds me of how on the farm we cured warts on a mule's leg. These warts would become large and very raw. The way to rid the mule of them was to sear the wound with a red hot iron. Just as they used to sear the stub of a man's leg when they had cut a portion of it off. But you can't hold a mule down in the manner you can hold a man when you apply the hot iron. So the thing to do is to make a noose, put it around the upper lip of the mule and twist it real hard. This makes the mule stand perfectly still.

Have you been reading *R.F. Illustrated*, published by the Rockefeller Foundation, that I have had sent to you? I'll bet you haven't! Well, throw it in the wastebasket if you wish. But it does contain some very interesting articles based largely upon research that the Foundation has supported. In the May, 1977, issue, for example, there is an article called "Teenage Mothers, USA." It is a factual discussion of the increasing number of teenage girls who become pregnant, who then face very difficult choices. They are forced to decide between having an abortion with its attendant emotional problems, or to have the child. To do the latter means suddenly being pushed into adult status and responsibilities, and losing all the freedoms, the parties, and the educational opportunities that come only when you are a teenager.

Another good article is called "The Times They Are A'coming." It is the story of Dr. Bannerman, a Black, who went to work in a county in Mississippi and became an instrument for social change. Shows what one person can do to change a community when he sets out to do so—in the right way. I enjoyed it because it reminded me of how we at Antioch College changed the community of Yellow Springs.

GRANDFATHER

P.S.: Have you read the book we sent you—*MS Goes to College*, by Jean and me? It includes discussion of the kind of subject dealt with in the RF article.

February 1, 1979

Dear Peter,

Boy, I'm sure glad this isn't the 2nd, because it is nice and clear, and the ground hog can see his shadow. If he saw it on the second, it would mean six weeks more of cold weather. It has been below zero, Celsius that is, for several nights—Broooooo.

Well, anyway, you are about to have a birthday. A big leap forward, as the Chinese say. You are becoming a teenager! I wonder if you will have the same kinds of problems I had as a teenager.

One of mine was girls. By the time I was thirteen I had become smitten with a girl in our school. My, she was beautiful. And nice. And all that. Gee, Wow, Jiminy Crickets. I was so smitten that one day I climbed up a black walnut tree and carved my initials with hers on a limb. When I deserted her for a more gorgeous gal, the tree felt so bad it fell over and died.

Her Dad's farm was catty-cornered to ours, although not nearly so good, because the soil was full of alkali, the result of poor drainage. It did have a pond on which we all went ice skating in the winter. And we had lots of fun. It's really more fun to swing a girl around the ice, holding hands, than it is to dance with one. For one thing, no danger of stepping on her toes! It's just too bad that you guys down there in Texas can't go ice skating, in the open air I mean.

Last spring I went for a visit to our old farm and to hike across it to the river where I used to go fishing. And swimming. And trapping. As I drove past the neighbor's farm, I saw my one-time girlfriend in her garden, so stopped to say hello. Here was this short, pudgy woman, 100 lbs. overweight, with a terribly big nose. Funny thing, I had not noticed her nose before. She sucked a toothpick the whole time we talked. Just picture yourself sitting across a table from that huge nose and that awful toothpick for 50,000 meals. Ugh, Ugh!

The fall after I became 13 I began to go to Solomon, three miles away, to attend school in the ninth grade. Almost immediately I fell for another girl. She sat right in front of me so I could look at her, smell, and sigh over her without being noticed; all of the while I should have been studying. My but she was pretty—even the back of her head. And she had a beautiful name, Haidee—isn't that a gorgeous name?

Her father started the first picture show in town. It was in an old store building in which chairs had been put. When the man had taken up all the tickets he would go in and start the projector. The pictures were small, only black-and-white (color wasn't invented until 15 years later), and they were all streaked with dots and flashes of light. But we thought they were great. We had nothing with which to compare them. And it cost only 15¢ admission. Someone down front banged away at a piano. The pictures were silent, because pictures with sound hadn't been invented yet. But they were moving pictures. At first there was always a reel about current events, then a lot of advertisements by merchants. Then the feature which was what we really liked. But I don't remember any of them.

Running the picture show was only moonlighting for my girl's father. His real job was manager of the ballast works along the Santa Fe railroad two miles south of our home. When the railroads were being built through Kansas they used ballast for the road bed. Rock was scarce and expensive to crack into small pieces and haul to the tracks. This ballast was made by burning gumbo until it hardened. Gumbo is a very sticky kind of earth much like adobe—you know adobe, don't you, living as you do in Texas where the Mexicans always used adobe bricks to make their houses. When the gumbo was burned into ballast, it could be loaded right onto the freight cars, and then dumped on the road bed wherever it was needed.

My romantic feelings about Haidee didn't last long because after a year and a half her father was transferred to some place in Missouri. And I never saw her again. Boo-hoo!

I was 19 when I met the young woman I presently married—Anne Cristy. I got acquainted with her through her brother whom I had come to know at the YMCA in Albuquerque. After walking home with her from a social I confided to my diary, "Anne is a very sweet little girl and quite friendly." But at that time I was smitten with still another peach, and it never occurred to me that one day, some three years later, I would renew acquaintance with Anne. Indeed, I might never have done so had she not written a "girl to soldier" letter when I was in the army. By that time I was infatuated with a girl from Florida whom I had dated in Washington.

Somehow I never stayed with girls merely because they had seductive eyes and bosoms. I learned, I think rightly, that successful marriage depends heavily upon mutuality of interests. For it is these that make daily companionships. Anne, your grandmother, had unusual intellectual abilities and interests, as has Jean (Granny) whom I married after Anne's cancer bout.

I was attracted to Jean because her professional interests paralleled mine. Then to my surprise she turned out to be a gourmet cook and a good home manager to boot. We have published two books and some articles as joint authors, and we've done a lot of travelling together. We've been having a very happy life together. And she brought into the family her daughter, Carol, who is both beautiful and does a marvelous job of teaching deaf children. Jean's most recent role has been as pregnancy counselor at the Cowell Clinic, the University of California. She has unusual empathy with young people; and her doctoral study coupled with experience as college dean have given her the technical competence with which to counsel those who are in need.

I guess the problem with falling for a girl is that you fall for one that you know. In your school, or at a party, or in the neighborhood. Now what does a boy in a country school with only eight girls in it, some of them scrawny little things, and others much older than you, all of them living in the same neighborhood and going to the same parties as you do, know of girls? Get smitten with a girl in Toronto? Or Hong Kong? Or New Orleans? How could you when you have never seen or heard of such a person.

One advantage of going to college, or perhaps of changing schools is that you then have the chance of becoming acquainted with lots of additional girls and boys. There you find new friends, lots more than you have had. Some of them are much more interesting than those you have known before. Most of my lasting friends came out of college, or through work that I was subsequently involved in.

I sometimes think that as we grow older and more mature, we are as much or more the products of our environment as we are of the education we have had. My first girl friend, the one with the toothpick in her mouth, never went beyond the eighth grade. For a while she was courted by a neighbor boy, but he was an alcoholic, and I suppose that is why she never married him. And since she played along with him for several years, she didn't get to know anyone else. In any event, in that neighborhood, most of the young men left to seek their fortunes elsewhere. She was in a rut and never got out.

My high school chum, on the other hand, became a great traveler, spent a few years in Africa, went to college and university. And became a college president; also a high official with UNESCO in Paris. I remained friends with him until he died. He had lively interests in lots of things and his conversation was never boring.

So, Peter, it is nice to know that you make such good grades in school and are coming to have so many interests. Pretty soon you will be in high school and then on to college and you will be learning all kinds of new things and meeting lots of new friends.

And, while sizing up the girls, think about what a wise choice your father made in picking Jerry as his wife—after waiting until he had found an intelligent, talented, congenial companion. And mother for you and Matthew.

GRANDFATHER

Carol

II

Life in a city today contrasts sharply with the experiences I had as a boy on a Kansas farm. A telephone, for example, is a "must" for a teenage girl; yet we lived without one. And what school boy today would even think of trapping skunks to earn money with which to buy a bicycle? Peter, Sabrina, I doubt if you will return to the self-sustained life of the rural pioneer, but I would like all of you to be aware of values and experiences you are missing.

May 2, 1978

Dear Sabrina,

    It was good of you to call me last week. Have you thought about what a great invention the telephone is? It is also a marvel to me how they can bounce our voices off a satellite that is way up there somewhere beyond the clouds, and have the sound land at a point thousands of miles away.
    I remember well when we got our first telephone on the farm in Kansas. Our number was five rings. You see, we were on a country line with about fourteen other farm homes. It was great fun to listen in on conversations; everyone did.
    What a marvelous change in our lives the telephone brought. Because earlier the only way to send a message was by saddling a horse or hitching one to a buggy, and riding or driving several miles. If we kids wanted to play with other children, we just had to wait until they dropped in.
    Of course the U. S. Post Office existed, but a letter had to be taken to town to be mailed and we went to town only once a week or so when we had eggs and butter to barter for groceries. Then there was a long wait for a return letter. No wonder people didn't write very often, even to their most intimate family. And to get a little perspective, compare the mail problem of my boyhood days with that of today. Now if mail is an hour late, we grumble.
    After rural free delivery was established, we had daily service. Our mailman, Fred Hall, made the rounds by horse and buggy, with a lighted lantern under his lap robe trying to keep warm. Even so, he froze his feet so badly one of them had to be amputated. I wonder if he got a pension? Guys today get pensions for the slightest disability, even imaginary ones.

Our telephone was in a large, long, fumed oak box, screwed onto the wall, with two bells at the top, mouth piece in the middle, a little shelf near the bottom, and the very necessary crank on the side. Goodness sakes, in this house we now have six jacks and three portable phones so we can talk from almost any room, and both of us can be on the line as we were when you called. Another thing, our monthly bills are much higher than in the good old days. Our phone was used sparingly, not like the way kids monopolize it today. And the phone is so demanding of attention. There is a germ of truth in Menotti's *The Telephone* when Ben has to propose to Lucy over the phone in his desperation to get her to listen.

So many things we have today weren't invented or available when I was your age. We got our first automobile in 1913. It was an Empire; did you ever hear of an Empire? If we had had sense enough to keep it, it might now be worth a fortune as an antique. I have a picture of our Empire with our whole family in it—Beulah, Bertie, Mom, Dad, Algo, Lee Merle, and Towser. We sure felt like big shots.

Until 1920 when we built a new house on the farm, the one your mother remembers, we had a house that my grandparents had lived in. It was two story, frame, with three porches. It had a dining room and kitchen where we lived most of the time, and a huge pantry with all kinds of places to store things like canned goods, flour, our drinking water pails, our overshoes and heavy coats, our shotgun and rifle.

The cellar, rock-walled with dirt floor, was for the storage of vegetables, canned fruit, crocks of milk, and had in one corner a cyclone refuge. This consisted of four heavy hedge posts at the corners and a top made of two inch planks, all of this below ground level so that if a tornado swept across the house we would be safe under this protection—that is, unless Mother's large square piano crashed through the floor on our heads. Many the night that we jumped out of bed, raced for the cellar, and huddled in this refuge until the storm had abated.

Our sitting room and parlor were seldom used. The parlor was never entered except for company, or when Mother felt like playing the piano. Occasionally we would sit in the sitting room. It had a double opening with the spare bedroom, so was a bit spacious. On the wall was a large framed picture of Grandmother Donmyer, looking very severe with hair parted in the middle and combed tightly back. When I see the teenage girls with their hair that way, I think of Grandmother. I liked her much better when she and Mom would sit in their rockers under the picture, their faces lighted up while they jabbered in German.

The upstairs consisted of three bedrooms and a small storage closet. Merle and I had one room and the two girls slept in the same room as our parents. The third room was for dressing. This was comfortable for us, but I wonder how my grandparents, together with their six to eight nearly grown children found places for their beds.

The spare bedroom was saved for guests or for when the children were born. It was always fascinating to have an itinerant peddler stop past. Frequently the folks would let one stay overnight—but not in the guest bedroom. If the weather was bad he would sleep with us boys; otherwise he would go to the hay mow. Can you imagine sleeping with a peddler? In exchange for food and a place to sleep, the man would give my mother yard goods, often beautiful imports from Armenia or Syria. A couple of times we also got a present of bed bugs. But this was a catastrophe for them, because we would pour coal oil into the cracks and the poor bugs would curl up and die.

We used kerosene lamps, the simple glass globed type. It cost only a few cents to operate them, a pint of coal oil lasting for weeks. The only problem was to clean the chimneys and trim the wicks, a weekly chore. Our ornate lamps were never lit, but were used for decoration. Alas, they no longer exist, having been given the heave-ho when we finally got electricity. Imagine the lack of foresight in throwing to the dumpheap a small fortune in future antiques. Did I tell you that a metal fireplace front that had graced the home of my Aunt Belle Winters was thrown into the dump heap, but later rescued by Helen Henderson's sister who is an antique dealer? Now it is again cosily decorating a living room fireplace.

I regret most that Mother traded her rosewood square piano for a modern one. But we discarded lots of other potentially valuable things, such as a grain reaper, horse collars and cruppers, the churn, and the milk crocks. All now prized antiques.

We had round bellied stoves in the sitting and dining rooms, and a large wood burning cook stove in the kitchen—and that was our heat. But it was OK. When we built the new house, we put in a furnace, and also a light plant—a direct current generator of our own.

We had our own water system, too. The system consisted of little Algie taking a bucket out to the cistern, pulling a pail of water up, dumping it into the water bucket, and then lugging it into the pantry near the kitchen. For hot water we kept a teakettle full on top of the range, and the stove had a reservoir that was kept filled with warmish water. What did we do for water for the toilets? Aha, why water? Our toilet was an outhouse, called by some a privy, located along the path beside the garden. You walked out there to do your thing and used the pages from a Monkey Ward catalogue for toilet paper. Or you went behind a shed, or in the barn, or out in the plum thicket. And there use a corn cob. Did you know that is why corn cobs are long, slim and round? You may wonder what we did at night. Well, under the bed was a nice convenient pot.

Do you know how the water got into the cistern? We connected the eve troughs and the down spouts from the house to the cistern. Of course, we had a well, too, for the livestock, but that water was salty. You see, that part of Kansas had once been an inland sea, so under the soil are these enormous beds of salt. One of the salt works was about two miles from us, and Uncle Billie was in charge of the plant. Salt from there won first prize at the Chicago World's Fair (1892?). So we couldn't drink the well water. In drouth periods, our cistern sometimes ran dry and we would have to get some barrels and drive ten miles to Sand Springs to fill them.

You know, I'm beginning to think that you grandchildren don't know nothing. You don't know how to skin a skunk, how to milk a cow, how to pluck a goose, how to butcher a hog, how to churn butter, how to cut a chicken's head off, how to break a wild horse, how to build a wheat stack, how to feed a calf, how to catch a rooster, how to cure a hide, how to fasten a crupper on the horse's tail. . . . You don't even know the difference between a cradle for babies and a cradle to reap wheat. MY, MY, MY!

GRANDFATHER

May 18, 1975

Dear Alex,

It's too bad that a snow storm drove you home from Albuquerque a day early. But you did start home in your auto at a lively clip over the paved roads. When I was a boy at your age we went places in a horse-drawn buggy, or in a carriage (surrey). When Mom would take us to Salina to shop it took us two hours to get there. Driving Little Daisy. How far was that?—just 12 miles. On one occasion we drove from Solomon to Newton, Kansas, to visit Uncle Jake and his family, just 60 miles, and it took all day to go there. So just imagine our going from Dallas to Albuquerque—by horse and buggy. What would we do? We would not go.

Only rarely did people travel any distance, and then of course by train. Mom and Dad made occasional trips to Kansas City, but that was a BIG trip. We had relatives come from Pennsylvania or Ohio, but such visits were the trip of a lifetime, to be taken only once. My folks did not go "back East" or to California, until after 1925.

The worst thing about the roads was that they were unpaved, not even gravelled. In the summer they were very dusty; in the winter, or after rains, muddy. During the muddy season they would develop deep ruts, and then these would freeze, and so the road would be very bumpy. The wheels of the buggy, and later—even much worse—the wheels of an auto, would get into one of these ruts and remain a captive.

The farmers would grade the roads—they did this as one way to pay their taxes—but then there would be huge clumps of mud and grass deposited in the middle of the road. These clumps kept getting stuck on the bottom of the car, and every little way we would have to get out in the mud, reach under the car and pull this stuff out. Otherwise we couldn't move. But then we would be all dressed up in mud. Once in a while a man would come to our house and ask us to bring a team of horses to pull his car out of the mud. One such person gave me $5, but usually we did it free. This is a description of how it was, not a complaint. Until the automobile was invented, roads had always been dirt—except in rare instances where primary roads and city streets were paved with cobblestones. The Romans had a few paved highways, as did the Mayans. But the ordinary person never saw a paved road, and being used to dirt roads, just took them for granted. It would never have occurred to anyone to pave the road between our farm and Salina or Solomon.

Isn't that the way we live most of the time, or most of us live all of the time? We are used to what we have and don't want things to be different. We get used to going to school or to work by auto, and resist going by bike or bus. Maybe I'm a little more flexible than many because I had four choices for going to high school in Solomon: by buggy, riding my pony, riding my bike, or, occasionally, walking.

Let me tell you a bit more about life on the farm, when I was a boy. Our fields were near the Solomon River, which flooded at intervals, depositing rich black loam soil on the place. So the land was very fertile. We did not use fertilizers, except a bit of manure from our sheds; and the region being new to farming had few bugs, so we did not have to use pesticides.

Our staple crops were wheat—mostly wheat—and corn. We also raised such things as oats, kaffircorn, and alfalfa. We sold the wheat, and some corn for cash, but fed the other crops to our animals and poultry. We had a large orchard for fruit—apples, peaches, plums, pears, apricots, cherries—and in our garden we raised potatoes, sweet potatoes, beans, peas, cabbage, onions, lettuce, radishes, and lots of other things. Some of the produce could be kept for winter use by storing or canning them. We would bury sacks of potatoes in the ground, putting hay and manure over the top of the pits to keep them from freezing. Mom always did lots of canning of vegetables and fruit. So we rarely had to buy any of these staples, even in the winter.

The farm yard and fruit orchard occupied ten acres. The road in front of our house was lined with maple trees; our farm was officially registered as "Maplelawn Farm." The rest of the road, a half mile in length, had black walnut and boxelder trees the full length. The other three sides of the ten-acre yard were also bordered with trees—mulberry and apple mostly.

Our apples were really super, and we had a dozen or more varieties. Every year we made lots of cider using our large mill. Have you ever tasted really fresh cider? Without preservatives and junk mixed in? We've tried to find some here, but none of the stores carries it. Only the insipid stuff. One year Dad made a whole barrel of cider for the owner of a packing plant in Salina. Then after all this work, the man didn't come and didn't come, much to our concern. In the meantime the cider began to ferment. He finally came, took a drink, and exclaimed: "Das ist gut. Yust like beer." My father was greatly relieved but hadn't realized that he was making beer in dry Kansas.

We had several large cherry trees, both early and Montmorency. These were not easy to pick—little Algie had to shinny up the trees for some of them. We sold them at a big price, such as $1 a bushel. Black walnuts are hard shelled and it is difficult to pick out the kernels. But they are delicious. You should have tasted the walnut cakes Mother used to bake. And the mulberry pies! Picking the mulberries was easy. Just wait until lots of them are ripe, then spread a cloth, one that won't hurt to be stained, shake the limbs, scoop up the berries, and wash them. Then what? Pies, pies, PIES. Did you ever eat fresh mulberry pie, made from freshly picked, fully ripe fruit? Yum, yum. And cherry pies. These really were great. Every Saturday was baking day on the farm. Six loaves of bread, two or three pies, and often a cake. Can you imagine such feasts as we had?

The biggest feasts were whenever we visited with the Donmyer or Henderson relatives. Visits were all day affairs, with Sunday dinners. Whether we entertained them or they did the same for us, the women went all out with food. Usually roast chicken, but on holidays, roast goose. Goose used to be the fare of farmers, but now it is a feast for royalty. It is such a treat always to have goose for Christmas at your house. We also had mashed potatoes piled high, with a cup of melted butter nestling in the center, vegetables, jams, pickled peaches or watermelon rind, pies and cakes. Everything was served family style, so these platters heaped with appetizing food were passed around and everyone helped himself to whatever and as much as he wanted.

Only sometimes, if there were several children, little Algie had to sit at a separate table with other children and eat drumsticks and wings.
Nobody had heard of freezers or refrigerators. If you wanted to freeze something such as ice cream, you bought a big cake of ice. We had an ice cream freezer, and having lots of milk and cream, had ice cream frequently; in the summer that is. A hand cranked freezer; and who do you suppose had to turn the crank? But there were big rewards. Because then we had all the ice cream we could eat. No dinky little cones costing 98¢.

The Donmyers had an ice house. During the winter when the Smoky Hill River was frozen, they would saw large chunks of ice, put them in their ice house, and cover them with sawdust. Then if they wanted ice cream they didn't have to wait until someone went to town. They just shoveled off some sawdust, and with big tongs took out a square of the ice.

Golly, the gustatory cells in my epithelium got so excited over those pies, fresh fruit, and ice cream that I went out in the kitchen and ate an apricot. But I felt cheated. It was soft and shriveled and not ripe.

We also had livestock and poultry—cattle, horses, mules, hogs, chickens, guineas, geese. Ordinarily we kept two milk cows and a few calves. It was sort of fun to run, accompanied by Towser, each evening to bring the cows in for milking. Sometimes I would pretend to be a coyote and yell like one. I would tell you how, but I can't yell on paper. It is sort of like the howl of a wolf; but you've probably never heard a wolf. Maybe you could buy a record that would give you the call.

Then you could go out on the Texas prairie and run as fast as you can, all the while howling like a coyote. And God would smile as he looked down, and say to himself: "There goes Alex, streaking across the prairie, yowling like a coyote." There is a sense of freedom in all that.

But did you ever milk a cow? UGH! I hated it. Let's not think about it. This is one area in which I am willing for the machines to take over. The cows have to be milked or they will be in pain from swollen bags. And we needed milk for food and to skim for cream. And churn butter. Did you ever churn for butter? Maybe you don't even know that butter had to be churned. Well, what some people don't know!

You put the milk in gallon crocks with narrow bottoms and wide tops, set the crocks on the floor of the cellar for a few days until the cream has risen to the top, then with a large spoon skim off the cream, put it in a churn, and churn for an hour or so. Then you can reach in with your hands, take the chunks of butter out and mould them into loaves about the size and shape of a bread loaf. You keep some, and sell the rest, or trade it for sugar, coffee, or yard goods. How do you churn? You just churn. Then imagine a little boy lifting that handle up and down, up and down, for about an hour. Maybe it was less but it sure seemed long. After a few years we bought a separator, and that helped, only the darned thing had to be taken apart after each use and washed thoroughly.

I neglected to say that when the cow is fresh—has just had a calf—the first thing is to wean the calf and start feeding it by hand. For a cow can give enough milk for her calf and for the family. So you can't let the calf drink it all. This is what you do. Separate the calf from its mother. Take some milk, maybe half a gallon or so in a bucket to the calf. Stroke it gently so it won't be afraid. Dip your fingers in the milk and let the calf lick them. Presently while this licking is going on, try to maneuver the calf's head into the bucket with its tongue in the milk. Be patient. Sort of like teaching a baby to eat spinach. Pretty soon the calf will be drinking heartily. And when it sees you coming, it will race toward you and try frantically to get its head in the bucket.

I'll bet there's something else you have never done. Like breaking a horse. Here's how you do it. You should learn, because it is much cheaper to buy a horse and train it yourself, than to buy one that has been trained (only I don't advise it). You select a mare that is real gentle and dependable and harness her in tandem with the wild horse. But first get the wild horse into a boxstall with sides high enough so the horse can't kick you, but low enough so you can throw a harness or saddle over it. Lay the harness on the colt's back. CAREFUL!! That colt will jump like wild; it is very frightened. But just keep trying until the harness can rest on the back. Now it is a bit tricky to buckle the hames and the surcingle, but keep at it.

You don't know a hame from a crupper? Golly. You put the crupper over the tail, not the neck, silly. OK, when you have the harness on, you get the old mare all hooked up on one side of the wagon tongue, then maneuver the colt to the other side tying it firmly to the mare. And hook the colt into the double tree. Now you jump into the wagon and take off. You are lucky if you can get out of the gate and onto the road. Don't worry about automobiles, they don't exist. Just try with your reins to keep the horses in the road, somewhere, and not in the nearest hedge. You'd be surprised; the old mare sort of takes the whole show in stride, and first thing you know that wild horse is trotting alongside. Only you have to do this with a wagon several times before you dare to hook up to a surrey or even a plow.

We always had several horses, each for a special purpose, such as working in the fields, pulling a buggy, riding, or as brood mares. We raised our own colts and they made very nice pets. We always had a few hogs, mainly to fatten for butchering. We thus raised and butchered much of our meat. We had a smoke house where we cured the meat for later use.

One winter Dad fed a carload of steers for market—as many small farmers did in those days. We put several hogs in the feed lot also, because we fed the steers on corn, and the hogs would eat the droppings and get fat. After three months of hard work Dad loaded the cattle into a freight car and took them to Kansas City and sold them on the open market. He brought me home my first watch. But he seemed disappointed, saying that he only made enough to pay for the expenses and wages for his time. That was the bane of the farmer, never knowing whether prices would be up or down. It was always a gamble to know when to sell steers, wheat, bailed alfalfa.

We had lots of chickens, two large henhouses. We would keep the pullets for eggs, eat the young cockerels, and sell off the older hens and cocks—they are called stewing chickens, and are usually a bit tough. You had to gather the eggs every day or they would go stale. We had large cases, twelve dozen eggs per case, in which to market the eggs. We also sold eggs for hatching.

Do you know how to dress a chicken for cooking? First you have to catch one. I used a long pole with a stiff wire which had a hook at one end. I would drop some feed and the chickens would come running. Then I would push this wire stealthily to a cockerel's foot and hook his leg. Having caught a chicken, you then take it to a stump or log, grab one wing and the legs with your left hand, lay the chicken's head on the stump, and with an axe, bingo, the head rolls off. Sounds cruel but chickens do have to be killed before you can eat them. Now you must have boiling hot water ready in a big dish pan into which you dip the chicken. This is to loosen the feathers so that you can pluck them easily. Pick them off real clean. Then light a newspaper and quickly thrust the bird into the flames. This removes the pin feathers. Next you open the bird and take out the intestines, heart, liver, and gizzard. The gizzard has to be cut open and all the sand and stuff removed. You simply pull the lining out. If you want fried chicken you have to cut it up, of course.

Alex, if you want to practice all of this you can doubtless buy a live chicken from somebody in Dallas—maybe in the Mexican section. Only insist on a young cockerel, otherwise they might sell you a tough stewing hen. Maybe you should wait until I can go with you so that you will pick out a good bird and use the axe with just the right finesse.

The main reason for keeping geese is that each spring you pluck the down off them in order to make pillows and blankets. Is your pillow made of down? Maybe your sleeping bag is? I'll bet it's filled with artificial stuff. Well, to get the down you must first catch the goose; don't let them bite you if they hiss at you. Then you have to hold them on the ground—better to have someone help you—and you simply pull the down off. It really is very easy. And an inexpensive way to get good pillow stuffing. You should sleep in a tick filled with down; it is sort of like a water bed.

The dumb geese quack the whole time you have them pinned to the ground. They don't realize how cool you are making them by stripping off the stuff that has kept them warm when it freezes. Sort of like taking off your wooly underwear that you have worn all winter. Or do you wear wooly underwear? I always did because we didn't have central heat, or heated autos, and all that sort of thing. On April 15 we could take off the wooly things and start to go barefooted. Do you go barefooted every summer? Isn't it great? To get rid of those old shoes and feel the soft earth under your toes and to be real cool? I could hardly wait until April 15.

Your great-grandmother, my mother, spanned the time between a log cabin and a house with flush toilets and central heat. What equivalent experience will you have before your feutrons run out? Perhaps a satellite ride in outer space with a stopover on the moon? Or a phone pal on Titan?

GRANDFATHER

October 12, 1974

Dear Sabrina,
    Fall is a time for feasting. Lots of vegetables, fruits, spring chickens available. In my boyhood we always preserved food in order to have something to eat in the winter. Like the bees and the squirrels.
    Our biggest event was to butcher a hog. I will describe the operation so that you can butcher—when the next depression comes along and other people are standing in soup lines. And so you will know how to make good liver pudding, sausages, and hams.
    We butchered as soon as the night froze. But first you have to raise the pig. Feed it scraps from the table, greasy dishwater, and corn. When it weighs about 250 pounds, butcher it.
    Get your 22 rifle, draw an imaginary line from right ear to left eye, and left ear to right eye, and aim at the intersection of the lines. When the hog drops, run to it with a long sharp knife and stab between the shoulders into the heart to make it bleed profusely.
    In the meantime prepare a rig in a tree so that with block and tackle you can raise the hog by the hind legs clear off the ground, head down. Earlier you should have built a fire under a huge iron kettle so that now you have lots of boiling water. The kettle must have been so placed that you can let the hog down into it to scald the hair. With sharp knives scrape all the hair off, wash the carcass, and hoist again.
    Now with a big knife slit the belly full length and gut it. Hey, what are you doing? Throwing the guts away? Gracious! Don't you know that you stuff them to make link sausage? Of course they must be emptied, turned inside out, washed, and scraped. Careful, don't slit them. Use the heart, liver, and other choice pieces to make liver pudding. Mixed with corn meal, this makes delicious scrapple. Do you know scrapple? Not the stuff you buy in cans—insipid, and never fried right in restaurants. And not served with pure maple syrup as we did. Scrapple! Yummm, yummm.
    Next you do a lot of cutting and slicing. Cut off the head and trim every scrap of meat off, except the ears and snout. If you like pigs' ears, however, turn to *The Foxfire Book*, page 205, to learn how to boil them in salt water. All trimmings are set aside for sausage meat. Cut the underbelly into squares or rectangles. This is for side meat (or bacon). Properly cured, it will last for months. Now cut off the front quarters to make hams. You can discard the hoofs unless you

have some way to make glue. But save the hocks. With lima beans they make tasty casseroles.

Saw the ribs and cut into useable chunks. Next the hind quarters as hams. Discard the tail because it is not so good for sausage and not long enough for a riding crop. Last is the backbone. The back is where the tenderloin is, choice meat that is usually eaten first.

Don't delay preparing the meat for smoking. Rub saltpeter over it. In the smokehouse you build a smothered type of fire and be sure to keep it going because you want to smoke the meat for a few weeks. Add hickory chips if you like the flavor. Your garage or your Dad's greenhouse just won't do, too leaky. Obviously you can't use the laundry room. I guess you'll just have to build a smokehouse.

Do you have a sausage press? You must get one, because you have to tuck the intestines onto the spout, turn the crank, and presto you have long links of sausage. Having put all the scraps of meat, after grinding and mixing them, into the press. Bury the sausages in tall ceramic jars, in lard, and store. Thus you can take out a link at a time and have sausage—real sausage, meat and not sawdust—for many weeks.

Now it is time to make soap. Take all the fat you have carefully saved, put in a big kettle, and cook until it becomes liquid. Throw in some lye. Stir. Presently let it cool and cut into slabs or squares. Good laundry soap. I do not recommend it for your bath.

Now you have enough hog meat to last until spring. So don't blame me if you neglect this squirrel-like thrift and starve to death.

GRANDFATHER

November 10, 1974

Dear Ilya,

Yesterday I was digging grass out from my rose bushes and got my hands covered with dirt. I also have six scratches on my right hand from the thorns. Very foolishly I don't wear gloves; but I find that I can get a better hold on the stems of grass with my bare hands and thus get more of the roots out. If you leave one tiny root, up comes another bunch of grass. But I have learned a good way of keeping nails from getting black. A farmer, as I used to be, nearly always has black nails because of the dirt and grease that gets under the nails. I have discovered that if you fill your nail tips with soap before digging in the ground, the dirt washes out cleanly. Do you think I could sell this invention for a million dollars? I could use a million.

I like to dig in the soil and so I like gardening. I suppose it is because I grew up on a farm and digging in the earth seems natural, and also a worthwhile thing to do. But at my age a person needs both recreation and exercise. Doing garden work provides both. Since the plants, shrubs and trees demand care, there is always a reason for going out of doors and doing something. It is also a way to get good company.

Rose bushes don't talk to you, nor do I say much to them—unless I yell "ouch" when they reach out and scratch me with their thorns. But they do respond to what you do with them. You prune them, cultivate them, do away with their enemies, and they in turn give you the most gorgeous flowers. My, how lovely they are. I feel grateful to them even though I don't say thank you out loud. It is fun too, to sow a seed in the soil, give it a little water, and then watch the tiny plant stick its head above the ground. Presently it will become a head of cabbage, a stalk of corn, a Catalina cherry tree, or a zinnia. Just think of all the things you can make happen in a bit of earth.

Do you know the difference between working the dirt and doing the dirty work? Working the dirt means things like planting seeds, nursing little plants, and fertilizing them as need be. Dirty work—well let me give you some examples.

My father always kept some milk cows, and of course raised their calves. We had a large barn, one part of which was a shed for the cows. We called it the cowshed. In it, the cattle were protected from the storms and they frequently slept in it at night. Now cows are sort of dumb and don't go outside when they need to. They have never seen a bathroom. Neither do they go into a corner to relieve themselves as dogs or cats do. So a cowshed gets real messy. And stinks. If you don't keep cleaning it out, the stuff can get knee deep.

Well, who do you think had to help clean the cowshed? One of the little sons, naturally. Of course, my father worked at it also. We used pitchforks. You take a pitchfork, or shovel if the dung is too fresh, push it under a pile of dung, then carry it outside to the manure pile. This sounds easy, but of course you had to walk around in the stuff and get your shoes all dirty and smelly—a bit of a problem when you returned to the house. Why are women so fussy like not wanting cow dung tramped on the carpets? And sometimes the barn floors are slippery—watch out! or you will get your arms, hands, and face all messy. Were you ever in a cowshed? I mean the old type, not the modern sanitized one. Oh well, farmers were used to dirt and smell and took it for granted. Barns had always been that way. In former times and in some parts of the world today the family lets the livestock come right into the yard and house.

We weren't finished when we had shoveled the dung onto the manure pile. Manure is too good to waste, because it helps make delicious strawberries, beans, and corn. We had a manure spreader and every once in a while we would pitch it full of manure and then spread it over the fields. But that was not too bad because it is necessary to let the manure dry before using it; otherwise it may rob the soil of more nitrogen than it provides.

My grandfathers had both moved to Kansas in the early days, the decade following the Civil War. Fuel was in short supply because there were not many trees and no easy way to bring in coal. So the settlers gathered up buffalo cakes for fuel. They make real hot fuel.

Do you know that in India, fuel is so scarce and expensive that many Indians use cow dung for fuel? Cows are sacred and wander around everywhere. In Calcutta, I saw a cow lying peacefully right in the middle of a major street intersection; the policeman just directed the traffic around it. I also saw women and children following after cows and scooping up the fresh droppings with their hands. They take the stuff home, mix it with straw to make a pancake, and then press it against the wall of their house to dry. Thus, they not only make fuel, but artfully decorate the walls.

When I was a senior in high school, I needed to work my way because I didn't want to spend so much time driving to school three miles each way. So I got a job as a porter in the Montezuma Hotel in Solomon. Hotels in 1913 were busy places. Most people traveled by train or horse and buggy so they had to stop frequently for the night. The grocery, mercantile, and hardware stores were small and independent, and there were lots of traveling salesmen visiting them. They stayed at the local hotel, usually in the heart of the business district. Also the hotel dining room was one of the few spots in town where one could get regular meals. The Montezuma was one of two hotels in Solomon, a village of 1,000 population. Today Solomon is still the same size, but the hotels have gone.

My job had some nice features, as well as earning me room and board. The hotel had a large lobby where one could read the newspapers. And it was instructive to talk to the people who gathered in the lobby in the evening—their rooms were small and unheated. One time a prosperous looking man from Kansas City asked me how to get to a certain farm six miles southwest of town. I told him and then asked if I could help him. He said he was thinking of buying it. I asked him how much he would have to pay. He said, "$145 an acre." I said I knew the farm, that the price was twice what it was worth, because the soil was alkaline and the buildings were shacks. He thanked me profusely. But no tip! Actually I never got a single tip as a porter. So why should I tip porters and waiters? Jean is always fussing with me about not tipping 15%, FIFTEEN PERCENT? Wow!

Have you read Charles Dickens' description of his travels in America? He was amazed at the way men chewed tobacco and how they would have contests to see who was the best spitter of tobacco juice into the spittoons or the fireplace. The lobby of the Montezuma was generously supplied with spittoons. In my day, some of the men were still taking aim at the spittoons. Each bedroom had a slop jar to take the water from the wash bowl, but guests were supposed to go out to the privy to relieve themselves. But they might use the slop jar instead, and sometimes a drunk would vomit all over it.

Each spittoon and slop jar had to be carried back of the hotel to the pump, washed, rinsed, and dried. With bare hands. Even when it was freezing. UGH! UGH! Well, you can get used to anything if you make up your mind to it. I had got the job myself and was determined to see it through. But between you and me I would rather clean up after cows. They don't realize what they are doing. Men do, although they don't seem to mind if someone else cleans up after them. This helped me to see how depraving and denigrating the jobs of servants and slaves can be. In spite of the distasteful features of this job, it did teach me to discipline myself so that I would not shrink from dirty and necessary work.

The pump at which I cleaned those filthy vessels was also the pump from which the hotel got its water for drinking and for the kitchen. This sort of thing would not be tolerated today because of the public health laws. But in this earlier period, really not so long ago, the small town hotel manager, the merchants, and the farmers didn't realize how important pure water is. After all there was lots of it everywhere. So we merrily washed the spittoons at the pump. Nobody complained; nobody got sick that I know of. Even if they had a bug, they would not have attributed it to the water. I'm glad we got rid of village pumps. I'm glad that schools now teach about bacteria and how to maintain good health.

The dirtiest job in the middle of the summer lay in the harvesting and threshing of the wheat. When the wheat gets about 30 inches tall, turns yellow, and the heads are full of grains, you cut and shock it. We used a binder that cut the wheat and tied it into bundles. Then these sheaves were droppped in a row. Dad drove a four-horse team and I followed after the binder and shocked the wheat. Shock? I don't mean an electrical shock, silly. Look at page 1196 of the American Heritage Dictionary if you want to know what shock means. Why do I have to explain all these things?

But that wasn't all. Not even the dirtiest part. Later when the wheat was real dry, we would stack it. I did the stacking, an art taught me by Uncle Billy. We built round stacks. You start at the center laying one bundle after another in ever widening circles, always with the head of grain off the ground. When the stack was as big around as you wanted it—maybe 16 feet in diameter, start at the middle again with more circles and extend them outward so the stack will bulge in the middle, then you begin to draw in until you reach a point at the top. Tramp, tramp, tramp the center of the stack to make

Stacking wheat

it real solid, but leave the outer edge loose. When the stack settles, the bulge will drop so as to create a slope for the rain to drain off. Now the stack is finished and there you are way up in the sky on top. How do you get down? Hmmm—that is *your* question.

Now you have to wait for a threshing machine, because no one farmer can afford to own one. The machines were huge, with a separator, a steam engine, a water wagon, and a cook shack. They traveled all over the wheat region, often from Texas to the Dakotas, and a gang of men went with them. The engine turned around to face the separator and the two were connected with a long belt. The flywheel of the engine operated the belt and the belt made the thresher go. You had to pitch the bundles of wheat into the big 36-inch mouth of the separator where the knives tore them into shreds, and presently out came the grain into a wagon, and the straw onto a stack behind the critter. The dust belched forth in great clouds, got in your eyes, nose, hair, and over your perspiration-soaked clothes. The sun beat down ferociously and there was no relief until the sun set. No seven-hour days or five-day weeks in the old harvest fields.

Then what do you do? Go home and take a nice, hot, soapy shower, you say. There ain't no shower. Not even a hot water tank. What I did was strip off my clothes beside the big water tank where the cattle and horses drank, and plunge in. After watering, unharnessing, and feeding my team, of course. Then I would put my grimy clothes back on. Sometimes I was so tired I just washed my hands and face. Why bathe? The next day, and the next, just buried you in more dirt.

Some farmers put the grain in bins in their barns, hoping that out of season the price would be higher. But Ilya, don't let your horses stick their heads in the bin and eat wheat. If they do when you aren't looking, be sure not to let them drink water for a long time. If they do, they will swell up and burst. It is always kind of messy to have a burst horse scattered around. One morning, when I was in the army keeping guard in a shell loading plant, one unit of the plant exploded. Soldiers had to go around with baskets picking up pieces of the men who had been killed. Made me glad that my liver and brains were still a part of me.

Another dirty job was to clean mites out of hens' nests. Have you ever done that? I suppose not, since you don't even have any hens. Or really fresh eggs. Or little chicks to play with. Mites are tiny and there are millions of them. They crawl on your hands, up your sleeves, onto your chest and belly. Crawly things all over your body. What a funny feeling! You clean the nest by sousing it with kerosene, but can a boy just jump into a barrel of kerosene? Or does he have to take the mites to bed with him? Well—there must be *some* way to get the pesky things out of your hair.

A friend of mine, Billy Leiserson, an economist, used to give a lecture entitled, "When everyone wears a white collar, who will do the dirty work"? He did not mean it that way, but the implication is that there should be a class of people who do the dirty work. I suppose that is the reason why in so many civilizations people kept slaves, and why in India there was an untouchable class.

So why shouldn't everyone be trained to do his or her share of the dirty work?

But why can't we humans learn to be more careful and thoughtful in discarding waste? Why do we permit the pollution of our air and water? Why do we foist our dirty environment upon our children, and their children?

But remember, working in the dirt is different. Ilya, learn to dig in the soil, plant things, cultivate and give them tender care and love. They will reward you.

GRANDFATHER

April 28, 1975

Dear Matthew,

One day while following like a puppy dog behind my father who with his plow was making a furrow in the earth, I found a tiny rabbit. Its eyes were barely open. At this tender age it was not afraid of me. I took it to the house to show Mother. Having done that, I poured some milk into a saucer and dipped the rabbit's mouth in it. After a few trials it got the taste and thereafter drank heartily. I decided to keep it as a pet. So I put it in one of the empty runways of Mother's chick incubator. It lived and grew and was a nice pet.

It used to come into the house, stand up, and beg for apple peelings. It also liked wall paper and when it found a loose strip, would pull it off the wall. Mom would yell: "Stop that!" but she never hit or scared my pet. After a year or so the rabbit disappeared. We hunted and hunted for it. Then one day we happened to look down a deep well in the yard and there was my poor rabbit. We fished it out and I buried it with great ceremony. If you will come with me I can show you the spot where my rabbit is buried. One remembers things like that so vividly.

Did you know that I used to trap animals when I was a little boy? On our farm of 120 acres there were lots of holes made by little animals, especially around the strawstacks. Every winter I would set out some traps, look at them once a day, take out any animals that had been caught, skin them, cure the hides, and then sell them. Do you know how to cure a skunk skin? I will tell you so you can do it next time you trap a skunk. Take a shingle—a wood shingle—and whittle the thin end to make it rounded, sort of like the prow of a boat. Now skin the skunk. Cut around the hind end and legs just enough to be able to pull the skin back over the body and the head, then cut it loose as close to the head as possible. Do *not* cut down the belly. Trim off all fat; careful, don't puncture the skin! Women won't buy furs with holes in them. Finally, slip the shingle into the skin, inside out, and stretch it real tight. Hang in the air until thoroughly dry.

Now you can sell it. Do you know that sometimes I got as much as 85¢ for a skin? You see, when I was your age, fathers didn't give allowances to their children. We earned money instead. One way I earned a lot of money was this: My father would give me a little pig which I would feed every day and keep until it weighed about 250 pounds, and then sell it. And it didn't cost me anything to feed my pig because it would eat garbage. Of course I had to collect the swill from Mother's dish washing pan and the scraps from the table and carry them out to the pig. Boy, I was really wealthy with all that skunk and pig money. On one occasion I was able to buy myself a new bicycle.

Be sure not to tell anybody, but one time I was visiting my grandparents and set a trap by the river expecting to catch a mink. A mink skin would make me rich. Next morning when I went to get my mink what do you suppose was in the trap? A chicken! I hid the chicken and didn't tell a soul.

My brother Merle and I sure had an interesting experience in school one day. On the way to school, instead of walking down the road—do you always ride? My goodness!—we cut across the fields to tend our traps. At one of the strawstacks we had caught a nice skunk. It was really beautiful. Black with white spots. The kind of pelt that women used to like to have fur coats made of. So we emptied the trap in the usual way and went on to school. It was a bitterly cold morning, probably below zero.

When we entered the school room we walked right up to the red hot stove to get warm. Do you know that that skunk had sprayed our clothes and we didn't know it? Out in that cold fresh air we had not smelled anything. But standing by that hot stove, whew, jiminy crickets, you should have seen the kids hold their noses. What do you suppose happened? The teacher yelled at us: "Now you go straight home, change your clothes and take a bath, and don't you dare come back here until you smell different."

I'll tell you the best way to bait a trap in order to catch a skunk. You take a male skunk and cut out his testicles. Now split them open and rub the parts onto the plate that triggers the jaws of the trap. You will be sure to catch a skunk. But don't give this secret away because we don't want just every boy to know this special way. Especially don't tell Peter.

But Matthew, I really think you ought not to trap any animals. When I was a little boy in Kansas there were lots of animals and the few that we trapped didn't hurt much. And when you are growing up on the frontier you follow the customs. Coyotes and skunks would catch chickens and eat them. So when you saw a coyote approaching the chicken yard, you would run and get a rifle or shotgun and shoot it, or at it. Nobody ever thought it wrong to shoot them.

In fact, the farmers in our neighborhood would have occasional roundups of coyotes. Our township was six miles square, and so made a nice area for a roundup. On a selected day the farmers would line up along the outer edges of the township, and at a given signal begin to walk toward the center, making lots of noise as they walked. When the men from the four sides came into the center, the coyotes and hundreds of jackrabbits would be cornered. There they were shot. To get rid of them. So they wouldn't kill chickens. Also turkeys, lambs and calves. The farmers didn't realize that coyotes also kept mice, rats, and vermin under control. While the men were hunting, the wives and children would come to the center with huge quantities of food. So here were all the people of the township celebrating the hunt and having a gay time.

Things are so different today. When you went to the Gulf for a vacation last year, did you see the whooping cranes that winter there? Did you learn that there are only about 40 of them left in the world? Because people have killed so many. The governments of Canada and the United States had to step in and protect them or they might all have been killed. Just last week, for the very first time ever, a whooping crane laid an egg while in captivity. Maybe more will do so. But it is nip-and-tuck whether the whooping crane will survive or become extinct. Just think of all the birds, animals, insects, fish, and trees that have become extinct. Forever.

But once in a great while, something that was thought to be extinct is found alive. From where I sit I can see a tree that I planted about five years ago, a Dawn Redwood. Everybody thought it was extinct. It had been identified in fossil form, so the scientists knew that it had once existed about 30,000,000 years ago. In 1946 a professor from the University of California traveled to central China to inspect a strange tree that had been discovered there. It was a Chinese coniferous, deciduous tree, Metasequoia Glyptostroboides, popularly known as Dawn Redwood. He brought home some seeds and cuttings and began to propagate the tree. As a result, we can now buy the trees in certain nurseries. I have one and it is already more than thirty feet high.

In 1965 when I was in London, I visited the Museum of Natural History where one can see all kinds of animals, fish, and birds that once lived but are now extinct. I asked to see the skull of a Toxodon that Darwin had found in South America and had sent to the Museum. As Darwin tells the story in his book, *Journal of Researches*, he was riding his horse one day when, stopping at a ranch, he found this huge skull, similar to that of a cow, but much larger. It was propped up against a fence and the men on the ranch had used it as a shooting target. Darwin recognized it as the skull of an animal that had been extinct for perhaps 100,000 years. So he bought the skull and sent it to the Museum. I said, "May I hold it in my arms"? So the curator lifted it out of the case and let me hold it. The poor Toxodon, not one still living. Isn't that terrible?

In 1960 I was driving across Montana, north from Yellowstone Park, and found some bones in the bank of a creek. It was near White Sulphur Springs, where I had been told to look for fossils by a curator in the Museum of Natural History at Denver. Denver has a very fine museum with exhibits of the skeletal remains of rhinoceros found near the border between Colorado and Wyoming. Did you know that we once had rhinos in North America? Lots of them. I took one of my bones from Montana to a paleontologist at the University of Michigan and he identified it as the shank bone of a prehistoric camel. Camels lived there during the Miocene period.

Granny and I visited Kenya and Tanzania in 1972 and drove through the wild country to see the animals. We saw great herds of elephants, giraffes, rhinos, hippos, wildebeestes, lions, cheetahs, buffalo, and many other kinds. In this part of Africa they still live just as they used to everywhere in the world.

But roads are being paved, and lodges built, so now tourists by the thousands are constantly driving among the animals. Pretty soon they will become tame, just as in a zoo. You should go there before this happens, because within a few years man will have penned up all the wild animals, never more to roam in freedom. Like the buffalo in the United States.

These nations are, however, doing their best to control the poachers. Do you know what a poacher is? Men who slip in among the herds and shoot animals in order to sell the ivory and hides. The natives have always hunted animals for food and skins for clothing; but now the poachers sell their plunder on the world market which is insatiable. If left to their own devices, soon most of the animals would become extinct.

Until recently we had passenger pigeons, millions of them. But people thought it fun to shoot them, and now not a single one lives. The last one died on September 1, 1914. The United States is trying to get the fishing nations to regulate the capture of whales. At the rate at which the Russians and Japanese are killing them—for oil—there soon may not be any left. The United States also makes it illegal to import certain things made of animal skins—alligator, for example, in order to discourage the killing of the animals. Wouldn't it be terrible if all of the alligators, whales, elephants, and cranes were killed off, so there would never, NEVER, be any more?

Some animals, such as the dinosaurs, may have become extinct because the food supply wasn't sufficient (that is only one of several theories). This could happen to people. The problem of population growth relative to the utilization of natural resources, including foods, but also oil, water, and minerals, is becoming acute. Maybe, if we don't find solutions to these problems, men will diminish in vigor and even cease to exist. Not right away, of course. But we should be looking ahead to understand the consequences of our acts.

So Matthew, tell all the children at school, and all other people, not to kill animals, or dig up plants, or hunt bird's eggs, unless they have a good reason. And tell all the kids not to pollute the water or the air, or to waste food, or to burn more gas than they really need. This is the way you can help ANIMALS, BIRDS, FISH, TREES, WILDFLOWERS, AND OTHER THINGS, TO KEEP LIVING. Also PEOPLE.

GRANDFATHER

May 12, 1975

Dear Peter,

So you're going to Canada again this summer. Will you do some fishing? It's too bad that the fishing isn't really as good as it was when we first began going there—when your father was a little boy. We always caught fish, huge ones, every time—bass that would weigh 2 ½ to 4 pounds, and pike. That is not a *fish* story.

But the most fun I've ever had fishing was on the farm when I was your age. We had a natural drainage through the farm that was grown with slough grass which stood about two feet high. In the spring of the year when it rained heavily the river would back up into this grassy area. A couple of times the water covered every inch of our farm, and also got into our cellar. We had an awful time getting rid of it, and the smell. Whew! Hold your nose.

Well, when the water was in this grass the fish would part the grass as they swam. So I, with pitchfork in hand, would spear it. Only my feet got very sore from being in the water every day for a week or so.

Another way to catch fish was in the corn field. We practiced dry farming, which meant listing a field when we planted corn. Do you know what listing means? We had a machine called a lister that had moldboards on both sides of the plow share which, when inserted in the earth made a deep furrow with a ridge between each two furrows. The seeds were dropped and covered in the bottom of this furrow. As the corn grew, we used a cultivator to turn the ridge gradually back into the ditch. This way the corn was kept well mulched and the earth retained moisture. Otherwise it would have been too dry to raise corn in that part of Kansas.

Do you get a picture of a big field made up of ridges and furrows?

When the river began to run over this field, the fish, going from one furrow to another would have to cross a ridge, and in doing so its back would stick out. So I would chase it with my pitchfork and capture it. Peter, don't smile like that; I'm telling you true stories. Don't you think I swim funny? Sort of like a dog. I never had any training such as you all get today. There were no swimming pools, the school didn't have any, and there was nobody around to teach swimming. We swam in the Solomon River. I learned to swim in an old river bed which had been left dry when the river changed its course. But when the river flooded, this bed would fill with water and remain as a lake for several months. While Dad was cultivating the corn, I would paddle in this lake. By clutching a board under my chest I was able to swim and presently I was swimming without the board.

Incidentally, it's just too bad that you don't have a field of corn to cultivate. You ride down row after row of corn, with the team of horses doing all the work. You just guide them a bit in turning around at the end of the row. The rest of the time you sit there and think. About things. About everything. And you daydream about all kinds of nice things that might happen to you. You can compose poems, or sing, or declaim, or what have you. Don't you think it's a good idea to learn how to amuse yourself? As Rodolpho, singing his love song to Mimi, said, "In dreams and flights of fantasy, and castles in the air, I am indeed a millionaire."

Back of the scratching shed where the chickens were fed when the snow lay on the ground, there was a grove of black walnut trees. One of them had been sawed off leaving a nice stump. I used to climb up on this stump and deliver orations—sort of like Demosthenes who orated on the shore of the Mediterranean, only I didn't put pebbles in my mouth. The only audience was chickens. When I had finished some rooster would shout "cock-a-doodle-do," and the hens would happily chime in with, "kak, kak, kak." When Demosthenes orated, the fish just clammed up.

Which reminds me that when I make a speech sometimes I am so intent in thinking ahead to my next topic that I forget what I am saying. That is real embarassing. However, I find that if I pause for a moment, maybe wipe my forehead as though I were hot, but all the while thinking back to where I was, I can recover my train of thought. But if I don't succeed, I just say calmly, "I've lost my train of thought, but this is the main point." Most people won't even know if

"ROME WAS NOT BUILT IN A DAY."

you don't get back to the exact place where you were. My friend, Billie Leiserson, a skillful labor arbitrator, had a trick of pretending to light his pipe when he wanted to hold the attention, but also reflect on how to steer the discussion further. He was very deliberate and so all eyes were on the pipe to see if the tobacco would catch.

This discussion of fishing and swimming makes me think of bathing. Do you know how I used to take a bath? I'll tell you so you can do it that way—if you want to. First, on Saturday night you heat up a lot of water in a kettle. Then get the big tub in which your mother washes the clothes (or does she?), put it in the kitchen, pour in the hot water, then some cold, close the door, take off your clothes, get in the tub—kind of hard to get your legs in all at once—and with plenty of soap, because you have a whole week's dirt on you, scrub yourself. If you don't you will stink like a pig. Now you need a good rinse. The method is real neat. Easy as pie. All you have to do is get a bucket of cold water, lift it over your head, and let 'er go. Actually you could let Matthew dump it on you if you wished. Of course, in the summer you could jump in the horse watering tank, but in the winter you would first have to break a hole in the ice.

Did you know that sometimes it is good to smell bad? When you go to school, hang a bag of asafoetida around your neck and you won't catch any diseases. Just try it. My father used to wear it when he went to school. It works because it smells so bad nobody would come near enough to you to breathe germs in your face. A wonderful idea; keep people away from you because you stink.

Speaking of watering tanks, let me give you a bit of advice. Never stick your tongue against an iron pump handle when it is covered with frost. It will stick and off will come the skin of your tongue. NEVER do that.

GRANDFATHER

September 15, 1977

Dear Matthew,

I know that you are in school now. I always liked school, but I didn't like getting ready. Mom would call, "Algo, have you washed your neck and ears"? Why wash my ears? I could hear OK.

I started school earlier than kids do now; in fact one year of school was over before I turned six. I remember how the teacher, Mike O'Grady, came to our door one day to ask if I was going to school. Mom said, "yes." He was making the rounds of the houses to meet his pupils. Can you imagine teachers doing that today? Or do some of them?

I went to a country school, just one room, heated by a round bellied stove. The teacher would arrive early, bring in a scuttle of coal, and start a roaring fire. Where we kids could warm our hands and noses. We all had to walk to school. I had only a quarter of a mile, the school being on our farm, but some, the Heath boys, for instance, had to walk two miles each way. This was in central Kansas where it was real cold and snowy in the winter. Don't you think you are lucky to be driven to school, and in a nice warm car? And not be pestered about your neck and ears?

We sat at school desks and had to ask permission to leave. Two fingers meant going to the outhouse; one finger to the big dictionary. We sure fooled the teacher on that one. She thought we were studying. Actually we often went to see what note had been left on page 374. One day a note from Loretta read: "Come up Sunday and we will fuck." She knew a lot more about the birds and the bees than I did.

We used the outhouse as an adjunct classroom—at least that was where Will Berrigan, an older boy, taught us about masturbation. One day when we boys were all crowded in there, fascinated by Will's performance, the teacher, Fred Delaney, rapped loudly on the door and said: "Do you boys live in there?" Whereupon we sheepishly filed out.

The one-room school served all eight grades. Actually it was not graded and anyone could go as fast as he was able. I was reading in the third grade reader by the end of the first year. We went to the front of the room to recite so I could hear everyone. I learned a lot from listening to the older kids and at the end of seven years I passed the county eighth grade exams. However, I was so young that my parents kept me there one more year. Even so, when I went to the high school the next year, I was the youngest member of the freshman class.

When my father was a boy, he studied the McGuffey Readers. They included lots of good literature and many moralizations, such as "waste not, want not." Over 100,000,000 copies of McGuffey were used. I have a complete set, reprinted by Henry Ford, who autographed the first copy for me. I think these readers made a strong impact upon the thinking and habits of the American people. The readers I studied were much the same as McGuffey.

We had lots of fun at the country school. The group was so small that in nearly all the games everyone got to play—baseball, fox-and-geese, sliding down straw stacks in the snow. On the way home we would throw stones at the glass insulators on the telephone wires. Why do boys like to throw at things? How long is your school year, Matthew? Ours was seven months and always ended the last of April. This was because the farmers needed the help of their sons and daughters all through the spring and summer. The month of May, for instance, was a busy time for cultivating corn, making hay, and putting out a big garden.

The public school was the one institution that brought everybody in the community together. We had a monthly "literary society" at which people contributed poems and essays they had written or memorized. And one of the most enjoyable features was the monthly paper which was made up of anecdotes about various people in the community. Everyone knew it was just for fun so there was much laughter.

A second major event was the box social to raise money. Each woman would make up a dinner and put it in a box, artfully deco-

Last day of school, 1905

rated with tissue paper and ribbons. The boxes were not marked so a man never knew whose box he was trying to buy. The auctioneer raffled the boxes to the highest bidder. Some of them might go for as much as $5. What a disappointment when you discovered that you paid that much for the box of some old maid and then had to eat with her! But everyone was a good sport and the food was usually super.

    The last day of school was a big neighborhood social event. A program was put on by the kids. Following this, at noon, a long table was set up on saw horses, covered with table cloths, and spread with food. My goodness, you should have seen the food. Always heaps of fried chicken, hard boiled eggs, home-made pickled peaches. Lots of pies, such as fruit pies. Cherries, Mmmmmm. Then banana cakes. In layers, with banana slices and a sprinkling of black walnut kernels between each two layers, and icing made of genuine egg whites. Help yourself boys. All that you can eat. After lunch there was a final ceremony—taking the group picture. All those well fed faces. What community spirit. What a happy event.

After country school I went to high school three miles away in Solomon. It was a small school with five teachers. My class had ten students, and eight remained to graduate. One day our class decided to organize and elect a president. Guess whom they chose—the youngest and greenest member of the class! I think everyone knew each other so well, that they picked someone nobody knew any bad things about. So there I was having to preside. I found it quite exciting. I guess I did all right because they reelected me in each of the remaining three years.

The most stimulating experience I had was in debate. The state university encouraged the high schools to have debating teams and to participate in a statewide contest. First we debated local high schools; then, if we won, on to the Congressional district and the state semifinals and finals. I was on the team for two years and each year we won everything up to third place in the state. The people of Solomon got so excited by our victories, they raised funds to build a special auditorium for the school.

I did well in my studies in high school and in the end was valedictorian. I also got a college scholarship. But I really think I got more personal value out of the debating than from any other thing. It was what I needed to overcome my diffidence, and our successes helped me to gain confidence in myself. I learned how to study a problem intensively and how to speak extemporaneously from a platform.

Our courses of study were the college-preparatory type—of necessity, the faculty being so small. But also the public high school was the successor to the academies whose purpose had been to prepare students to go on to college. In my day only about 10% of the youth went to high school; and they tended to be those who were the "smarter" ones, and who were not content to stop school in order to become farmers, or clerks in a store, or what not. Today, virtually all youth go to high school. Thus it becomes necessary to give attention to subjects that are practical or vocationally oriented. But it is too bad that so many kids who are intellectually able, do not get encouragement to go into courses that are in the liberal arts and sciences.

I went on to college, but not without difficulty. It had not been the tradition in my family to attend college; my parents didn't discuss this possibility with me, and had no money for the purpose. So I messed up the first year by staying out a while, and then going to a business college. It was associated with Kansas Wesleyan University, so I was able to use my scholarship. There I did quite well, and after completion, at age 18, got a job teaching commercial subjects in a country high school. While on this job, I resolved to go to the state university, but shortly after entering the university I had to quit. The first World War had started and all the young men were enlisting. So my real start in college had to await the end of the war.

After World War I, veterans did not get college-going bonuses; but I had saved money during the war. Indeed, I worked my way all through college, graduate and professional schools; seven institutions, ending at Harvard. It took 14 years.

In retrospect, it is clear to me that I should have continued into college right after high school, but at the time I did not comprehend the value of doing so. I had very little counseling about my abilities or my potential development. As a consequence I lost much time—for example, by learning secretarial and bookkeeping skills instead of diving into intellectually challenging materials. For a long time I scorned the idea of writing, failing to understand that intellectual development comes through acquiring vocabulary, expressing oneself, and developing one's reasoning skills. It was after age 40 that I discovered that I could write for publication; and as a result I have published ten books, four booklets, and perhaps two hundred journal articles, chapters in other books, and survey reports.

So, Matthew, you and Peter, and the Pratt girls, all have this wonderful opportunity—to go to a first class school, with your parents' full support, with excellent counselors, and with your tuition and expenses all paid. Just think how much better you can do than I was able to do.

GRANDFATHER

February 12, 1975

Dear Ilya,

Thank you for correcting my spelling of weird. My mother, your great-grandmother, would have a fit if she knew that I loused up a word. In her day they had district and county spelling matches as incentives to learn to spell better. One year while she was in school, Mom won the championship of Saline County where we lived. Actually I think I spell pretty well—until one of my grandchildren catches me up. We had regular spelling drills the whole time I was in grade school.

Maybe that is why I thought I would never want to be a teacher. Teachers were drill masters. Or was it because all of the kids in my day talked about the teachers behind their backs and often said nasty things about them. I remember one teacher, a Miss Whittel, whom we didn't like, so one day a bunch of us kids cut down a thorny hedge tree and started dragging it into the school yard. We were going to thrash the teacher. She saw us coming, came rushing out of the building yelling at us, "Where are you going with that hedge tree"? Whereupon we turned tail and dragged it back where we had cut it.

To my surprise I became a teacher. I'll tell you the story. When I had graduated from high school, I went to business college for a year, and then looked for a job. I had two offers. One was as a helper in a lumber yard—doing office work and waiting on customers. It was attractive to me because I liked lumber, and it was a good business. The other job was as a teacher of commercial subjects in the Rawlins County (Kansas) High School. It paid $75 a month whereas the lumberyard job paid only $60. I had pretty well decided that I wanted to go on for more college, but I needed to work a while to save money for the purpose. Since the teaching job paid the most, I accepted it.

At the end of the year I announced that I was going back to college. Whereupon the high school kids circulated a petition throughout the county asking the Board of Education to be sure and keep me, and to raise my salary enough to entice me to stay. An amazing number of people signed it. The Board invited me to stay and raised the salary to $90 a month. I stayed. Now I think this was foolish because it set me back a year in college, and then the war came on and set me back still more. But at the time I was flattered at what the kids had done and the response from the parents. I have the petition among my treasured possessions. Dreaded thought, I got a kick out of teaching.

After two years (1915-1917) I did go back to college, this time to the University of Kansas. But war had been declared, I felt patriotic and quit after one term, and was gone for a year and a half serving in the army.

In January 1919, after the armistice, I was discharged from the army and immediately enrolled in K.U. In the spring of 1920 I took the state examination for certified public accountant. During my two years while teaching at Atwood, I had taken correspondence courses in accounting—this on top of what I had learned in business college. The examination was difficult and lasted three days. The man in charge was the chairman of the Economics Department at the University. I had not known him—although I had taken some courses in economics—but during recesses he talked with me. He seemed impressed with the fact that I had studied accounting enough to take the exam, and also that I had taken some courses in law at Georgetown School of Law. One day he asked me if I would consider being a departmental assistant in economics, grading papers and helping the professor of accounting. So there was another invitation to teach, although in a rather menial capacity. Grading papers, of all things!

Shortly after returning to college, I had obtained a job part-time with the Edgar Car Seal Manufacturing Company in Lawrence. The company made steel seals for freight car doors. You see, there is much stealing from freight cars and there is always a question of whether the stuff was really stolen or whether the company that loaded the car just claimed that they shipped more stuff than they actually had. So the insurance companies wanted some way to tell whether things had really been stolen when they were asked to pay the claims. Car door seals were invented.

There were two principal types, the Tydon and the Edgar. The Edgar was a slender piece of steel about eight inches long with impressions in it at two-inch intervals. When the door was closed, the steel strip was slipped through the hasps, then three of the two-inch lengths were folded into a triangle and the fourth strip folded back. Anyone opening the car door had to undo the seal but the dents in the wire caused the seal to break. Thus the thief could not replace it. The thief wasn't caught but the claim for damages was fixed on the right party.

All of this was very interesting to be a part of. I kept the accounts, wrote letters, filled out sales bills, and so forth. Another interesting thing about the job was that during lunch hour I would take my sack up to the loft over the factory and eat with a paleontologist, Charles Sternberg, who had his laboratory there. He was mounting huge fish taken from the chalk cliffs of Western Kansas.

But in spite of how interesting my part-time job was, I was flattered by the offer from the university and accepted it. So there I was back in a kind of teaching situation. But wait until you hear what happened! I think I was born under a lucky star. That summer I was following a threshing machine to earn money for college when one day I got a telegram that read something like this: "Professor Ferguson has resigned to accept a job as Professor of Accounting at the University of Pittsburgh. Do you think you could teach two of his classes"? I wired back I could! That was a lot of brass because I had never had a real university course in accounting. However, I had taught American History in high school and had never actually had a course in *it*. What had happened was that I had read lots of history and in high school had asked permission to take the final exam in American History just to see if I could pass it. I had made 100!! So I taught it at Rawlins and of course learned a lot more.

So there I was suddenly a regular instructor in the Economics Department of a university. And because of lousing up my education, I didn't even have a bachelor's degree. I taught the courses in accounting and business law. In the meantime I also studied and worked out my degree in law. The task was easy for me, and I liked it. Later when the Alumni Association polled alumni about who they thought the best teachers at the university were, some alumni named me.

Well, I taught at K.U. four years and then went to Harvard for some graduate work. I had decided definitely by this time that I wanted to practice accounting and law in subjects where they overlapped—taxes, estates, trusts, administrative laws and procedures. During the first year at Harvard I received an offer to return to Kansas as an Associate Professor, which was a nice promotion, but which I did not accept partly because the salary was not too high, and because I wanted to try professional practice for a while.

While at Harvard I received an enticing offer on the Harvard staff. Here is how it happened. A professor, William Morse Cole, gave our class a problem to solve—and also gave us the answer. It was in the mathematics of annuities. When I worked out the problem I got an answer that was different from the one that Professor Cole had given us. This surprised me very much, yet I thought I was right. So I stayed up half the night studying and restudying the problem. I proved over and over that my answer was correct. The next day in class, all other members had found the answer that the teacher had given us. I still thought I was right. So I asked permission to step to the blackboard and demonstrate my solution. I did so and the professor agreed that my analysis was correct. What had happened was that there were two possible answers to the problem and not even the teacher had discovered one of them. The answers were ratios and the correct ratio depended upon which base you chose.

Well, I got two rewards from the extra effort I had put in. I learned something about original approaches to thinking—that is, always think a problem through yourself, and then prove your answer to yourself; and the professor offered me a job beginning the next year as his assistant. This was flattering and if I had accepted I might have worked my way up to being a professor at Harvard. Many young people would give their eye teeth to be granted this opportunity. But I was venturesome and had a lot of self-confidence at that point, and decided that it was too long and confining an effort to go through the treadmill of becoming a professor at Harvard.

A few years later, 1936, when I was president of Antioch College, I attended the tricentennial celebration of the founding of Harvard. While seated in my academic robes on the platform, I glanced down to where the Harvard faculty was gathering and spotted Professor Cole. So I jumped up and went down to say hello to him. We chatted for several minutes and then I resumed my seat. Months later, I was a speaker at the Dayton Harvard Club and during the program a film of the celebration was shown. When the camera focussed on the Harvard faculty, there was Algo Henderson squarely in front of the camera! So I will go down in history, documented by film, as a professor at Harvard. One seldom can eat his cake and have it, too.

One day at Harvard, the Assistant Dean of the Business School, Deane Malott, called me on the phone and asked if I would go for an interview with Arthur Morgan, President of Antioch College, who was looking for a teacher. "I'm not interested in teaching." He cajoled me into making an appointment nevertheless. So I took the tube to the Parker House and talked with Mr. Morgan and his assistant, Helen Greene. Morgan told me the story of what he was trying to do at Antioch and Miss Greene, a delightful Bostonian type, represented it as a fascinating place.

Morgan suggested that I set up an office for practice in Dayton; the college encouraged its faculty to keep in actual touch with the practical world. They were so persuasive that I asked if I could get my wife so that she could hear about the place. After lunch we talked again for a long time. I found Morgan and his ideas inspirational. He had great charisma. It also interested me that he had attended college for only one term at St. Cloud State College, Minnesota, and so, in a way, his background resembled mine. I had learned a lot "by doing" which seemed the heart of the Antioch idea.

So, in one day my whole future got shifted. I accepted his offer of an associate professorship at a considerably higher salary than the one at K.U.—$3100. Also with the freedom to practice part time in Dayton. I did maintain an office there for a year or two in partnership with Denton Magruder, representing a Chicago firm, Frazer and Torbett. But I got so busy at Antioch that I could give the office no attention. So there I was in a teaching job again.

In late August, Anne and I arrived in Yellow Springs a little ahead of school opening so that I could prepare for my classes. I went to see Mr. Morgan to discuss more specifically what I was supposed to teach. I had barely sat down when he said he had an idea for an art bronze foundry that he wanted to discuss with me. He asked if I would investigate the idea and recommend to him whether to launch the project. We talked about this so long that we never did get down to discussing what I would teach. I did, of course, teach for a few years, but my first job turned out to be to study bronze foundries and get one started at Antioch. Thus, from the beginning of my career at Antioch I was an administrator. Shortly I became business manager, dean, and president.

That is the way I got into education, first in high school, and then in college. I had said I wouldn't choose this vocation, and then worked in it for most of my life. And I liked it very much.

I think that part of the reason why I began to like teaching when I had said I wouldn't was because people told me I was a good teacher. People respond to praise, don't you think? This morning while I was driving to the village, I listened to a radio talk show. The man was asking people to call and tell him about good teachers they had had. A lot of kids called and described teachers that they thought were especially good. The man read all of the names of these extra good teachers. I thought that was a wonderful idea. Just think how good it would make these teachers feel. And since they will feel good about teaching, they will try to be even better teachers in the future. It pays to say nice things about people. Say it to them or so that they will hear it.

GRANDFATHER

III

Pen portraits of three persons whom you grandchildren never knew, but whose genes you have inherited.

June 7, 1977

Dear Ilya,

Did you know this is my wedding anniversary, June 7, with Anne Cristy, your Grandmother? If she were still here, we would be celebrating our 54th. It was a church wedding, followed by a reception at the Cristy home in Albuquerque. She was a lovely bride, and had prepared an elaborate trousseau, so she had lots of nice new dresses. They would look funny now because the styles have changed so much, but they looked great at the time.

After the wedding we took the Santa Fe night train for Colorado Springs where we stopped to see the Garden of the Gods and the other sights; then on to Denver with similar objective. Next we stopped at Solomon to visit my folks. It had rained heavily and the river was in flood. So much so that Dad had to meet us with horse and buggy rather than the automobile. In those days the roads were dirt, so in rain they became terribly muddy. Also there were places in the road where the river had backed across the road and it would have been dangerous to try and drive a car through. So Anne got a first hand taste of the old horse-and-buggy days down on the farm. After a little visit, we went on to Chicago where I entered the summer session. So we had a whole summer of honeymoon.

We needed it, for our courting had been largely by mail. I was on the faculty at K.U. and also finishing Law School. She lived in Albuquerque, but was teaching in high school at Holbrook, Arizona. I had met her in 1916 when I spent a few weeks in New Mexico. She sang in the choir of the Presbyterian Church, why I don't know because she didn't sing especially well. One Sunday Hi Waters, a friend of mine, pointed her out, saying she was an unusually nice person. So I began to look at her with different eyes. Her brother, E. J., worked some at the YMCA where I was staying, and I had come to know him well. I played tennis with him, and in doing so borrowed Anne's racquet. I also walked her home from one social. However, I wasn't there long enough to start anything.

During the winter of 1918-1919 I was in the Army, and one day to my surprise I got a letter from Anne Cristy. She said she thought she should write to some boys in the Army, and E. J. had suggested that she write to me. So without realizing the consequences we began to exchange letters. They were on an intellectual plane, and I began to appreciate the quality of her mind and the types of interests she had.

We didn't meet again until 1921. I was taking the famous Model T trip to San Francisco, and arranged to visit her at Long Beach where she and her father and mother were spending some time at the beach. I remember she was very beautiful with a large broad brimmed hat that set off just right the delicate lines of her face. We spent a lot of time together, lots of it on the beach. After that things began to get more serious. I visited her at Christmas time and also in the summer of 1922. So we decided to marry.

It took a little time to work out adjustments, especially relating to sex since neither of us was experienced. But it doesn't take long to learn when you are in love.

We spent a year at Lawrence where I had become an Assistant Professor of Economics and Commerce; then went to Harvard for a year. To get there I bought a second hand Ford Model T, and a bed that fitted over the seats. At the farm I bolted a red board to the front and rear fenders so the running board of the car would hold cooking and camping stuff. Dad gave us an old hay stack cover that we used as a side tent in which to dress. We started out gaily enough, but in crossing Missouri, I had to change tires three times—and repair them of course. It took three days to get across that one state.

Our journey took us through Ohio, then north by way of Canada, the Adirondacks, Green and White Mountains, and finally to Cambridge. On a brow of a mountain in Vermont I was enjoying the beautiful green sweep of the valley, bordered by tree-shrouded hills, when Anne remarked: "How monotonous!" "What!" "Nothing but green." Obviously none of the delicate shades of lavender, yellow, red, and brown of the painted deserts. In Cambridge we sold the car; I was in graduate school, street cars were available, so what use would we have for a car?

Anne Cristy

    Anne was a very modest person, but I learned that, although she lived at home, she became quite active at the University of New Mexico where she majored in Spanish and French. She joined Phi Mu which gave her a better social situation than she had living at home. She became editor of the senior annual; she was elected to Phi Kappa Phi, honor fraternity; and she was the valedictorian of her class. After graduation, she taught in high school for three years at Holbrook, Arizona.
    During our years at Antioch College, she became very active in the community and in college affairs. For several years she was president of the League of Women Voters. She served on a committee that reorganized the village government. During the whole time I was president, she was president of the faculty women. In these positions she was always working for the best interests of the group and of society, and in a completely unselfish way. And she was very intelligent about her programs.
    We did a great deal of entertaining—visitors to the college, faculty, students, trustees. Each September we had an all inclusive reception for the returning faculty and their wives and husbands. We

made a point of always having all members of the senior class each year to dinner. Anne was very effective at planning and managing, also hosting these social affairs.

In the earlier years she also taught Spanish at the college, but this was interrupted by the coming of Joanne and Philip. By the way, did you know that your mother's name is a composite of Alg(J)o and Anne?

Anne received a bit of shock when I proposed moving on to New York State, but took only a moment to say OK. I had been going to Albany for several weeks and had become quite engrossed in the reforms being undertaken there; she had not had this preparation. I had been so busy I had not fully communicated my enthusiasm for what we were trying to accomplish in New York. I was also fed up with the chore of money raising at Antioch, and I was reaching age 50 when all men seem to have a restive period. In retrospect I am sure we made the right move, although after 22 years involvement in Antioch it was hard to leave.

We were in a high state position, so were immediately drawn into the social swim where we made lots of friends. Anne continued her League of Women Voters interest, and presently was elected to the State Board in New York.

After three years we moved to Michigan. We found Ann Arbor a delightful place to live, and again made good friends. Once more she became active in the League of Women Voters, and shortly was made the president. She worked hard on state and local issues. Indeed, she was so consumed by an effort to get a revision of the State Constitution that she neglected to get her regular gynecological exam, and it may have been this delay that resulted in the cancer infection having penetrated the lining of her uterus before it was discovered. Anne also became secretary of the Women's Faculty Club. We entertained a lot, especially our graduate and postdoctoral students and their wives. This activity meant a great deal in creating fine morale in the department.

During one year Anne had a temporary appointment on the faculty of the University of Michigan—to fill in during a leave of absence—to teach Business English in the School of Business Administration.

We had an unusually nice time the summer before she was stricken. I taught at the University of Colorado, and we would take our lunch and some reclining chairs into the mountains nearly every day. Also trips to other places such as the Rocky Mountain National Park. After summer school we toured through the parks: Yellowstone, Glacier, and Waterton; and then drove east on the Canadian Transcontinental Highway. Taking the boat across Lake Superior, we continued to Appegesamok Nodin where we ended our vacation.

In November, 1960, she discovered that she had cancer. Operations, radiation, chemicals, nothing stopped the growth. She passed away January 13, 1962. A few weeks before you were born. I received a huge number of letters from her friends and admirers. Several memorials were created in her name—books at the library at Gore Bay, Ontario; funds at the League of Women Voters, the Presbyterian Church of Albuquerque, the University of New Mexico, and the American Cancer Society; also a book fund at Antioch College set up by Joanne, Philip, and me.

Because Anne had been so helpful to me at Antioch, and so prominent in village affairs, I though it was appropriate to scatter her ashes under a young oak tree in Glen Helen.

When tragedy strikes, we must know how to turn the leaf and begin a new page.

Maybe this letter will help you feel acquainted with your Grandmother Henderson even though you never saw her.

GRANDFATHER

March 7, 1974

Dear Matthew,

Did you celebrate your birthday yesterday? You must have been five years old. I guess I was five once upon a time, but I do not remember it well. I do remember at that age sitting on the lap of my Grandfather Robert Henderson on the front porch of his home. He had a long beard; I suppose he never shaved.

Do you know that my father, your great-grandfather, was born on March 5? Almost the same day as your birth date, only a century earlier, 1868. He died on March 9, 1947. He was a nice man—would you like to hear about him?

His name was Calvert Columbus Henderson. Everybody called him Cal. He was born on a farm near McConnelsville, Ohio, son of Robert and Mary (Rowland) Henderson. My grandparents had had

Robert Henderson

Calvert Ella Algo Bertie, 1898

nine children, then there was a lapse of five years before Dad was born. One can speculate that they had decided not to have more children. Suppose they had really stopped, where would you and I, and the rest of us be?

Robert's father was George, his mother Mary (Glenn), who was born in Donegal, Ireland. George Henderson's father, also named George, had migrated from Northern Ireland, landed at Philadelphia, then moved farther west in Pennsylvania. Isn't it too bad that there are so few family records. I would like to know why they were in Ireland, for they were Scotch. I theorize that they were part of the Scotch who were moved from Scotland to Ireland by James VI of Scotland (James I of England—son of Mary, Queen of Scots) around 1600. Philip has the boards of a walnut chest that was used by the Hendersons to move some of their personal effects from Ireland to the United States.

Cal was brought from Ohio to Kansas when he was eight. Although his father had been a farmer, he had run a nursery near Zanesville just before they moved to Kansas. I have his pruning knife. When I was a boy we had ten acres of fruit orchard and beautiful shade trees, a very unusual thing for that part of Kansas. Robert had brought the trees with him. Dad later bought a lot of peach trees. He and I used to pick peaches and cherries and peddle them in Salina. We would drive along the streets in our spring wagon, calling "PEACHES, PEACHES, CHERRIES." And women would come running. Dad always sold nice ripe peaches and asked a fair price, so the women liked to buy from him.

On October 19, 1893, Cal was married to Ella Cora Donmyer. My sister, Beulah, has a copy of the wedding invitation. It must have been a big wedding because they got all kinds of presents. I remember several large, much decorated oil burning lamps, and beautiful china and glassware. Just think how valuable they would be now, but the lamps vanished long ago. We have a mantel clock that Robert and Mary gave to the newly weds and it still runs well. Jean and I have put in it a card saying that we want you to have it some day, so take good care of it.

I don't know how Dad and Mom got acquainted, but they had gone to the Salina Normal at the same time—maybe they had planned it that way. It seems probable that Dad's older brother, Jacob, who became a lawyer, and had married a Dorflinger, neighbor to the Donmyers, got Dad involved in the romance.

Dad and Mom raised Silver Laced Wyandottes. When I was in Salina recently, Beulah showed me a box full of prize ribbons they had won at shows. I brought one home because I remembered it well. We had a cockerel that Dad and I thought was unusually good (I had learned how to judge chickens), but it was disqualified at the local show because of a tiny white speck in one earlobe. We still thought it was good, and so sent it to the State Fair at Wichita. There it took second prize in the state.

Dad liked horses and always owned several. Earlier he had had a fast trotter and a racing cart, and I remember him driving up and down the road going liketysplit. At one point he also had a pacer. Do you know the difference between a trotter and a pacer? A pacer moves both feet on one side at the same time and in the same direction, whereas a trotter alternates the feet on the two sides. A pacer needs special training and glides along more smoothly than a trotting horse. Dad took excellent care of his horses, currying them, brushing them, and feeding them well. When I was about eight he began buying me ponies. One was a bit frisky and the moment I got on its back it dashed under a tree and brushed me off. I was disgraced! Later I rode ponies to high school, three miles away. A pony is lots of fun.

Dad was a good farmer and proud to be one. He introduced a type of Russian hard wheat into the area. He was the first farmer to use a manure spreader. Our family was the second in the vicinity to have an automobile. Dad was an alert community worker, perpetually on the school board and its treasurer; he served as Township Treasurer; and as a Trustee and later Elder of the Presbyterian Church.

I think of my Dad as a very kind man, always in good humor. I think he never punished me. On the other hand, I now wish that he had helped me more with the kinds of problems boys have, such as going to college. He was very permissive, almost too much so, and I had to figure out so many things by myself.

Wouldn't it be nice if you could know your great-grandfather? I remember all of my grandparents, and also a step great-grandmother. Wasn't I lucky?

GRANDFATHER

March 6, 1975

Dear Alex,

The information about what you read in school was much appreciated. I was quite impressed. One hears so much about deficiencies in the reading programs of the schools that we become concerned about deterioration of the schools. However, you are getting a much better education that I got.

You write especially well. By this I mean you are analytical and not merely descriptive; you discuss ideas, thus going beyond describing activities; you are thoughtful, and you express your thoughts in phraseology that communicates with your correspondent.

You should see the Magnolia tree just outside my window. It is loaded with blossoms, gorgeous pink blooms. The rose bushes—fifty of them—in full view, are sprouting new branches decorated with fresh green leaves; just beyond the fence the pine trees are showing their new yellow-green buds; and the creek is alive with croakers busily squawking. Isn't spring wonderful? All this burst of energy taking place just in front of me! All I have to do is to be observant.

You asked me where in Alsace our Donmyer ancestors came from. The Donmyers (then called Dormeyer) came from the Dukedom of Nassau, which was situated between Phals, Zweibucken and Alsace-Lorraine, in the villages of Drulinger and Assweiler. When our ancestor, Jacob, came to America he was listed as being from the Palatinate which is the same general region. The Donmyers were German but of course Alsace has been conquered by the Germans and the French alternately several times.

Jacob came the first time on the sailing vessel Phoenix, landing in Philadelphia in September, 1749. Since he was born in 1734, he was only 15 years of age when he migrated. He had to sign his name with an X.

Jacob may not have been able to write, but he was good at some things. He fathered eleven children, and it has been estimated that his descendents now number 3,600. The name Dormeyer got changed to Donmire by one school teacher, and to Donmyer by another. Dormeyer meant "gatekeeper," so maybe I should really be Algo Gatekeeper Henderson.

The doctor who presided at my birth was Dr. Algo Donmyer, a

cousin of my mother's. He told my father he would give me a suit of clothes if they would name me after him. I have often been asked about my distinctive name, which I didn't like as a boy. I once asked my mother to change it to Joe Dan, whereupon she reminded me that was the name of a notorious drunk who lived up the river from us. Every Saturday night he went past our house asleep in his buggy, the horse knowing the way home. That ended that. But later, Dr. Algo got drunk one day, fell off a train and was killed. I never got my clothes.

Are you a Patriot? Well then you will want to know that Jacob served in the Pennsylvania Militia during the War of the Revolution. So you can belong to the Daughters of the American Revolution—a prize some women would give their left hind leg to have. You are one of a privileged few. This is the organization that prevented Marian Anderson from singing in Constitution Hall in Washington. When our Constitution was adopted, Negroes were slaves, so why should a Black sing in Constitution Hall? Might desecrate it. Well, Eleanor Roosevelt, a marvelous woman, came to the rescue and arranged for Marian to sing from the Lincoln Memorial steps.

Don't you think that superpatriots of the flag-waving sort are the greatest? During World War II at Antioch I defended some conscientious objectors to war and also made some pronouncements on free speech. Some people decided I was a Communist—who ever heard of Communists favoring free speech? At any rate when I made speeches, there was a patriotic woman following me and taking notes. If you want to join the Daughters of the American Revolution, go ahead; but don't follow me around or I will snap at you.

Jacob settled in Whitehall Township, Pennsylvania, and in 1763 Indians raided the settlements, murdered 18 persons, and destroyed the houses, barns, and fences. So the settlers got together and destroyed the Indians. Sounds like Vietnam. Thereupon the Donmyers moved to Lancaster County.

However, the fear of Indians didn't stop just then. It was still much in the air a century later in Kansas when the first Donmyers arrived. Indeed, in my boyhood, the only good Indian was a dead Indian. But Indians didn't kill any Donmyers at New Cambria. They would walk into a house without knocking, and take anything that appealed to them. They didn't know the Commandment "thou shalt not steal." For that matter, the guy who stole some rings from us didn't know it either.

The house the Donmyers first built in Kansas wasn't really designed to keep out strangers. No locks, bolts, or burglar alarms—isn't it too bad that we now live in more civilized times? When my grandfather, Lewis Junior, came to Kansas in 1869, he and a brother, with their families (15 in all) lived in a two-room house. My mother was only a few months old. When Lewis erected a house for himself, with logs hauled from the Solomon River, he caulked it with cakes of dirt on the inside. Lewis Senior had a similar house, and one day a snake came wiggling through the dirt; whereupon his wife made him build her a real house. Lewis Senior lived to age 87. Too bad he didn't live to 90, because then he might have had 20 children instead of 18. Just think how many more relatives you would have had.

Lewis Jr. and Sarah Custer Donmyer

When my parents were married, they had a nice house, but entirely nonmodern. No electricity, gas, running water, central heat. I often think how hard Mom worked. She did all the house work, all the laundry, much of the chicken care, some of the garden work, and she made many of her own clothes and most of those for the two girls. She processed and preserved much fruit and vegetables, and helped with the butchering of meat. When we had chicken for dinner, she had to start with stripping off the feathers and cleaning out the guts. The purebred poultry and egg business was really hers, although Dad took much interest in it. Mom advertised in farm journals in Kansas and Iowa; we packed the eggs in candy buckets and shipped them, by parcel post, to several states—and none was ever broken!

Mom was highly intelligent, the county spelling champion, she spoke two languages, had been a country school teacher, played the piano beautifully, taught piano, and made patchwork quilts and goose-down bedding. She gave herself to her family and to the homestead. A generation later she would have become much better educated and would have been relieved of many of the physical burdens of managing a home. It is pleasant to be nostalgic about the "good old days," but they had their drawbacks.

One grows up taking his mother and father for granted; only later as one looks back can he see clearly what wonderful people they were.

GRANDFATHER

PS: Benjamin Franklin was a wise man; but in 1751, two years after our ancestor, Jacob, migrated to this country from the Palatinate, Franklin is reputed to have exclaimed: "Why should the Palatine boors be suffered to swarm into our settlements, and, by herding together, establish their language and manners to the exclusion of ours?" In retrospect, this sounds funny, doesn't it?

IV

Making a Model T Ford out of junk, building log cabins in Canada, a box seat at the start of World War II, tea at the House of Commons and again in Kyoto at the tea house of the First Shogun, writing for UNESCO—by relating my adventures to you grandchildren I hope you will want to do more when traveling than just hopping from one Hilton to another with packaged tours.

March 29, 1975

Dear Ilya and Peter,

    Now who do you suppose went on an Easter vacation to a place where it snowed all the time? And to a place that had tornadoes that knocked all the windmills down, uprooted trees, and blew sand in your face? Why Ilya and Peter, of course. You both must have had an exciting time. Tell Granny and me all about it.

    I got to thinking about trips I had taken, and although I usually didn't pick a place where there were tornadoes, or snow and sleet storms, I did think of one unusually exciting trip that I had made when I was a young man in college.

    In 1921 four of us, Bruce Campbell, Marshall Havenhill, Ed Philleo, and I, decided to make a trip from Lawrence, Kansas, where the university was, to San Francisco—by way of Yellowstone Park and Seattle. Only we didn't have enough money for train fares, there weren't any planes, and we didn't have an automobile. In those days no student in college ever thought of having a car as everyone does today. They couldn't afford it and it wasn't necessary. Why do all kids think they have to have an auto of their own the moment they turn 16? I think they should spend their money on more important things, such as getting a better education.

    So we decided to get an automobile for the trip. Only we didn't have enough money to buy a new one. We looked around for a second hand one and found it, a really good one. And we got it cheap because it had been in a fire, only $100. Now we had a fine car. A Model T Ford.

    It would have run fine except there was something wrong with the tires. They had been so badly burned that they wouldn't hold any air.

Crossing the Kaw

Well, we bought a set of new tires from Monkey Ward. Now we had a car with brand new tires, one that would run like greased lightning.

Only there was another little matter. The fire had burned the top off. This was in the days before hard tops had been invented; the top was made of fabric, so naturally it burned. We couldn't pay for a whole new top, so we bought some top fabric from Monkey Wards and made the top ourselves. Now we had a really grand car, as good as new, with new tires and a new top—new from top to bottom.

There was another small item that wasn't so good. The body had been so badly burned that if you leaned against it the side would cave in. This was a real predicament because we couldn't just be under a new top, on new tires, with nothing to sit on all the way to San Francisco—by way of Yellowstone and Seattle. So we had to buy a body. We didn't have enough money for a new body. *What* were we to do? Well we went to a dump heap where people had left old cars, and, what do you know, we found a Model T that had a body just the kind we needed. How much? The junk dealer said he'd take $20. OK. So now we had a new body. Almost. The paint was scratched and marred, and full of rusty spots. But we smoothed up the surfaces, and then painted the body. Now we had a classy looking Ford that would run like a jack rabbit. And people would think we had paid a thousand dollars for it.

Then we discovered one more thing. The engine block was cracked. However, we cranked it up—it had a crank on the front end and you had to stand in front of the engine and turn that crank around to get the engine started. Charles F. Kettering had not yet invented the starter. Sometimes you had to crank and crank and crank, all the while making adjustments with the magneto and the air mixture. And maybe examine all the spark plugs to see if they were still attached to their wires, or fool a bit with the carburetor.

I remember one night when another man and I drove in an old Model T Ford from Lawrence to a town about 50 miles south of Topeka to judge a high school debate. On the way home, about 11:30 at night, with the temperature −2 degrees, our motor suddenly stopped. There we were, freezing, a long way from nowhere. We got out of the car and started fiddling with the wires and adjustment screws, a couple of college teachers turned mechanics. Would you believe it, after about twenty minutes we got the darned thing started and then sailed merrily home. Not even our toes froze. Well, to get back to the subject, our new motor ran in spite of the crack, and it didn't spout oil or water, so we decided to just leave it alone. Our beautiful car, with fresh paint, new tires, new top, and all, tearing along the countryside with a cracked motor. But it worked and that was all that mattered.

Then horrors, we discovered something else amiss. The steering gear was defective. It would function OK while going forward, but when we attempted to back up the wheels would wobble one way and then flip over and wobble the other way; we never knew whether we would end up on the road or in a ditch. But if you are driving to San Francisco, by way of Yellowstone and Seattle, who wants to back up? All you need to do really is to keep going forward. To get there. If you drove backwards you might land in New York! We decided that the steering gear was fine. Now we were all set to leave on the journey.

We didn't have enough money to stay in motels. Furthermore there were none, so what good would money have done? We found a couple of tourist camps enroute, but no motels. So we borrowed a tent and a few pots and pans, and bought a box of matches. We took along a small hand axe. Now we were all set. Except that we needed sleeping bags. Only people didn't use sleeping bags in those days.

What you did was just take an old blanket and roll up in it at night. Can you imagine all the tramps that used to come for work in the harvest fields each carrying a sleeping bag? Don't be ridiculous. How could they steal rides on top of the freight trains if they were lugging along a sleeping bag and a lot of blankets, towels, soap, and all that sort of thing? The freight trains used to have maybe a hundred men riding on top of the cars, and of course they had to be near the middle of the top or they would be blown off by the wind. If they had sleeping bags they would bump one another off the train. But sleeping bags didn't exist, so what am I talking about? No, we each had a blanket and that was enough.

After leaving Lawrence, we drove to the farm at Solomon, stayed over night, got the last full meal, and borrowed some blankets from Mother. Our new auto, with its bright and shining paint and new top and tires worked fine. So off we went. To San Francisco. By way of Yellowstone and Seattle. First we headed north toward Nebraska. None of the roads was marked and so we had to feel our way. But we thought the best way to go west was to go north first.

Near Delphos, Kansas, a couple of small white dogs came barking at us and ran after the car. I don't blame them for barking, although why should they bark at a beautiful new car? Well, anyway two of the boys picked up one of the dogs and decided to take it along. I didn't like the idea, but recently had come from the army where taking things that didn't belong to you was common, and I did not protest. So here we were, four men and a dog, sailing along in our new car at 30 miles an hour.

That was about as fast as you dared drive over dirt, mud, and washboardy roads. We encountered dust, or mud, and lots of chuckholes that one tried to dodge to avoid hitting them with a big bump. We went straight north into Nebraska. Not having any road markers, such as I 90, or US 64, or anything else, we didn't always find the right road. In cutting across Nebraska, we came to some sand hills, where the sand in the road was real deep. We got stuck. Stuck real good. However, our car was not heavy as they are today, so three of us got out and pushed while one man steered; and the dog sat in the back seat like a real kingfish. By pushing hard for a couple of hours, we finally got over the hill and we were again on our way.

We had barely turned west on the main road through Nebraska when something happened. We were running along at the fast clip of 35 miles an hour, when suddenly we hit a big bump—kerbang! It was a chuckhole. You see, it being a main road east and west, it had lots of travel on it. Not only automobiles, but buggies, hay wagons, horse riders, and cattle. So the road was rough, real rough. Our new auto sagged badly in the rear end. We got out and looked. Sure enough our rear spring was broken. There we were in the middle of Nebraska with a broken spring, and a long way from town.

Now the springs in those early days were made of a series of loose leaves, and what had happened was that one leaf had broken in the middle where a long bolt held the leaves in place, and had dropped out. So naturally the car sagged. But there were some spring leaves still in place. Not like today, when a spring breaks it is all broken. You just call the AAA and they send a tow wagon out, and in a couple of hours you are on your way. Well, there were no AAA services, and I'm not sure there were any tow trucks. But we could drive the car. It was new and in good shape, and all that. Except it had one spring leaf missing. So we shifted weight by putting a third man in the front seat, leaving the dog and one man in the rear, and drove slowly to the next town.

There we bought a spring leaf to fit the spot. Also a stout rope. Next we drove around until we found a tree that had a limb sticking out front from its trunk strong enough to hold an automobile. We ran the car under the limb until the rear end was even with it. Then we slung the rope over the limb, attaching one end to the body of our car. Two men lifted on the car and two pulled on the rope. The dog just stood and watched. He never once on the trip earned his bones or travel. But he was nice company. With the car hoisted in the air, it was easy to unbolt the spring, fit the new leaf in place, rebolt the body to it, let the car down—and there we were not only with new tires, new top, new body, but part of a new spring. And it had cost us only $1.50 for the leaf. In a garage today this repair would cost $50, maybe $100.

I'll bet you can't guess who was elected chief cook? I knew how to boil water and fry eggs, which is more than the others knew. Anyway by the time we got to Wyoming we had our first real problem. How do you cook sage hen? You see, we went hunting and shot some sage hens. But we didn't know how to cook them. So I heated some water to a boil and put them in it; and after a bit I greased a frying pan and browned them nicely. Yum, yum, yum. Have you ever eaten sage hens? Or prairie chickens, or grouse? WELL, where have you been all your life! When you go camping out in the Panhandle, or in the

Big Bend, don't you hunt sage hens or pheasants and have a great feast?

But I would advise against cooking prairie dogs. Have you ever seen a prairie dog? They used to be thick all over the prairie; we had lots of them on our farm. Only we never tried to eat them. But now we thought we should try them. We fried them like the rabbits that we shot. Do you like rabbits? They are good. Especially in the winter. You skin them and then hang them up where they will freeze over night being careful to hang them so that dogs or coyotes can't snag them. But these prairie dogs, were they tough! Ugh! We went hungry that night. You see, we didn't have much money, so we would go hunting for our meat. Two fellows would hunt while the other two would gather some wood, start a fire, and get the water boiling. Like the Indians, we would eat whatever the hunters brought in. Only we never fried rattlesnakes.

Making camp wasn't too difficult, because all we had to do was lay our tent on the ground and throw our blankets on it, thus making a nice, solid bed. If there was a stream nearby we would wash up a bit. In the mountains we nearly always camped where there was water, beautiful scenery, and gorgeous odors of pine trees.

I should mention that we broke our springs three more times—just think how smooth our roads are now. But they were easily fixed. Kind of annoying though to be sailing along at 30, sometimes 35 miles an hour, and kerbump, out goes a spring leaf. Then the rope stunt all over again. And the dog just sitting and watching.

Out in the middle of Wyoming we were jumping from chuckhole to chuckhole, much like a jack rabbit runs, when we passed a truck stranded beside the road. About a mile farther along we passed a man trudging along the road. We though he was the truck driver going to the next town for help, so we invited him to ride with us. He got in, squeezing the dog over to find room to sit.

When we got to a town, we asked him where he wanted out. He said he didn't want out, he wanted to go with us. Have you read Huckleberry Finn? How Huck and Jim on their raft, sailing down the Mississippi, rescued two men who came running to the river with a possee chasing them? And then Huck and Jim were unable to get rid of them? They were con men. Well we had picked up a tramp and couldn't get rid of him. Not only was he taking advantage of us, but he made it very crowded for the dog, and he stank.

We drove on and shortly came to Hell's Half Acre, a spectacular badlands of brightly colored earth needles. Naturally we all got out to see the sights. While there we devised a scheme to dump our unwelcome guest. Ed, an expert shot, set up a marker; then fired at it a couple of times, hitting the bullseye each time. Then we all climbed back in the car. At the next town we said to the tramp, "Get out!" He got out.

Beyond Casper we hit our first large mountains. Going up one of them we ran out of gas. We really were not *out* of gas, we still had some in tank. But in these old cars the gas tank was under the front seat and the gas ran into the carburetor by gravity. When you were on a steep hill, and the front of the car was high and the gas tank low, the gas wouldn't feed into the engine. Lots of people knew the trick of turning the car around and backing up to the top of the hill. But if we had tried to back up, we probably would have run off the road and crashed down the mountain side. Because our front wheels would have flipped and flopped. Now we were really stuck. The next gas station might be 25 miles or more away.

One of the boys got a brilliant idea. Eat the tomatoes in a tomato can, siphon some gas from the tank, unscrew the plug in the top of the carburetor, and with one man steering and another pouring gas into the carburetor we could climb the hill. In those days the autos had wide running boards, like buggies, to serve as mud guards. So Bruce lay on the running board and poured gas, while Ed steered, and we went merrily up the mountain. And as luck would have it, at the bottom of the mountain there was a gas station.

We were surprised when we came to Thermopolis because as one might expect from the name, it had hot springs. Also a tourist camp and HOT SHOWERS, and a place to wash clothes!! We stayed two days, mostly in the hot showers. Once again we and our clothes were spic and span, and the dog smelled as sweet as a rose.

We also enjoyed Cody, named for Buffalo Bill. This was a special treat because we had seen Buffalo Bill at the circus, with his white pointed beard and riding his white horse. We thought that the Cody Museum which was devoted to the Wild West was good. We found a bakery and bought a couple of pies. We smacked our lips.

Then we headed for Yellowstone Park. In our beautiful car now affectionately called Laverne, after a girl we knew. Laverne was purring along like a cougar when suddenly she coughed and stopped. We were out of gas. And it was at least 20 miles to the Park. Where to get gas? We were sitting disconsolately beside the road when a GAS truck came along. We frantically waved him down and told him if he would give us gas to get to the next station, we would give him a piece of the finest pie he had ever tasted. He said "OK." So we lost a part of the pie, but we were able to travel again. Fortunately there was a gas station at the east entrance to the Park, so we could climb the 8000 foot entrance with a full tank.

At the altitude at which we camped we nearly froze—we with our skimpy blankets. We kept our clothes on, built a big fire, but in the night I got up and sat in the car. Brooooo!

We were already so high that we decided first to take the eastern trail which goes above 9000 feet. After driving a ways we ran into snow. The snow kept getting deeper and deeper. We had new tires, but no chains. The road was too narrow to turn around. Then all of a sudden, round a sharp curve, came a snowplow headed right for us. Hey, you!! They saw us in time or we might have been scooped to the bottom of the canyon. Now how do we get past the plow? After conferring, the plow men decided that if they hugged the wall and we drove at the very edge of the cliff, we could pass each other. We let the fellow who stands on his head on the edges of cliffs, Ed, drive. We made it OK. Then we had nice sailing because the snow had been plowed off.

I had heard lots about the Park because Uncle Than Henderson used to drive a coach with a four-horse team taking tourists on sight seeing trips. Later he did that in Yosemite. He was one of the early stagecoach drivers, and I thought a very romantic figure. One winter he and his wife, Laura, remained all winter in Yellowstone, in charge of some properties. Imagine being snowed in for several months, along with the moose and the bears. So I was fascinated by all that I saw, as were the other men. Have you seen the geysers, the mud vents, the yellow gorge, the fishing bridge, the herds of buffalo, and all that? You must, and of course you will. Only take more than one blanket. Even in July.

We stopped for a while on the fishing bridge and dropped some lines into the water. We could see trout swimming around as thick as fleas and we easily caught a mess for dinner. In a later year I tried again, but there was not a fish to be seen or caught.

In Montana we came onto some primitive roads through the mountains. They were not only strange, they were also beautiful. They wound through the woods, virgin timber, trees with huge trunks, much gorgeous shrubbery, countless wildflowers. But the roads were dirt, mere trails, because not many people traveled there. It is quite different today with so many automobiles, with all that smog and the cars crashing into each other. Have you read about Fairbanks, Alaska, since the oil pipe line boom? This fair city on the banks of the Tanana River, with air that was almost pure oxygen, is now one of the worst smog covered cities in the nation. Imagine that—Fairbanks, which you think of in association with snow, and glaciers, and forests, and Eskimo dogs. Now as bad as Los Angeles. In our mad rush for oil.

Some of the Montana trails were quite steep, with sheets of water running across them. So they became real slick. So slick our tires wouldn't hold. Of course, we had new tires, or at least they were new before they had run over the chuckholes of Nebraska and Wyoming. But we had no chains. Well, there was nothing to do but for three men to get out and push. So there we were, chauffeur and slaves, pushing the dog up the mountains of Montana.

In Idaho we had a pleasant surprise near Coeur-d'Alene, an irrigated, vegetable region. Being a bit fed up on rabbits and potatoes, we now could be vegetarians. We were just in time for ripe strawberries. We picked some; guess how much we paid for them. You could never guess. For 25^e we got six—6—boxes. We gorged ourselves on berries.

I forgot to mention that on one of those steep mountains we ran out of gas again. This time we really found a solution. We should have got a patent for it. We cut a hole in the lid of the gas tank, fitted the tire pump to it, and pumped the tank full of air. Do you know the magic that followed? The air pressure forced the gasoline into the carburetor. So, when we ran out of gas on a hill, as we did again in Oregon, one man just sat on a front seat and pumped air into the tank. Just like autos now have—air pressured gas tanks. We had thought up a million dollar invention but alas didn't know enough to cash in on our luck.

In Seattle I as chief cook bought a large ham thinking it would taste wonderful after all those rabbits. Just then Bruce came up and asked what I was going to do with it; it was not cooked. I hadn't thought of that. I guess there were no cooked hams as there are today. So back to the rabbits.

In Portland we toured the city admiring the gorgeous roses, the like of which we had never seen before.

When we got to San Francisco, we settled our accounts. The car had cost a total of $232.22. We charged ourselves each $40 for depreciation, and turned the car over to Bruce and Marshall for the trip back to Lawrence. Our other expenses are interesting in the light of today's prices: food, $45.30; gas, $66.90; oil, $9.34; repairs, $25.82; tire replacement and repairs, $25.10; and miscellaneous, $29.61. We had left Lawrence on June 9 and arrived in Oakland July 2, 24 days. Our expenses other than the cost of the car, had averaged for each of us $50.52. Total. Not per day, sillies.

After sight seeing, calling upon Aunt Laura, Uncle Than's widow in Sunnyvale, and Uncle Sib and wife in Fresno, I traveled by bus on South.

While in the army I had been corresponding with a young woman whom I had met in Albuquerque in 1916, and now she and her parents were spending the summer in Long Beach. It seems they went there for their summer vacations. Naturally I went to see her. The beach was clean, the surf musical, the swimming great, the sunsets romantic. She was as nice as her letters had sounded. Her name was Anne Cristy. By the way, Ilya, isn't your middle name Cristy? How come?

GRANDFATHER

July 28, 1975

Dear Alex,

You think you are the real cat's whiskers to be going on a backpacking trip to Colorado. Well, that is wonderful. But don't think you are the only one who ever did that. Let me advise you about some of the best places to go, based upon your Grandfather's personal experiences.

I am most familiar with two spots in Colorado—the Rocky Mountain National Park (Estes Park), and the region just west of Colorado Springs. Both are beautiful, and include some of the highest mountains in the United States.

Estes Park is a favorite recreation spot for people from the plains of Kansas. To escape the summer heat and winds. In their later years my parents went out there nearly every summer. I started going there when in college. There was a large YMCA camp in Estes, and a cheap place to stay. If you go there be sure to climb the mountain called

Teddy's Teeth. It is a good one for tuning up your leg muscles and lungs. My friend, Ed Philleo, would walk out to the very edge of the 2000-foot cliff and stand on his head. I do not recommend this for you. You can, of course, climb Long's Peak, the highest in Colorado, 14,290 feet. I never made it to the top but don't remember why not.

In 1960 I taught in the summer school of the University of Colorado, sharing an office with Homer Rainey, former president of the University of Texas. Anne and I lived in an old Chautauqua camp in Boulder. My classes began at 7 am, were finished by 10, and then we had the day free. We would put a couple of lawn chairs in the car, head for the mountains, find a spot by a stream, and lunch and read there to the background of water gurgling and birds twittering.

One day we decided to have a picnic in Estes Park. So we invited to go with us Mrs. Marston Bates. Marston was the author of semipopular books on biology, and also editor for biology for the New York Times. He was in Boulder as chairman of a commission that was revising the high school texts on biology—part of the American attempt to catch up with Soviet Russia, they having just launched the first Sputnik.

We had our lunch on the shore of a lake that was so blue you could see the reflections of all of the mountains in it. All five peaks of the continental divide were visible. I began to take pictures, and asked Nancy if she would stand and point to the peaks. She did. I remarked that we could take a picture just like the ones that appear in the National Geographic with some member of the Bell or Grosvenor family in the picture pointing at the subject. Then it dawned on me that she was always called Nancy *Bell* Bates. I said: "You aren't by chance a relative of the Geographic Bells, are you?" "Yes, I am; I'm a granddaughter of Alexander Graham Bell." So I got a picture of the continental divide just as the National Geographic would show it. Of course you know that it was Bell who invented the telephone. Or was this too long before your time?

Incidentally the area west and north of Denver is rich in paleontological interest. North of Denver along the border of Colorado and Wyoming they find skeletons of rhinoceros, which lived in the Miocene Epoch. If you are in Denver, be sure to visit the Natural History Museum where you will see fossilized rhinos, camels, oreodonts, and other mammals and fish now extinct. Strange, isn't it, to realize that they once wandered over Colorado, Wyoming, and Nebraska.

Will you be visiting the Air Force Academy? It has exceptionally fine architecture. Under one of the mountains the US-Canadian Strategic Command has a network of tunnels supposedly invulnerable to attack. Maybe ordinary visitors can't get in, but I was escorted by a general from Wright Field, as his guest in an air force plane.

My prize trip to Colorado was backpacking west from Colorado Springs. Warren Pearson, a red-headed, jolly, graduate student at the University of Kansas and I made our blanket rolls and got food packages at Manitou, and then headed into the mountains. We were aiming toward an abandoned railroad right-of-way and shortly came to it. The railroad had been active in the gold rush days, running from Cripple Creek to Colorado Springs. Grandfather Lewis Donmyer and his oldest son, Clarence, had prospected for gold in this region, but came home empty-handed. In Alaska, any one who had a grandfather in the Klondike gold rush mentions him as a hero. All that I remember being told about my grandfather at Cripple Creek was that one day a bear confronted him in his path.

One day while we were exploring in the mountains we came upon a white-haired, bearded man sitting in the sun in front of his shack. He showed us a tunnel which he was digging into the mountain, hoping to find gold. We chatted a while, then discovered that his name was Clemens. He was a cousin of Mark Twain! He looked just as you expected a hermit to look.

We were a bit late in starting our trek, what with buying vegetables, making sure we had matches, and arranging things so we could carry everything. And we dallied on the upgrade because the views were spectacular—we climbed the ridge slightly to the southwest of Manitou. After a couple of hours it began to rain, which disconcerted us because we were not used to camping in the rain. Late in the afternoon we found an abandoned water tank along the rail tracks. By cuddling close under its rim we found a partially dry spot. We were so hungry that we ate nearly all of our potatoes the first meal—we had expected the food to last three days! Why we carried potatoes I don't know. We were greenhorns, of course. But also concentrated food of the kinds developed during World War II was not available.

The next morning I ached all over. Boy, was I stiff, and uncomfortable. By noon the second day we had arrived on a mesa about 8000 feet high, and discovered a ranch where we could buy milk. It was owned and run by a woman who invited us into the living room. What was our surprise to find the walls completely smothered with books. She learned that we were people who also read books, so we hit it off right away. She not only had milk, but also a stock of groceries; and she was the official postmaster of the region.

We had noticed a couple of cabins along a stream as we neared the ranch house, so we inquired about them. She owned them and they were not in use. "Could we stay over night in one?" "Yes, stay as long as you like." No charge. So we established ourselves in one of the cabins.

That afternoon we climbed Mount Baldy, over 12,000 feet, just south of Pikes Peak. Not a difficult climb. From the top gorgeous views of mountains, forest and several lakes. The top of Baldy is bald. We sat on a big rock and ate a can of beans. Presently about a million red bugs crawled from under the rock and took over. On the way down by a different path, we came to a beautiful lake. On the inspiration of the moment, and having need of a bath, we jumped in. Broooooo! My but it was cold! We got out in a hurry. It's a good thing we did, because two years later, Pearson dropped dead. I've often thought, what if that icy water, at 11,000 foot elevation, had given him such a shock he had passed out right there.

The ranch hands suggested we try fishing and loaned us their equipment. Also one of them was the fish warden, and he winked at us. So we tried. It was really unbelievable. For about three weeks we caught an average of 20 brook trout a day, and kept the ranch supplied. This was in 1922; seven years later, in 1929, after the rail bed had been made into a highway, the Algo Hendersons, Cal and Ella, my father and mother, and Bertie, Oliver and Dale Miller, drove over that road and tried to fish. There wasn't a fish to be found. We had to go to a private fish pond for our dinner. Changes in environment can certainly take place fast when droves of people get access to wild places. Alas!

The ranch had lots of horses and cattle, and they gave us each a pony, saddle, and cowboy chaps to use. One day the owner decided to take a carload of cattle to Denver to sell. She wanted the cowboys to go with her, so she asked: "Would you mind tending the ranch, sell groceries, and take care of mail?" We would do so. We helped drive the cattle to Colorado Springs where the railroad was, and the woman then took us to the post office and Warren was sworn in as Postmaster. We got the mail, some supplies, and headed back up the mountain. This time in style on our ponies, with cowboy hats, chaps and all. No sleeping in the rain under a leaky water tank. No potato dinner. So there we were running a big ranch, a store, the post office, and having the time of our life fishing.

The old railroad ran near the ranch house, and here the rails were still in place. We had discovered a huge patch of wild raspberries up the track a mile or two. And now we found an abandoned section hand car. What is a section car? Golly, you kids don't know nothing. A railroad track has to be kept clean of weeds, the rail ties have to be replaced as they rot, and the rails must be gauged repeatedly to be sure they are level and straight. All this work is done by section hands. They ride to work each day on little flat cars that are either operated by hand pumps, or pushed along by hand.

So we decided to go raspberrying on the flat car. It was a bit of a job pushing it uphill, but we got there OK. After picking a bucket full of berries we got on the car to roll down hill. How to brake the car? By the time it got to the ranch house it would be going like greased lightning. Well, we got a long pole, rather stout, and used it as a leverage against a wheel. That did the trick.

One day we were sailing along down hill, thinking what a glorious life this was, when what did we see puffing up the line but an engine. Great Scott! Imagine having a confrontation with a steam engine on an abandoned railroad, at 9,000 feet, fifty miles from nowhere. Luckily our brake held.

So we had deliciously ripe raspberries bathed in fresh cream, and freshly caught mountain trout every day. Often three times a day.

Time came for the annual rodeo in Colorado Springs and the cowboys decided to enter a pony. We drove to town down a winding mountain road, leading the pony. At the entrance to the rodeo grounds, I, dressed as a cowboy, led the pony to the corral, then the other fellow came in with a ticket he got free for entering a horse. So both of us got seats in the stand occupied by the performers directly over the chute where the wild, bucking animals were released.

After three weeks at the ranch, we had to leave. What an interesting, exciting turn our backpacking trip had taken.

I neglected to mention how I got to Colorado Springs in the first place. I had been visiting Anne Cristy in Albuquerque, and then headed north via the narrow gauge D & RG railroad that ran from Santa Fe to Salida. There were only two or three passengers on the train. I liked to stand on the rear platform of trains so I could see the scenery well. I was standing there while we chugged slowly up this steep grade when the conductor came out where I was and said: "We are nearing the top, and then we start down an equally steep grade. Will you help me keep the train from going too fast?" "What do I do?" "Well, you see that hand brake?" pointing to a long lever with a handhold on it. "You keep your hand on that lever and pull back on it as we near a curve so as to slow the train." So there I stood easing the train down the mountain. It's easy as pie.

GRANDFATHER

February 2, 1975

Dear Peter,

Granny and I have sent you a gift which we got in the Hopi Reservation in Arizona. At a famous trading post founded by Mr. Hubbell. Did you know that when your Grandmother Anne was teaching in Holbrook (1920-23) she went with Mrs. Hubbell to buy rugs, pottery, and jewelry from the Hopis and Navajos? Near Keams Canyon. We have some rugs and pottery that she kept.

A moment ago I was in the living room and saw a deer in the yard. It ambled around exploring things for about ten minutes. One day I saw three of them. They are so graceful; wouldn't it be nice if people were as graceful as deer. Perhaps they could be if they practiced. Hey, why don't you get out on the beach at Manitoulin and practice running like a deer?

Saturday night we went with our Et Al eating club to a restaurant, and then invited them to come here. We showed them our slides of Iguasu Falls and Victoria Falls, the two largest in the world; and then some pictures of our camp in Canada. Showing these pictures made me feel nostalgic. They display ideas and activities that say a lot about my life, especially with my family. You see, I was already a college dean when your father was born, and I was terribly busy— virtually every day in the week. But at camp we could all do things together and have lots of fun. Fathers who work hard should have a hideaway without telephone where they can play with their children and talk with their wife.

I will tell you the story about how the camp got started, and how it was built. In 1930, when Philip was only three months old, his

mother and I decided to go to Michigan for a vacation.
We chose Mullett Lake near Cheboygan. We had a good time, but there were only rock bass fish, the lake was shallow, and the country around had been denuded of its forests. Isn't it horrible the way we let the loggers and the farmers strip our land of its magnificent trees? In central Michigan is a small tract where some virgin pines have been preserved. A thoughtful lumberman did this. We used to stop there to walk among and hug the trees.

The next summer, 1931, we decided to try to find a good place in Ontario. So I wrote to some postmasters in towns along the North shore of Lake Huron and also on Manitoulin Island. Several of them answered. Can you imagine postmasters today doing that? From the names of camp owners they sent to me, I contacted one on Kagawong Lake, Manitoulin Island. After getting details, we rented a cabin for two weeks. It was a new cabin, located in a nice grove of maple trees. The beach was OK except that the man's cows came to it every day to drink and left their calling cards.

While we were there some Antioch families—Mathiasons, Owens, and Magruders—came also and set up their tents in a pasture nearby. We had lots of fun, including one big birthday party for Edith Owen. We bought some chickens from a farmer and fried them, and Eunice Mathiason baked a cake. In those days people carried lots of camping equipment, including stoves, and also staples of food. They lived in tents and cooked on fires made of brush. Every day was a picnic. Today we drive like mad on a freeway, fouled with exhaust fumes, from motel to motel, then tired out plump in a chair and turn on TV. Presently we eat at a fast food restaurant. This is because we are affluent and always in a hurry. The more affluent we get the more we chase dollars and the less we enjoy life. Or so it seems. Maybe you don't buy that? Well, wait until you get the perspective that age gives one.

One day we all decided to go fishing and hired Mr. Wagg to guide us. We went first to the fishing bridge between Lake Wolsey and Bayfield Sound; but the water was too rough to go out in a small boat. Do you remember how angry the waves become when there is a northwest blow? Mr. Wagg then described an inland lake near the Coburn farm. So we went there—Stone's Lake near the second barn. Shortly Mac caught a small Northern Pike. He yelled "a snake!" He was furious because we were supposed to be fishing for the small mouth Black Bass. So we left. Our day seemed to be ruined! But on the way to the cars we noticed a small section of road that had just been graded and asked Hugh Coburn where it went. He said: "to Lake Wolsey." Richard Tappenden of Cleveland had recently bought 80 acres on the lake, built a cabin, and was starting to grade a road to it. We decided to investigate. After a long walk over logging trails in the woods we came to the cabin.

Lake Wolsey was large, beautiful and enticing. Mac and I took off our shoes, rolled up our jeans, and started to wade south along the shore, the others trailing along on the beach. We liked everything so much we just kept going. After a mile or so Mac and I came onto Ed Titus and his father cooking a meal in front of a logger's hut in which they were staying. They owned part of the land and in answer to our questions said it was "great." By this time Mac and I had fallen in love with the place, and on the spot decided to try to buy the tract between Tap's and Titus'. As we walked back through the woods we even picked out places for our cabins—the very ones on which we later built. The Mathiasons were not interested, but the next year the Owens joined us and began developing their tract.

Mac, Hester, Anne, and I stopped in Gore Bay on our way back to Kagawong and talked with the Smith Brothers, owners of the shore. They had 100 acres, including three-fourths mile of shore line. Yes they would sell. "How much?" They held a whispered conference and then said that they got the land in settlement of a grocery bill of $500. We could have it for that amount. We nearly fell over. I immediately asked for a sheet of paper and using their grocery counter wrote an option to buy which the Smiths signed. After we got back to Yellow Springs we sent them a check and received the deed. In 1931, with the depression already being felt, we didn't have money to throw away, but we thought that $250 for each of us in payment for that gorgeous lake shore, and 100 acres of land covered with white cedars of about 60 years growth, was too great an opportunity to be missed. In any event it was just what we wanted.

After getting the option to buy the land, Anne and I sent a telegram to Tappenden asking to rent his cottage for two weeks. He wired back OK. So that same summer we shifted from Lake Kagawong to Lake Wolsey. The Taps had not as yet used the place so it was completely bare. The Magruders could not remain, but loaned us their camping equipment. Coburns hauled us down to the lake in a wagon and later brought us a row boat. We hung sheets as curtains and made beds on the floor. The cabin, built by the Coburns, had been made of green lumber; so after it had dried out there were big cracks in the floor. The mice had a jolly time running over us at night. Also in the early days at camp we could hear the wolves howling at night.

Every day I would row down to our cabin site and during the two weeks I cleared out much brush, staked out a site for the cabin, and dug a well. I also fished and caught bass and pike. The fish were large, beautiful and plentiful. During our first 20 years on the lake, Mac, Billie Owen, and I had many great days on fishing trips. Coming home in the evening, our families would gather on the beach for a fish chowder party. The lake was so clear and unpolluted that we drank the water. How delicious water and air used to be before they became polluted with waste.

During the following winter we had Hugh Coburn build the frame shack that we now use for storage—for $85. The next summer Magruders lived in our cabin while having one of their own built. We fitted the cabin like a trailer, and with a fold-under bed and a not-a-bolt wood stove. Philip slept on a cot and I built for Joanne an upper bunk made of cedar poles and canvas. We got a fish box, set it in the ground, brought chunks of ice from town, and thus had an ice box. The Ocean House, a hotel that has since burned, had an ice house where one could uncover the sawdust and help himself to ice—the same as my grandfather had. We had lots of fun and were always busy. It was quite a change from the grind at the college.

The shack was 9 x 11, and of course we cooked, ate, and slept in it. And also had parties. Usually the parties were held on the beach with a huge bonfire going, and with Mary Magruder leading us in singing "Down By the Old Millstream" or "Out in Arizona." But one night it was so cold and blowy that we all assembled in our shack, about a dozen people. This was all the place could possibly hold, but in the midst of our gaiety in walked the Coburn brothers. We were always glad to see them—they helped take care of our camps—but on this occasion, with a hot wood fire in the stove, and about 15 people in the room, their pungent odor became something else!

During the first few years we would park our cars near the second Coburn barn and have the Coburns haul us to the beach on an old lumbering trail. We then had them build us a road. In determining where it should be, Hugh stood on the ancient sand beach near the barn, sighted to the lake, cleared a path, put cedar poles over a swampy place, then dumped gravel. The road has lasted well, with frequent repairs. But Hugh's sighting was not too accurate. The road departed from the right-of-way, and left a strip of our land on the north side. After the swath was cut through the trees, Hugh looked for the survey stakes and found them. Later he showed them to me and I marked the locations.

Within a couple of years we started to build the bunk house. Ed Titus had had a one-room cabin made, with the logs standing on end. I decided I could do that. So I drew a plan. I used white cedar logs which a farmer cut for us, at 10¢ a log! We peeled the logs and I made a mitre box 7 feet long in which to cut square ends. From the lumber mill in Gore Bay we got boards, window sash and screen; and from the mills making shingles from the huge cedar logs that had been discarded from the lumbering some 70 years earlier. Our cabin cost $60. So then we had a place to sleep—two bunks down and two up. The old shack became the cook house and a refuge from rain and cold winds.

The post cabin is easy to make. Use large cedar logs for the foundation boxing them on both ends with a spiked 2 x 12 plank. Under this structure place flat rocks. On the outer rim on top of the logs, make a sill in the form of a rectangle of 2 x 6 planks spiked to the logs and the end plank. To get the logs level all round, adze them as needed, then nail to their top sides a 2-inch strip, shimming it as necessary to get a level floor. This becomes the base for the floor.

Then make a second rectangle just like the first. Place posts at each of the 4 corners and mount the second rectangle on top. Between the upper and the lower rectangles stand the wall logs, each 6 to 10 inches in diameter, and the window and door frames. But before doing this make the roof structure. Fashion the roof rafters, working on the ground, by making them fit the sill frame. Then they can merely be lifted in place on the top of the wall structure. The sheathing and shingles are easily added. I always let the framed building sit from one summer to the next so it will be well dried. Then I would caulk between the logs on the interior with small cedar saplings, and chink on the exterior with a cement-lime mixture.

Newly peeled logs can become badly mildewed when handled. But if washed with chlorine bleach they regain their silky sheen. It is such a pleasure to lie on your bunk and look at those white cedar logs, which after 45 years look just as they did when they were erected. One of the most satisfying things in life is to create something yourself. What people *do* miss when they do not have this experience! With my axe I almost cut Billie Owen's leg off one day. We built our boat docks by driving cedar posts into the sand, then fashioning a planked walkway on top. I was chopping away one day, standing in water with a wet axe handle, when suddenly the axe slipped from my hands and went flying through the air straight toward Billie's legs. Boy, was I scared. It just missed. Whereupon Billie gave a nervous laugh, "*that* was close!"

We were imbued with the woods and early decided that the out-of-doors should be the living room. We made chairs out of cedar poles and canvas. We built a rock fireplace on the beach and often did our cooking there; also popped corn. And we erected a windbreak out of cedar posts and canvas—the post butts are still there as an archeological excavation would show. Thus with a fire we could sit on the beach late in the evening. Fires look so nice and cheerful at night. Why do people sit in a room at night instead of on the beach with a nice fire? Think of the Northern Lights that they miss.

Presently we *did* build a living room cabin, with logs cut by Carl Slomcke. First I built a fireplace. The whole family hunted rocks on the beach and with these we designed the face of the fireplace. Billie Owen came over one day and asked me how I was going to build the smokeshelf. My grandfather had five fireplaces in his house in Ohio, but I didn't know that you had to have a smokeshelf. So I borrowed a pamphlet on cabin building from Tap and followed its directions for making a smokeshelf. In the woods I found a log with a blazed burn on one side and from it hewed out a mantel with the streak facing the cabin interior. One day Connie Sontag asked if the mantel had caught on fire. I said "no," but I should have said: "yes, about a hundred years ago." This cabin took four years to build and cost about $350.

Started when your father was 1 year old, the camp expanded as the family matured. A couple of other families were admitted to the group, the first being Lillian and Valdie Carlson and their two children. After a while Philip was old enough to plan and build a cabin of his own. We made this one in the Maine style—logs laid horizontally, with a hog-trough of 2 x 10s and 12s standing erect in each corner and into which spikes were driven to hold the logs in place. You don't know how to make a hog trough? It's like a quadrant. Again the whole family worked on the project. Anne peeled logs, Joanne did shingling, and all of us drove nails between the logs to hold the chinking in place. This time Philip split some old cedar logs and made strips to use as caulking in the interior. It is a nifty cabin, don't you think?

Last we built the kitchen/dining cabin. Philip, by now in architectural school, designed it. He also helped to build it, the work running through four summers. The materials cost about $900. One day I saw a pile of birch boards at a farm that had a small sawmill. They were long, some were 14 to 16 inches wide, and all were over an inch thick. I asked what he would take for the pile and he said $25. I bought them on the spot, carried them to camp on top of my car, then stored them so they would dry thoroughly. Later we had them dressed at the planing mill in town.

These were the birch boards with which we built the counter tops and the dining table in our new cabin. Not many cabins have such luxuries. Philip designed them, and I prepared the assembly parts in my workshop at Ann Arbor. The summer we assembled the counter, Charles and Betty Odegaard, and their daughter visited us for a week. In 1974 I wrote to him (President Emeritus of the University of Washington) saying how proud my daughter Joanne, and my daughter-in-law Jerry, were to be able to get meals behind a counter with birch tops, designed by a prize-winning architect, fabricated by a college president, who in assembling the structure had the assistance of a helper who became the president of a large university.

By this time we had electricity. Thus we could put in storage the kerosene lamps, and install an electric stove and refrigerator. How lucky you kids are that you can read by an electric light, reading being one of the principal diversions at camp.

We also put in a power-operated pump for water, which was then piped to the kitchen. And to a flush toilet, outdoors so one could walk to it in the rain, conveniently located among the cabins. But the original privy still stands as an extra accommodation, or an unique experience for those who like to sit with the door open, enjoying the woods that surround it and meditating on the meaning of life. After I had become acquainted with General Eisenhower, I dubbed it the Dwight D. Eisenhower Cabin—out of affection, not disrespect. Somehow it portrayed the same image as Ike, being content with the status quo.

Peter, some people vacation at a resort where they sit around on their fannies, loll on the edge of a swimming pool, and eat and drink too much. I'm glad you like our camp, because there you live in the

Cabin building

Joanne, sailor

Philip, architect

Pratts firing pottery

Hendersons—bass for lunch

woods, play on the beach, swim in a clear lake that has no chlorine in it, hunt butterflies, pick wild raspberries and cherries, catch frogs, dig clay, and make pots which you then fire on the beach, go fishing and sailing, design and make chairs, take pictures of wild flowers and lady's slippers, spy on beavers and humming birds in the Indian Paint Brush swamp, feed peanuts to chipmunks, listen to loons on the lake at dusk, watch the shore in the morning for wild ducks or otters, climb the second bluff, look for rocks, fossils, corals, and polypody, also osprey, herons, and pileated woodpeckers, thread your way through the cedar woods to see the huge logs left when the timber was cut, make apple pies—my goodness, how busy we all are! Maybe someday you will build a cabin for yourself and your family —we left room for it.

One of the principles of living is to be a participant in creating your own life and the life around you. The alternative is to be a parasite, absorbing what others set before you. The creative life is the route to happiness. One of the things I am most proud of having helped to create is Appegesamok Nodin, an Ojibwa expression meaning Land Where the West Wind Blows. Hester suggested this as the name for our place.

Incidentally, the last of the Ojibwas in our region, Indian John, was still living in a shack a bit north of Tap's cabin when we first arrived. I once took him to town with me. Tap has his snow shoes, the remaining relic, except for the cemetary near the fishing bridge, of our predecessors on Lake Wolsey.

On Manitoulin, archeologists have found Indian artifacts mixed in glacial drift, indicating that Indians were on the Island 9,000 or more years ago. Some experts think they date back 25-30,000 years. We have been there only 45 years, haven't we?

GRANDFATHER

February 17, 1975

Dear Peter,

So now you are nine. Your father remarked the other day that his ninth year was one that stood out in his memory. Some great things happened to him that year. He went to Europe for the first time, and spent several weeks in England, Scandanavia, and Scotland; he lived in Palo Alto for several months; and his Uncle E. J. gave to him his Grandfather Cristy's architectural instruments.

The year was 1939 and a gigantic war was threatening. I had a sabbatical year and we had planned to spend it in London, making a special study of civil liberties. At the time of making plans we had no idea that the year would be so exciting. Let me tell you about the European experience. We literally had a ring-side seat for the opening of World War II.

Anne and I thought it would make a stimulating beginning if we would accompany the American Seminar, led by Sherwood Eddy. Because we had the two children with us, we asked permission to join the group only in London and Moscow. This Sherwood permitted us to do.

We traveled by boat, as everyone did those days. On the way over we had about seven days of relaxation, but also daily meetings in which prepared leaders discussed with us some of the political, economic, and social problems that we would be further examining in Europe. One amusing incident sticks in my mind. Eddy explained that we would be meeting very important people, so should always keep our shoes shined. Whereupon we were each presented with a small brush-rag of a size to fit in a pocket, and which we were to keep at hand for last minute shines. Can you visualize 20 congressmen, lawyers, ministers, and college professors and presidents gathering before the door of an office, and everyone pulling the shine rag from his pocket and giving his shoes a brush? For years afterwards I called every shoe brush a "Sherwood Eddy."

It was a distinguished group. I have kept up with only one member, Andrew Cordier; he later became the assistant to Trygve Lie, the first Director-General of the United Nations, and still later, President of Columbia University. Eddy had led such a group for perhaps twenty years in succession, and had contacts in the highest places. His leadership was especially valuable in Moscow where all tourists are in the hands of Intourist. We had the advantages of both services.

An illustration of the kind of conferences we had was the one with Lord Halifax in London; he was then Foreign Minister in the Chamberlain cabinet. We assembled in his conference room around the usual table. Almost immediately, Lord Halifax appeared. A distinguished looking man, tall and slender, his slightly withered arm was somewhat noticeable. He sat at the head of the table and after a few pleasantries, drew from his coat pocket a paper. Then he said:

"Here is a speech written by my assistant which I am supposed to read. However, I know that you are professional men and women and I would welcome the opportunity to discuss problems with you. If you will promise to keep the discussion confidential, and not quote me, I will throw this paper aside and we will just talk." Everyone exclaimed "Yes."

Halifax talked about many aspects of the political situation quite frankly. For example, he told us about negotiations that were taking place with Soviet Russia. One of the things Russia wanted was British recognition of their right to remain in the Baltic States— Estonia, Lithuania, and Latvia. Britain, on the contrary, felt that these countries deserved to continue as independent entities. So the two nations were deadlocked over the issue. Among other topics, Halifax mentioned the problems of the African colonies. He said that the European nations that administered the colonies should find some way to establish an international fund to be used for the economic development of these countries so they would no longer be subjected to the bleeding of resources that had characterized the imperial rule. I came away with the feeling that Lord Halifax was a man of integrity and had a sensible approach to the geopolitical matters that were bringing Europe to a new crisis.

One of the most interesting meetings was with Harry Pollitt, leader of the Communist Party. We had sessions with the leaders of the Liberal and Communist parties, the assistant leader of the Labor Party, and some of the cabinet members of the governing party, the Conservatives. Pollitt gave us a talk on the British tradition of freedom of speech. He cited the phenomenon of his appearance, as a Communist, before us, a foreign group, at a time when war was brewing, yet he could talk freely without restraint or censorship.

During the question period, one person asked: "Mr. Pollitt, you have spoken of the freedom of speech that you enjoy; what freedom would you permit the opposition if the Communist Party came to power?" Pollitt gave a short laugh, as though he were caught in a trap, then answered: "If our party gets the power, as we intend to do, our program for England will be terrifically important. It is essential that it become well established, and hence it will be in the interests of everyone to suppress opposition to the program for the time being."

We had a panel of speakers on "the Palestine question." One side was represented by Malcolm Macdonald, son of the former Prime Minister, Ramsey Macdonald, and himself on the way to becoming a distinguished diplomat in the Middle East. The debate centered on the Balfour proposal to create a Jewish state. Both the pros and the cons were well analyzed, indicating that the British leaders were still puzzled by the proposal, and uncertain what the best course of action should be. At that time none of our group sensed the future importance of the issue to the American people.

I recall that a year or so later, Lessing Rosenwald, head of the Sears store in Philadelphia, asked me what I thought was the solution to the Zionist problem. The question caught me unprepared, and I said that I thought it would be best for the people of the world if they became assimilated, and that Jews everywhere had set a fine example of becoming assimilated nationally but preserving their identity, religion, and culture. This was before the murder of millions of Jews by the Nazis. I did not intend by my answer to take a stand pro or con Israel. What was my astonishment when I was quoted publicly by Rosenwald as opposing the creation of a Jewish state—which I assumed was the position he took.

Among my mementoes of the London seminar is a picture that I took of Lloyd George, the great Prime Minister during World War I. With his flowing white mane, he still looked the part of a man of unusual self-assurance and experience. One of our speakers was Harold Nicholson of later fame as a writer. An event that stood out in the minds of Anne and me was when Lady Astor invited us all to a tea on the terrace of the House of Commons, to which she also had invited several of the outstanding intellectuals of England. Anne was pleased when she was asked to pour the tea.

During these ten days or so, in order to free both Anne and me for the seminar meetings, we had arranged for Joanne and Philip to stay with a woman in Wellwyn Garden City. We took them out on the train. With sinking feelings we watched as they drove away from the station, in a tiny English motor car, top down, with Joanne perched on the back rest, her right hand gripping her broad brimmed hat to keep the wind from blowng it off. The plan of having them out of the city worked well, and they had an experience of their own.

Following the period in London, our family traveled alone because we wanted to go via Sweden where we had arranged to leave the children in a Swedish camp while we were in Moscow. We took the cross channel boat to Esbjerg, Denmark; then the train to Copenhagen. Both boat and train were very nice, but between the islands of Fyn and Sjaelland the train runs onto a ferry to cross the water. As soon as the ferry started, everyone jumped up and ran out of the train. It took us a few minutes to realize what was happening; there was no one left from whom to get information. Then it dawned on us that they were going to eat dinner. So we followed.

Sure enough, there was a dining room on the ferry. But every seat was taken! We waited. After an interminable period we got seats. Not knowing how long the ferry trip was, we were much concerned that the train might leave us. So we gulped our food and then made a run for it. We got on the train, but barely. As if that incident were not sufficient, when we got off the train in Copenhagen—it being then quite dark—a man told us that the hotel at which we had reservations no longer existed! Consternation! Late at night; a foreign city; nospeaka da language. The man offered to take us to a good place, and for some reason we trusted him. The place was O.K.

My memory of Copenhagen is principally of Tivoli. The children and I took a ride on a roller coaster that was the real thing. The dips were so steep that we could hardly catch our breath. But loads of fun.

One day we took the electric train north to Elsinore. I wanted to get an understanding of the adult education program in Denmark, and more especially the plan of education used by Peter Manniche at the International People's College. Manniche received us cordially, and invited us to listen in on his classes. He gave me a copy of his book, *Denmark, A Social Laboratory*, and autographed it.

The plan of education was significant for two reasons: one, it was concerned with the education of all people; and two, the aims were for the cultural, economic, and social development of the people of the nation. In other words, the good of the whole of the people was involved, whereas much of the education in the United States has been focussed on the vocational or cultural education of an individual. Some people think this approach has helped spread the good life widely and prepare for the exportation of products, as for instance, bacon to England.

Going to Sweden we deposited the children at Syljanschölen on Lake Syljan about 100 miles north of Stockholm. The Lynds, famous sociologists, had left their children there the previous year and had recommended the place to us. Anne and I traveled by boat from Sweden to Finland, staying in Helsinki a couple of days. The Scandanavian cities are delightful, partly because they are so clean. I recall on the train north from Stockholm I had carelessly put one of my feet on the opposite seat, something one thinks nothing of doing in the United States. The conductor asked me to remove it. I felt ashamed.

The Finns, of course, enjoy saunas. It was our first experience, and we were surprised at the luxury of the baths in Helsinki—we having a mental picture of the stone-heated sheds where a sweaty bath is followed by a plunge in icy water. We took in everything, as one should do while traveling. Following the sauna and a dip in the pool, I enjoyed a rub down. The woman was very efficient, and since she was about 65, I didn't get any particular thrill out of the nude experience. We made special trips to see some of the elder Saarinen's architecture, including his famous railroad station.

The change from a Finnish pullman to a Russian one at the border was startling. The former was spic and span, with picture windows through which we had been enjoying the scenes; also the heavy fortifications on the Finnish side of the border. The Russian pullman was dark, dreary, cramped. We shared it with a couple of men, although that really caused no problem. The men very politely left the room while Anne and I got ready for our berths. It is surprising how easy it is to adjust to customs such as nudity, or a nonsexist pullman room if one takes changes in stride.

At Leningrad a young woman guide who spoke excellent English-English was at the station to meet us. The guides we had in Russia were always informed, courteous, and agreeable as companions. They seemed to show us freely anything we wanted to see. I had heard about Russian shadows and secret police, so to test it one day, I took my camera into the Red Square in Moscow, and as conspicuously as possible photographed the Kremlin and other buildings. Nothing happened. The customs officers did make all of us get our film developed in Russia, and the processing was poor in quality, alas, but all my pictures were returned.

In Moscow we stayed at the Metropole, and again picked up the seminar group. We did lots of interesting things—the Park of Culture and Rest, a children's camp run by a labor union, a court room, social service agencies, an interview with high officers of the Ministry of Education, and other men and women most of whom, however, ranked below the top echelon. The man from education made us smile because he related how Soviet Russia had extended education to all the people, which was true; but he added that for the first time in history, common schooling was compulsory and free. In the history of Russia, yes indeed. But he was taking in the whole world, ignoring or ignorant of our policy since the days of Andrew Jackson and Horace Mann.

Our most amazing encounter with Russian interpretations of history was at a reception the Ministry of Cultural Relations gave us. The tables were laden with heaps of goodies and bottles of vodka. Eddy sidled up to me and warned me not to drink too much, me a recent emigree from prohibition-minded Kansas! As part of the entertainment we were shown two moving pictures. One was of the first World War when the Bolshevik army was trying to hold the line in the West. The picture showed Trotsky, the Minister of War, ordering the beaten armies to retreat; but at that moment a young officer named Stalin rushed to the fore and led the armies to victory.

The other picture was a portrayal of a collective farm in the Ukraine. It was very romantic, with huge tractor-drawn gang plows, and a beautiful young woman dashing around on a motorcycle as a messenger. Suddenly one of the plows turned up a spiked helmet, obviously a German helmet, presumably a relic of World War I. Then the commentator digressed to say that the Russians were surrounded by enemies and that they should be ready to convert their tractors into tanks in order to protect themselves.

Following the reception we invited the Russians to join us for dinner at the hotel. They accepted, and at the table I happened to be seated beside the young man who had interpreted the films. He had a Master's degree in history from Harvard. So I asked him why the first film portrayed the roles of Trotsky and Stalin so different from that as known from historical facts. Without a moment's hesitation or batting an eyelash, he said: "You know how a painter in sketching a landscape will portray a true and beautiful picture by putting in the authentic elements and leaving out the bad. We know now that Trotsky was a traitor, even then, so we portray him as one."

From a later incident we realized that the German helmet theme showed that this particular ministry was not up on the latest Russian line. We knew from our meeting with Lord Halifax that the Russians and the British were negotiating for a treaty, and somewhere we learned that the Germans, under Ribbentrop, their Foreign Minister, were also in Moscow for the same purpose. About two weeks after the film was shown to us, the Hitler-Stalin pact was announced. The Germans had not only conceded all of the Baltic states but had also agreed to divide up Poland in exchange for assurances from Stalin that he would not move against the Germans when they invaded

Poland. Germany had suddenly been transformed from enemy to friend. A couple of years later, Hitler invaded Russian, but Stalin claimed that the pact had given the Russians a time period in which to prepare themselves for war. What a sadistic business diplomacy can be!

We walked around Moscow freely, and included a visit to a Russian Orthodox Church. It was full of elderly people. The chanting is beautiful, but the custom of kissing the icons by the long line of worshippers was repelling to me. Most repelling of all were the beggars that swarmed over the front steps. Since we saw no beggars elsewhere we decided that they were permitted at the church to cast aspersions on religion.

On the way back to Sweden, we stopped in Leningrad to visit the museums. These museums contain the royal treasures, and some of the finest art in the world. In a way, it is saddening to look at, because it makes so clear the royal pomp and splendor that existed when the people lived in such poverty and ignorance. Such divergence between affluence and poverty leads to revolution. The Russians got one in good measure. So did the French a century earlier. So will we, if we permit too much concentration of wealth and power, with consequent inequalities of opportunity and in the administration of justice.

While dining one evening in the Leningrad Hotel, Anne said: "That white haired man, obviously an Englishman, looks lonesome, why don't we ask to sit with him." This we did, with most interesting consequences. He was Sir Charles Trevelyan, who had been Minister of Education in the Labor Government. On a visit to Russia he was now on his way home to Morpeth, near Newcastle in England. After passing through Sweden and Norway, we planned to take the boat from Bergen to Newcastle. When Sir Charles learned this, he said: "When you get to Bergen, send me a cable giving your time of arrival in England. I will meet you and you must come visit us at our country home for a few days." We did just that, and the week was perfectly fascinating.

But first we stayed in Sweden about three weeks, and in Norway a few days. In Stockholm Anne and I attended a seminar on Sweden, visiting new housing, inquiring into their adult education programs, and visiting museums and castles. Sweden at one time had been a militaristic nation, making invasions far into Central Europe. Today it is a reasonably prosperous, self-contained country, with many enviable features. The Scandanavians seem to have learned how to combine industrialization with a system of distributing the products and benefits to the general run of the people. This makes an interesting and instructive case to study.

We felt secure about Joanne and Philip, but presently Joanne wrote us urgently requesting that they be permitted to join us in Stockholm. The camp was OK and they were well treated, but they were fed up with sour milk soup, none of the boys with Philip could speak English, Philip had not been given the woodworking (sloyd) that we had paid for, and I guess they were just homesick. So we arranged for them to be put on the train and we met them at the Stockholm station.

The Swedes enjoy formality. We were invited to a reception honoring a former Consul General, but always addressed as "General." I introduced Joanne to him and was amazed to see her curtsy—obviously the thing to do!

After an inspection of the ancient Viking boats at Oslo, we took a train across Norway and a boat ride in a fjord. The scenery was magnificent. Then at Bergen we took the cross-channel boat to Newcastle. For the next hour or so it was nip-and-tuck whether the immigration officer would let us into England. We were coming after a period in Soviet Russian, and without too clear a purpose for wanting to stay in England a while. I got so fussed it took me several seconds to recall the name of Harold Laski with whom I had decided to study at London. By this time the British knew how serious the war outlook was. Perhaps it was the fact that Sir Charles was meeting us that finally enabled us to pass through the gate. But Sir Charles was nowhere to be seen. Again we were much concerned. But presently we found his chauffeur who had come to meet us.

Sir Charles' "little summer home" proved to be Wallington, a French Chateau style structure that measured 120 feet on each of its four sides. The stairs we climbed to our bedrooms were from the Tudor house that had preceded Wallington on the same spot. Wallington itself had been built in 1688. It had housed Lord Macauley (a cousin), Sir George Otto Trevelyan, the historian of the American Revolution, John Ruskin, Sir Joshua Reynolds, who had done some of the paintings, and countless other famous people. Now *we* were there, ah ha! Lady Trevelyan was very hospitable, and on August 20, Joanne's birthday, gave her some buttons of historical significance. She had a famous sister, Gertrude Bell, an authority on

Arabic lands and cultures.

While we were at Wallington the Hitler-Stalin pact was announced. Whereupon Sir Charles sent for a panel of civic leaders, among them Julian Huxley, to think about what British policy should be. Probably this had no effect because the Chamberlain Government had got itself into the vortex, and it was late to extricate. Things were daily becoming more serious. We found time one day to go picnicking on the old Roman Wall, which Hadrian had had built from Newcastle across England. I visualize Philip running on the top of the wall. Walls, just like moats and Maginot Lines, crumble when mad men try to settle their differences by fighting.

Other stimulating experiences included a "shoot" and some sheep dog trials. The shoot took place on the moors near the Scottish border where George Trevelyan, Master of a college at Cambridge and brother of Charles, held the right on some 3000 acres. Six gentlemen armed with shotguns, accompanied by a dozen servants, a pack of dogs, and buckets full of lunch materials, gathered at the foot of an imposing hill. The gentlemen, including me, climbed to the brow where we hid behind a series of blinds.

The beaters and the dogs at a signal came up the hill beating, yelling, and barking loudly. The poor birds, scared to death, flew straight into the guns where they were mowed down. I had done lots of hunting in my youth to get rabbits for dinner, but I had never seen or imagined British sport being like this. I was equally puzzled at lunch time when we ate in a long narrow building that had a solid partition in the middle. The gentlemen were in one end and the servants in the other. Since the latter had all the food, they had to keep running around the structure in order to feed their masters. Not quite like the harvest field of my youth where a hungry man was a hungry man whether he was an itinerant tramp or the owner of the land; all sat at the same table.

Sir Charles bequeathed Wallington, and the estate, to the National Trust to be held in perpetuity for the benefit of the people of Britain. It holds many treasures and is now open to the public. One of the items is a huge tapestry depicting the history of the Trevelyans which Lady Trevelyan had taken 23 years to do. Sir Charles gave to me, and autographed, a copy of a book he had written about Wallington.

We visited Edinburgh, the castle where Mary Queen of the Scots had reigned, and the genealogical library. I wanted to check out my theory that the Hendersons were among those moved to Ireland by

James I, but found the task too imposing.

The war situation became more intense with the invasion of Poland by Germany. War seemed imminent since England had a mutual assistance pact with Poland. All Americans were instructed to report to the nearest consulate. The Consul in Edinburgh tried hard to persuade us to take passage on a boat, the Athenia, that was to leave Glasgow within the week. We refused. We had a trunk and a car stored in Wellwyn, and we were not yet ready to give up our plans for the winter.

A couple of days after this boat had set sail, 2-inch headines appeared on all the newspapers: ATHENIA SUNK. It was the first passenger liner torpedoed by the Germans. Fortunately, *we* were not floundering in the sea, but riding third class in a train for London.

We spent the next month in the quaint cathedral town of Wells, well away from possible air raids and the commotion. The swans on the moat rang the bell for their food, and we wandered the countryside. With gas rationing we had very little petrol, and no one answered our ads for the sale of the car. Finally we booked passage on the liner United States. We drove to Southampton, sold the car to a junk dealer for $20, and boarded the ship. England had been in the war a month, so the harbor was festooned with large balloons to prevent dive bombing.

The boat felt its way through the submarine nets. Everything was completely blacked out. However, once outside the harbor, our ship became ablaze with lights, evidently to display that it was American. We retired to our stateroom—being a party of four we had a room to ourselves, whereas other people, wrapped in blankets, were lying in the recreation rooms, making out as best they could.

When we awakened the next morning, thinking we were well on the way home, we heard a lot of banging and scraping, together with the noise of trains. To our astonishment we were in the harbor at Bordeaux, taking on refugees from France and the continent! We remained there for three days while train after train brought suitcases, trunks, boxes, and people to put on our boat. Also dozens of carloads of French wines. Nothing overt happened, we sailed again, and after the usual seven days landed in New York.

The dock in New York was stacked high with whiskey and scotch. Either the Americans wanted to hoard a drinking supply, or the British and French were establishing credit for war materials. In any event that was our welcome home. The war went on and became worse and worse. All the brains of Europe had been unable to stop it; no one could stop it until it had consumed enormous physical resources, murdered 6,000,000 Jews, and killed millions of fine young men and women.

Is it any wonder that your father remembers his trip to Europe when he was nine?

GRANDFATHER

May 27, 1975

Dear Sabrina,

I recall with much warmth the letters you wrote to me from places like Iran and Afganistan when you made your trip around the world—at age 11, was it not? In return I want to give you highlights of the one I took in 1956-57, with emphasis on Kyoto and the Far East.

Kyoto treated Anne and me most royally. From various sources—the Asia Foundation, the Institute for Democratic Education, and the Japan Committee for Intellectual Interchange, I had letters or contacts to the presidents of three universities: Kakuichi Oshimo of Doshisha, a private Christian University, oldest in Japan; Morikawa of Ryukoku, the best of the thirteen Buddhist Universities in Japan; and Takikawa of Kyoto, a national university which everyone rates next to Tokyo U. for strength and prestige. At the latter, too, I was especially welcomed by Dean Kosaka of the Faculty of Education who had invited me to give a lecture at Kyoto University.

We arrived at 4:30 at the Miyako Hotel, coming by train from Tokyo. At 8 PM a committee consisting of two presidents, Dean Kosaka, and about ten other professors and officers called on me to ascertain how we wanted to spend our time in Kyoto. I invited them to the bar room and ordered tea and beer, for which I signed the check but never received the bill, so I guess they paid for it. I made some preliminary statements about my mission, and they in turn had a long discussion in Japanese which ended by presenting us with a program of events.

The first one was the next morning at 10, with Dean Kosaka and Dr. Nagai of Kyoto University, (Dr. Nagai is now the Minister of Education in the Japanese Cabinet), in a university chauffered car, to see the Imperial Palace and grounds. This was the home of the Emperors after the Meiji restoration in 1868; doubtless you saw it. In the afternoon, the same car arrived, with Mr. Miura, a high school teacher, as our guide. We then went to the Shugaku-in, a palace with extensive gardens.

The next day the car appeared again with Mrs. Sagaro, the wife of a professor, in charge. She took Anne shopping for lacquer ware. Then the president of Doshisha took me to his university where I found assembled the chancellor of the eleven units, the chairman of the trustees, Leeds Gulick who had been on the faculty for some years, and other officials. They showed me the campus, and we spent two hours discussing the problems of higher education. Following this, we went to lunch in a skyscraper restaurant.

Next I visited Kyoto University where I upset plans a bit by innocently arriving before the president was ready to receive me. However, he spoke enough English to be polite until "communication," as he called it, arrived. The Japanese are always polite. Immediately one arrives, so does tea, and this is replenished frequently. No matter how many offices one enters there is always tea. Sometimes it is green tea, sometimes black, and occasionally a vile sort of stuff made of some tree bark—served cold. There is an immediate exchange of professional cards, a nice custom since it helps in remembering names. I had had cards made up with my LHD and LLD degrees prominently displayed, as is their custom, but I didn't have enough for such large delegations. Then, to proceed with the manners, the host knits his brow to think of the right English words, and invariably begins: "*When* did you arrive in Japan?" "How *long* will you stay in Japan?" "Oh, is that *so!*" Then it is time for the interpreter to take over.

First we visited the library (1,800,000 volumes) and the archeological museum. There I distinguished myself by identifying one collection of artifacts as being Swedish (they were so labeled in German). "Oh, is that so?" whereupon one of the men read the Japanese label which said they were Swedish. All agreed that I was an expert. I then went to a lecture room for a 2-hour meeting with some 200 professors and students. I talked about the philosophy underlying the American curriculum and teaching methods. The old universities in Japan were modelled after German ones. After the war, the military government had been changing them into the American pattern. So they were much interested in the rationalization behind the American pattern. There were many questions from the professors, but none from the students; students do not ask questions in the presence of the teachers.

After this lecture, we had another meeting, this time with a chapter of the Institute for Democratic Education, along with much tea. The Institute was an organized effort to counter the moves by conservatives who wanted to return the universities to the former curricula and methods. I spoke at several of the chapters in Japan and had a paper published in their journal.

Then we went to the Faculty Club, the former house of a Prince. Here were the president, the ex-president, three deans, and a few others. Mrs. Sagaro and Anne had also arrived. Anne and I sat with our backs to the tokonoma, being the distinguished guests. We had an elaborate six-course meal with saki and beer. At the conclusion, they presented me with a flowered lacquer bowl, a copy of one that is a fine example of Japanese art.

The following morning the car arrived again with Miura as guide. We visited the Katsura Palace, and the Ryoan-ji Garden—famous for the symbolism of its 15 rocks. At the moss garden we had the school principal as our guide as he was familiar with the 26 or so kinds of mosses, and the 14 ferns.

In the afternoon President Morikawa showed us Ryukoku University. One of the temples on the campus has famous wall and screen paintings. The garden is famous in Japan, being the site of the house of the first Shogun of Japan, predecessor of the Tokogawas. The president and a professor of English took us into the tea house for the tea ceremony. I thought to myself, here we will have the real thing. What was our disappointment when they served American style; but they did present to me the cup from which I had drunk. We saw also the bath tub in which the Shogun took his baths; it and the tea house are now national treasures.

Later, in the library, they brought out some rare Chinese scrolls, Buddhist, about 2500 years old. They had been found in Western China near Tibet. I unrolled one gingerly, much afraid that I would tear it. I then tried to plant a new idea in their minds by reciting how the University of St. Louis had microfilmed the ancient documents in the Vatican, thus making microfilms available for inspection without danger of damage to the originals. After the men had listened most politely to my little lecture, the librarian asked if I would care to see their optical laboratory. We accompanied him, and there we saw the very latest microfilm equipment from Switzerland, Germany, the United States, and Japan. I was utterly humiliated, having overlooked the Japanese prowess in optics.

Ah, Kyoto! One departs so reluctantly.

After Kyoto we visited Nara, and, favored with a university car, went to see the temples, the deer park and the pagodas; and we also had conferences at the University. From there we proceeded to Okayama, and to our surprise the President of Okayama University and a delegation were awaiting us in the VIP room at the railroad station. Again we received a program for our visit, one of the features of which was a drive around the province in Governor Miki's car, with chauffeur, guide, and telephone. Among other things we visited two museums, one of them a famous folk museum, and a harbor that was in process of being developed.

When we returned from this all-day tour, ready to hit the sack, we instead found ourselves at dinner, Japanese style, the Governor on one side of me, and a Geisha girl on the other. The dinner was delicious and I helped myself generously to everything. After the Japanese meal had been concluded, Governor Miki said: "Now we will have an American style meal." Whereupon in came huge steaks, vegetables, and what not. I felt like General Grant did when the Chinese treated him to a 26-course meal, and he had gorged himself on the first three. He remarked that "there I sot full of soup." But Miki, who was about as round as he was long, ate heartily. Unfortunately I was weary by this time and the Geisha found it difficult to entertain me. Don't you think that was too bad?

We spent about a month in Tokyo and there, too, enjoyed a whole series of pleasant and exciting happenings. One of these occurred when we received an invitation to attend a banquet being given by the Government of Japan in honor of the Vice President of India, Dr. Radnakrishnan. The banquet tables were lined with Japanese, together with about forty Indians. About a half dozen Western guests were included, so we felt quite honored by being invited. A curious thing about the dinner was that all of the toasts and speeches of the evening were given in English! I saw the same thing happen in Delhi on the occasion of the celebration of the 2500th birthday of Buddha (1956). The audience included thousands of Indians and only a handful of others. But the seven speakers, with only one exception, spoke in English. The exception was Nehru, even though he could, of course, speak excellent English. President Prasad spoke in Hindi and then repeated his talk in English. These two occasions demonstrated so well how English has become an international language.

One of the speakers in Tokyo was Arnold Toynbee with whom we became slightly acquainted. A couple of days later, the Toynbees and we made a trip together to see Nikko. We went up on the electric and spent the whole day there.

The day at Nikko provided an interesting sidelight on the Japanese character. While taking pictures of the magnificent scenery from a brow overlooking a canyon, I had laid my briefcase on top of a stone wall. Some thirty minutes later I realized that I had not picked it up when I left the spot. Retracing my steps, lo and behold there was the briefcase just where I had laid it. Probably several hundred Japanese had stopped there during the interval. At home I feel I have to keep everything under lock and key.

In Japan we did a lot of other sightseeing. We visited Kamakura, Hakone, Ise, and the Mikimoto pearl farms, to mention some highlights. We also stayed at a Japanese Inn, the Kawaroku, at Takamatsu on Shikoku Island, complete with typical Japanese style bath, sitting and sleeping on the floor. Did you have a Japanese style bath? Your grandmother and I thought it was lots of fun. Our room at the Inn was delightful in that it opened onto a small brook of unusual beauty.

I also talked with many educators and visited several universities, collecting ideas for my research project and carrying through on the intellectual exchange program.

Our adventures involved a stop in Taiwan and a several days visit to Hong Kong. The Asia Foundation had inquired of me whether I would be willing to give some help to a group of colleges in Hong Kong that were trying to consolidate their programs by becoming one institution. I had said I would. But we weren't prepared for the rush that was given to us. Two presidents were at the plane to meet us, and before even depositing our luggage we were involved in a planning luncheon. From that moment on we had virtually no time on our own. Instead there were meetings with faculty, a dinner with the governing boards, and many conferences with individuals. I have a red silk scarf on which the guests at the trustee dinner inscribed their names.

The problem was that two crises had come to a head at the same time. One was a tremendous increase in interest in higher education on the part of Chinese young people, and they were not being admitted to the University of Hong Kong. The other was the presence in Hong Kong of refugee scholars from mainland China, who had no way to continue their professional work. The University of Hong Kong was a typical British institution. It had some 800 students, but according to the Chinese admitted only 25% Chinese. Although Hong Kong is a great port city with much banking, insurance, and commercial business, the University had only one professor in the area of economics and business.

Furthermore, this university had a monopoly on degree-granting powers, one result of which was very curious. The refugee colleges were arranging with the National University of Taiwan (a foreign university) to award degrees to their graduates. So these refugee scholars had started some little colleges, mostly in garrets and store buildings. The man who took the lead in working with me was Dr. Chen Ping Chuan, president of one of these colleges, and who had been president of the University of Canton.

One objective was to find a way of uniting and building up an institution that would have degree-granting powers and become viable in operation. It sounds easy but there were many complicating rivalries, much lack of funds, and great unevenness in the programs. However, five of the colleges did unite and become the United College of Hong Kong. It is now one of three major units in the new Chinese University of Hong Kong. When Jean and I were in Hong Kong in 1973, President Li Choh-Ming held a reception in our honor. It was gratifying, indeed exciting, to see this new university with a modern plant overlooking the channel, and with an enrollment of over 3000 students. During our visit in 1956 we didn't get much time to do the usual shopping. However, it was tremendously interesting to have this close-up look at the Chinese problems.

Our visit to the Far East was part of a 10-month, round-the-world trip made during a sabbatical year from the University of Michigan. Anne and I continued on to Cambodia/Angkor Wat, Thailand, Burma, India, Sri Lanka, East and South Africa, and several countries of South America, studying their university programs, and also sightseeing.

My visit was sponsored by the Committee for Intellectual Interchange, and my fare around the world was supplied by a Rockefeller Foundation grant. I felt quite honored because among the recipients of the grants were such persons of distinction as Eleanor Roosevelt and Walter Gropius.

Founding United College of Hong Kong

In India I was sponsored by the Ministry of Education and visited nearly all the principal universities. We were lucky to have seen Angkor Wat in Cambodia before it was ravaged by the Vietnam War. In Sri Lanka we were joined by Myra and George Cooley, and while staying for a month at the Queens Hotel in Kandy, explored the whole island. In Kenya we enjoyed a game safari in Amboselli. At Montevideo I substituted for Hedda Hopper, noted gossip columnist, as a luncheon speaker—what a switch for the audience! We arrived in Santiago in the midst of a revolution and were confined for several days in the Hotel Crillon while the machine guns played rat-a-tat-tat at the street intersections.

Sabrina, some day I'd like to read your diary of your trip around the world.

GRANDFATHER

October 23, 1979

Dear Alex,

Once again I shall try to get the enclosed letter, written in September, to you. It keeps coming back to me. This time I shall use an address supplied by your Mother, who certainly must know where you are, otherwise how could she send you the checks that keep you alive? And did you get a card mailed by us in France? Drat the P.O., or did I copy your address wrong when you gave it to me in July? I should think just Yale would suffice. Doesn't everyone know about Yale?

The card was a picture of the beautiful building occupied by UNESCO in Paris. Did you go there when in Paris? When I visited it, I ate in the dining room which has a grand view of the Eiffel Tower. I'll bet you went to the Tower instead. You climb the Tower and look out over the Seine and Paris. So what? At UNESCO you can also do this; but in addition you look out over the whole world—the world of education, science, and culture.

I was at UNESCO to confer with Dr. Balbir, a Pakistani, who sponsored the research publication I did in 1970. UNESCO wanted to be of help to universities in various parts of the world, especially those in the developing countries. When I did my sabbatical project in 1956-57, I visited some 14 such countries, making comparisons between the types of universities that in colonial times had been modeled after the British, French, and German universities, with newer ones that were being modeled after the American land-grant type of institution. The former emphasized elite enrollments of few students, the humanities, and preparation for the civil service. The colonial powers wanted natives who would get a veneer of Western culture and with whom they could converse in a Western language.

When I was helping the refugee colleges in Hong Kong launch what is now the Chinese University of Hong Kong, I had lunch with an educator from Britain, W.H.G. Armytage, a really progressive man judged by his writings, and asked him why the University of Hong Kong had such a limited enrollment and narrow curriculum. His answer was that if Britain educated large numbers of Chinese in Hong Kong, they would return the favor by driving the British out.

But the American type of university emphasized both general education and technical education—for example, liberal arts, engineering, agriculture, and business administration. Also the enrollment of students from all economic-social strata of society. On my trip I found that many of the older universities, after independence, had been reconstructing their policies and programs, modeling them after the American pattern.

In some cases the government had to take the initiative. For example, a representative of the Ministry of Education in Turkey consulted me about the bases for establishing a new university in Turkey at Erzurum. But before he would discuss the subject, he asked me to keep the conversation confidential, for he said if the faculties of Istanbul and Ankara learned what the Ministry was planning, they would defeat the project. This was because the Ministry thought that a new university to be located in a mining and agricultural region should be based on the study of engineering and agriculture rather than on the classical studies, law, and medicine. They went ahead with these plans and selected the University of Nebraska as their model.

A country like Ghana—I had a young man from Ghana as my assistant in the UNESCO study—newly independent, and heretofore a pawn in the hands of the industrialists and bankers of Europe, who were interested primarily in raw materials, now desired to develop its natural resources and human potential for its own benefit, to educate the people, and to raise the general standard of living in the country. How does one do this? A principal means is through the education and research that universities can bring to the situation. The development of human resources must come first. Consider Japan—no oil, and a scarcity of minerals and forests; but having trained and educated its people, Japan has become a major industrialized country.

In many countries this has required the founding of many new universities, and a considerable change in focus and an expansion of the older universities. One stumbling block is that college faculty in these one-time colonial countries have been educated at British and continental universities, and so have become indoctrinated with the older concepts of education. This has been changing because so many of these countries more recently have been sending their young people to the United States to study. And many of them have become teachers in their home countries.

Another problem has been that the administrators that have been available to organize and run the new and revised institutions have also been trained in a limited way. What UNESCO wanted me to do was to develop a manual for the training of university administrators, which would teach them some new concepts about education and new methods of organizing higher education and administering the institutions.

So I prepared a 90-page document entitled *La Formation des Administrateurs d'université, Le development de l'enseignement superior*. It was published in French and in English, 1972.

At our conference in September I was able to bring Balbir and his attractive assistant, a young woman from Tunisia, up-to-date on some reference materials.

Then while in the dining room, contemplating all the international figures who streamed in and out, I thought to myself, "Wouldn't this be a great place for Alex to work!" She has all the best qualifications in languages, intellectual interests, and also personality. I should think that a person on this staff would have the feeling that he was serving a real mission in the world—a world that so badly needs improvements in education, science and culture. Get people of the world thinking together about how to achieve the best life and work in collaboration in order to achieve it. A better approach than through tanks and bombs.

And I think the way to get rid of the war machines and the war mentality is through some such approach as UNESCO. In fact, that is the very reason why it was set up. If only people, countries, would put their funds into this effort rather than wasting it on things that can only harm and kill people.

We were disappointed in Paris to find a line of people a mile long waiting to be served in the restaurant atop the Pompidou. But we got a window seat in a restaurant from which we could study the blue pipes that swirled round and round as though they were going somewhere. I found the building "interesting" as the architects say when they are not yet ready to be enthusiastic. But if I saw it a number of times I am sure I would get used to it, and probably like it. Or at least admire its ingenuity.

One thing I really liked was a visit to a bronze bell foundry, Cornille-Havard in the village of Villedieu-les-Poëles, Normandy. It is several hundred years old and has been in the same family most of this time. It makes bells, church bells, on orders from around the world. Using the lost wax process, same as we used at the Antioch Art Foundry.

We had a really great trip through Normandy, Brittany, and the Loire Valley. Two couples in a station wagon, with an excellent driver/guide. Followed by a night train ride to Madrid and a tour through Andalusia.

Alex: make a mental note—UNESCO, and my friend Balbir; education, science, and culture to displace war.

GRANDFATHER

V

Antioch College loomed large in my life. As you approach college age I should like Alex, Sabrina, and all of you, to reflect upon differing philosophies of education and to know of innovations that we tried at Antioch. Also by telling you about how we at the college transformed the community of Yellow Springs, I am suggesting that you can *help change the environment that surrounds you.*

February 20, 1975

Dear Sabrina,

I recall how artistic you are. Winning first prize at the Texas State Fair, and all that. I wish I had that kind of talent. I think sometimes that I probably do have the talent, that is, the sensitivity and the ability, but in my school we had nothing—nothing—in the arts, so I grew up ignorant of the possibilities in creative art and undeveloped in skills. Today you all have a curriculum that is so much richer than I had. I envy you.

But I did foster art at one time. For a couple of years, Walter Abell, an art teacher and I ran a little business in Yellow Springs. We imported from Europe pottery, etchings, prints, and similar things for household decoration; held exhibits, and made sales. Our purpose was to stimulate people to have better art in their homes. We distributed a lot of art and we broke even financially, but after a couple of years of effort we decided that we were not accomplishing too much. I retained some of the pottery and etchings. Just recently a guest said the etchings were among the best he had seen.

The importing effort was a small one compared with one to establish an art bronze foundry. The story begins in 1925 when I first came to Antioch College. Have you learned how to do bronze castings? By the lost-wax process? This technique is necessary when you cast objects from a model that has undercuttings. It is a very ancient art. Somebody discovered that if you add copper and tin together you get a beautiful metal. About 15% tin makes the finest bronze, although you can use anywhere from 5% to 20% tin with the copper.

The Chinese a few centuries BC began to make art bronzes, as you can see whenever you visit an art museum. The Shang dynasty, dating before 1500 BC is rated a high point in artistic skills. Just think for a moment what our Western ancestors were doing at that time—probably living in miserable huts, tending sheep, spinning yarn from wool, and trying desperately to keep themselves warm and fed.

I know you have been around the world—you world traveler you—but you didn't stop in Taiwan. When Chiang and his followers had to leave mainland China in 1949, with the Communists at their heels, they gathered together the finest art objects in the homes and museums and took the collection to Taiwan. Now they may be seen in the National Museum in Taipei, one that the Japanese had built up during their occupation of the island. Because of the combined efforts of the Japanese, who are great museum creators, and the Chinese, this is one of the great museums of the world. In any event, the bronzes there are magnificent.

Cellini, the Italian, 1500-1571 AD, "perfected" the lost-wax process, *a'cire perdue,* and built a great reputation for his art bronzes. Have you ever read his autobiography? Please do, for it describes well events of the Renaissance Period, his own life and activities, and for that matter his escapades with various women. He describes in detail the techniques he used in making some of his famous castings. Did you visit Florence on your trip? The museums there have Cellini's art on display, a noted bronze being his Perseus.

Well, I arrived on the Antioch campus late in August. Shortly thereafter I asked to see President Morgan about the courses I was to teach. However, as I entered his office he immediately launched into a description of an idea that he had to start a little bronze foundry. The previous summer he had had a portrait bust made of himself by a sculptor named Paola. The sculptor told him how the bust could be cast in bronze, describing the Cellini lost-wax process. Morgan's imagination immediately caught fire about the possibilities of starting such a foundry.

In reorganizing the college in 1920 he had introduced a plan of having the students alternate study and work as their education. As a part of this plan he began to start some small industries near the campus. Through them the students would learn how to initiate and manage small enterprises. Morgan was also concerned about the tendency in America for everyone to drift to large cities, where inevitably they would become mere employees of large corporations and lead submissive lives. He thought education should develop people to become self-reliant, and that it would be best for them and indeed for the country if college graduates would remain in smaller communities and create there a good life for themselves.

Morgan thought that a bronze foundry would give students employment, would add an interesting laboratory to those of the art department of the college, and also provide opportunity to do research on bronze casting. This last objective was important not only as a research activity of the college, but because the Cellini method was out of date. Cellini, using the ancient Chinese method, had done such beautiful castings that no one wanted to change the techniques. Sculptors who had their objects cast into bronze would stipulate the Cellini method because they wanted to be able to say that the art work was by the Cellini process. This had prestige value.

Morgan said to me that any process that had been kept the same for 400 or 4000 years surely could be improved. Much has been learned in more recent times about chemistry, physics, and technology. For example, the Cellini method still called for telling how to judge when the molten metal could be poured by looking at the color of the flame. Today, this can be done by using a thermometer. Brick dust put into the plaster to strengthen it used to be measured by pinches and handfuls, instead of by precise quantity or weight.

Let me illustrate further the advantages of modern technology as compared with practices that are handed down from workman to workman. During the World War II the Lockheed Corporation came to us with a problem. In building and testing aircraft for use during the war, the company was having numerous failures in the stress parts of the planes. Using an x-ray technique they had determined that the failures were due to irregular molecular alignments, but the cause was a mystery. No one had found the answer.

So the company asked our foundry to try to solve the problem. It proved to be simple. To get regular molecular alignment and thus adequate strength in the casting, all of the metal had to be poured at exactly the same temperature. Workmen in the big aluminum foundries had carelessly let the heated metal vary in temperature when being poured. So they got castings that were good enough for most purposes but that would crack when put under the kind of strain that occurs when a plane banks and turns.

At this initial conference with Morgan he asked me if I would study the question of whether the college should start, and could operate successfully an art bronze foundry. I began the very next day. I took the electric traction to Dayton, staying two or three days, and interviewed several knowledgeable persons and also visited some foundries. These were "sand" foundries doing flat work rather than art objects, but I needed information about foundry practices and equipment. Within a week I made my report to Morgan, including a recommendation to go ahead with the project. Morgan then asked me to take general supervision of it.

We began by searching for a bronze artist. Through Paola we found one in Sicily. This man, with wife and five children, was brought to Yellow Springs. He knew how to begin in a simple way, which was fortunate because we had no special money for the project, and the college really had none to spare. The Italian made a kiln out of bricks, and we attached a gas line to it. We employed a student as his assistant. The enterprise was housed in an old horse barn, long since burned to the ground. So we were ready to make castings.

The first one naturally was the bust of Arthur Morgan. There followed similar Paola busts of Charles F. Kettering and Colonel Deeds, prominent Daytonians. Morgan had the notion that the Dayton Engineers Club would be happy to have the bronze busts of the three men, and so would reimburse the college for the costs. That was still in the days when men's clubs were decorated with the stuffed heads of moose and the plaster or bronze busts of prominent members. Well, wouldn't you know, the club wasn't interested, and neither were Kettering or Deeds; so we had done all that work for nothing. But we had made a start with our little foundry. The Sicilian knew how to make bronzes—by the Cellini method.

One of the problems in casting is to keep air bubbles from distorting the metal, because wherever a bubble exists there will be a blemish. Just give a Cellini-made casting an acid bath and it will uncover innumerable imperfections that had existed, and which had been cleverly concealed with patina. Every hole in the casting has to be filled with bronze, and every imperfection on the face has to be filed smooth. This repair work is terribly expensive because of the hand labor; to the extent you can reduce this expense, you reduce the price of the completed object. You also have a better casting. This was one of the reasons why we wanted to research ways to improve the casting process.

The pouring is always exciting. Read what Cellini says about some of his pours. The one I remember most vividly at Antioch was the pouring of the bronze flag pole bases and capitals of columns for the National Archives Building in Washington. Doubtless you saw them when you visited Washington, but didn't know that I had a hand in making them. Everybody goes in that entrance because it is just inside where the original of the Declaration of Independence is kept.

These bases are huge. It really took an enormous amount of preparation to make a plaster cast that would hold the weight of the metal as it was poured into the space where the wax had been. I was an onlooker, and Morris and Xarifa Bean and Amos Mazzolini did the pouring. Things seemed to be going well when suddenly a crevice appeared in the plaster casing and a small stream of molten metal shot out through the crack. A drop of it landed on Amos' cuff and hit his foot. He jumped and howled with pain; but this was such a crucial operation that he stayed right at the job until the pouring had been completed. So, when you look at these bronze flag pole bases next time, just think, a part of Amos Mazzolini's foot went into that casting.

But I am ahead of my story. The Sicilian knew how to make castings, but only in one way. Just as Cellini made them. He held two hard-and-fast views: (1) Cellini's way was the only way; and (2) to learn the process takes seven years of apprenticeship. That was the way he had learned the art and any person who worked with him had to do it that way. Imagine what that attitude did to our ideas. We wanted to train students, and we wanted to do basic research on the methodology. We were stymied on a point that had not occurred to us—one of personnel and not of technology. It was a battle between the old Central European frame of mind and the inquisitive, venturesome attitude that Americans have.

We had to take action in spite of having imported and become responsible for an Italian with a big family, and who could speak only a few words of English. We resolved the matter by employing a youngish German-educated Italian, Amos Mazzolini, who was a plaster moulder and sculptor. We made him the technical assistant to the Sicilian, and also gave him a teaching role in the college. Our instructions to Amos were to watch like a hawk everything the older man did in order to learn all of his tricks as fast as he could. Amos was a good natured but serious, intelligent man, who knew the fundamentals excepting the bronze process itself. Within six months he said he thought he could make castings.

Thereupon Morgan found a job for the Sicilian in a New York foundry, where he had lots of agreeable companions and fellow bronze casters. At one point I visited all six of the art bronze foundries in New York and found that all of them were sticking closely to the Cellini process. They had made advances in patinas but that was all. So our man could feel right at home.

Amos did OK right from the start. This of course debunked the idea that it took seven years to learn a few relatively simple skills. The delaying tactics involved in an apprenticeship have other motivations, such as controlling the number of people who become proficient and eligible to practice a trade. During World War I Great Britain took much longer to convert its production facilities to war production than did the United States. Their apprentice trained employees could not adapt easily to new production techniques. Since the war, Britain has shifted largely to our methods of training personnel, through schools and colleges.

The foundry was of some interest to students of art; in teaching accounting I required the students to design a cost system for the foundry; and we gave a series of students experience in managing foundry operations. After a bit we employed two students, a husband-wife team, Morris and Xarifa Bean, majoring respectively in mathematics and chemistry. Because of their training we were able to begin some research. Working together, they achieved some outstanding results. The most basic discovery was a method whereby the plaster mold, through baking it, could be given enough porosity to absorb air and moisture. This meant that there was less need to place numerous vents in the mold with the result that there were fewer air bubble defects in the finished bronzes. It was they who solved the problem for Lockheed. They found a way to assist Goodyear in making tire molds with 2 negatives instead of 32. They assisted General Motors in perfecting a nonferrous air compressor for its two-cycle diesel motor. Many such research results flowed from their efforts, much of it coming during the years after they had graduated from the college. Morris became president of a successor company called Morris Bean and Company, and Xarifa is now the president. So the use of students did work out well in their case and the research was a big success.

With Mazzolini and the Beans working at the job, the Antioch Art Foundry made progress in producing quality castings, and in reducing the labor involved in making them. It did casting for artists, on order, from various parts of the United States; perhaps the most famous artist was Milles, much of whose work was cast there.

The foundry, alas, was not at that time a profitable venture, and indeed in most years required what was for us considerable subsidy. For example, the casting for the National Archives was terribly interesting but cost us several thousand dollars over the contract price. Along came the big depression, and it became especially difficult to include the foundry subsidy in the budget. At the same time we were reluctant to close it.

In the meantime the inventions, which had been patented, made the process applicable to nonferrous metals, especially aluminum and magnesium. This introduced some commercial opportunities. In 1936 Goodyear came to the foundry with the tire mold problem and provided a subvention for research. The success in this effort led to additional opportunities, and so the aluminum branch of the work began to outshine that of the art bronze.

The bronze project continued to get interesting orders for castings and Amos maintained it until his death. We incorporated the Bean Company as a project under the leadership of the Beans. It grew steadily and rapidly. It continues today as a major economic enterprise with two production plants, employing several hundred persons.

The Bean project exemplifies several points: the importance of having an attractive and viable idea; the attention that should be given to the motivations and the quality of the people involved; the need for sustained, and often long endured support through the infancy stage; the importance of emphasing quality of production; the need for imaginative leadership; the determination not to take "no" for an answer. It also demonstrates that a free enterprise, in a small community, is still viable and possible to create.

Well, Sabrina, artist that you are, I trust that you will now respect your Grandfather's creativity in art.

GRANDFATHER

June 19, 1977

Dear Sabrina,

My, what an inspirational site the Kauai beach is! I'm sitting on my verandah looking out upon the Pacific Ocean, watching the surf play unendingly upon the sands. No wonder Robert Louis Stevenson did such beautiful writing while at his cottage in Samoa.

Now that you are going to college, I want to explain to you a concept of education that was basic to our program at Antioch College, where I spent twenty-two years.

Experiential learning is based on an age-old fact of life. If you experience something, physically or emotionally, you will assimilate it better intellectually. In the simplest form it means that if a child touches a red hot stove, the experience will register with him for the rest of his life. Ah, I forgot that you have never seen a red hot stove, much less have touched one! OK, substitute a glowing coal in a camp fire. If you pick it up, you will yell bloody murder. Same thing. You have learned a lesson, haven't you, with an intensity of experience that you will never forget.

Now to the extent that you can experience your education in college, you will better assimilate the knowledge. It is easier to do this with some subjects than with others. For example, you can study French for four years, learn a lot *about* it, but not achieve much facility for using French. To gain a full knowledge of French it is necessary to practice it, practice it a great deal. Or if you want to learn music you can acquire knowledge about music that had been written, and you may qualify yourself to be a music critic. But in doing so you are always learning what others have created. If you wish really to become a musician you must learn to play instruments or to sing. Or to compose. This takes a great deal of practice.

It is less easy to see this principle at work in an abstract subject like philosophy. You can read and study philosophy and acquire knowledge. But the real test of your understanding is your ability to philosophize. This means discussion of ideas with your teachers and your peers. In doing this you make ideas become your own based upon your experience and your perceptions. And you learn to express yourself orally or in writing fully and with clarity. As a consequence of this assimilation process your personal philosophy will become apparent in your daily life. You will be refining your atti-

Antioch Towers

tudes toward life and restructuring your habits and acquiring new skills of thought and action.

I am speaking of practice such as writing, or experimenting, or applying principles in field studies. But that is not the whole of experiential learning. In one sense, the latter means making some bit of knowledge your own, assimilating it in a manner that causes it to become a part of *your* knowledge and wisdom, making it a tool for future use in your own life. This may be contrasted with an alternative—studying always to be able to recite well, or to pass an exam, or to please a teacher. In school, have you learned to regurgitate, or to assimilate knowledge?

It is the carry-through that is so important. Learning to solve problems is sort of like this: (1) you identify a problem and define it carefully so that it has a clear focus; (2) you work on it and get a solution; (3) you test the solution to determine its correctness; (4) you derive from your work some principles and procedures; (5) you then apply these principles and procedures to novel situations. In this way, the solving of the one problem prepares you to solve other problems. This is a process of developing your mental capacity. And that is what college should be about, certainly the Vassar kind of college.

You see, most students are satisfied when they pass step 2 or possibly step 3 above. So are many teachers, unfortunately. Whereas for developing your brain power the last three steps are highly important. The first two steps may be called training, that is, you are being coached to find a solution that the book or the teacher says is the correct one. Like getting skill in multiplication or division. It is the other steps that really educate you, that is, develop your mental capacity to solve problems when there is no answer book available.

Now let me analyze the concept of experiential education a bit further. I shall give the analysis that we used at Antioch College because Antioch has done more with this idea than any other college. Doubtless you know that Antioch provides a program through which the students gain various kinds of experience. Among other things, the students are placed in realistic jobs, alternating study on the campus with work for some employer or in a community other than the campus one.

However, any job or campus or class activity will provide learning benefits. But only to a point. A job or an activity can remain elementary or be repetitive. What is needed is progression from a narrow experience to broader ones, and from elementary situations to the more complex or sophisticated ones. These results will be achieved best if there are definite educational objectives, accompanied by repeated evaluation of the experiences in relation to those objectives.

At Antioch we sought four objectives: (1) vocation exploration and progress in finding the right vocation; (2) application of theories studied in class to practical situations; (3) observing society—in general and also in specific situations—as it is, in order to learn better how to apply the wisdom of the past to the problems of the present and anticipated future; and (4) making progress in clarifying and maturing one's aims in life. These educational objectives might well be those of any good college, or of any individual going to college. Antioch differed mainly in creating more situations through which the students might seek the objectives.

Vocational exploration means trying a number of occupations as a basis for knowing them better and finding one in which your talents and interests best fit. The initial choices can be narrowed by taking some interest and aptitude tests. Then try one or more of those for which you seem best qualified. It is easy to romanticize about a future vocation; you get excited about all the good things and overlook or blind yourself to the bad aspects. One reason our students did so well later in schools of medicine was that the ones who were less fitted psychologically or otherwise for the practice of medicine decided on the basis of preliminary experience, say in a hospital, that they did not want medicine after all. Observing the doctors as they treated the patients either reassured the student about his choice, or persuaded him that this occupation was not for him.

The second objective is to make the theory studied in the books more meaningful. I am referring to the specificity of meaning to you of the things you study. A theory is not merely a statement to memorize; to be valid in your thinking you must know just what it means. If you find some way to apply it, and then test the results, you will have learned what the theory means.

I recall a student working in a factory who failed to be precise as to the temperature at which some metal was to be poured. As a result the melt was spoiled. And he got thoroughly bawled out. What might have been close enough in the college to "get by" was not precise enough in practice. The student said he had learned a lesson, he would never make that mistake again.

As for the third objective, it has commonly been said that a liberal education consists of passing down the cultural heritage. More educators than not subscribe earnestly to that phrase. Superficially it is true that our common heritage is passed down from generation to generation, much of it through education. But the study of history, literature, art, and music, can lead to the acquisition of a cultural veneer, not an education in depth. Much depends on how the teacher teaches and how the student learns.

Men differ from lower animals in that they can store up knowledge and through books and otherwise make it available to oncoming generations. Thus each of us can begin where others have left off. In invention, for example, a chain of knowledge is built through a sequence of discoveries; based on this foundation the next step can be taken. If man had to start afresh each time, he would have a very slow and painful journey in his intellectual and social development.

The atomic table, for example, wasn't discovered overnight. First, when making a chemical experiment, Lavoisier noted an addition in weight for which he could not account. He called this addition "phlogiston." Then Priestly identified the weight as a chemical and named it oxygen. So oxygen became the first item that began the discovery of the atomic table. Over the decades and centuries other atoms were identified and the atomic structure determined. And presently we learned how to explode the atom. This in turn opened an array of subparticles that placed a whole new light on matter and energy. The point is, knowledge grew by increments, but students today do not have to start from scratch. They can learn about a neutron without waiting to discover it. Such knowledge composes the wisdom of the past, a phrase I like better than cultural heritage.

But knowledge of the past is useful also as a guide for the improvement of the future. To comprehend most fully what the past means, it is necessary to consider the present. Students therefore should become keen observers of the present as a basis for really understanding the past. Hence we have the two-fold objective of finding how the present got as it is, and secondly how to apply wisdom in trying to improve society as it now exists. So, Sabrina, look around you critically, observe the environment, the way people behave, the way institutions, governments, business enterprises are organized and perform, the way in which wealth, health, employment are distributed. Or, if you have a job, as Antioch students do, use it as a base from which to study your environment. Then seek the knowledge and wisdom that will help you to deal with the problems you have identified.

The fourth objective, to learn how to live the good life, should be common to all of higher education. But usually it is taken for granted. Antioch tried to make it more specific. For example, students were required to write life aims papers and major autobiographical analyses of where they had been and where they were going—in life, that is. To find out who they were, to use a phrase popular with students today. To make them think about how they educate themselves, about their personal development. To cause them to do some planning for themselves. Effort was made at Antioch through written reports, and counseling interviews, to cause the students to relate their vocation to a way of living. The aim was to show that a vocation is both a way to earn money with which to live, and a means through which to accomplish many of one's goals in life.

The point is, most people spend much of their time and energies on their jobs. The rest of their time they want to be entertained, say by TV, or to be on vacation. Presently retirement comes and what have they accomplished? They have fed and housed themselves, raised some brats, and watched a lot of TV. Is that the life for an educated person? A Vassar alumna? There is a fundamental principle here—if you want to live a good life in the future, you must begin *now*. Now while in college. In college is where you should get the motivations, learn the skills, and acquire the habits. You must change yourself while in college, or it will be too late. You must make choices, and experience the better quality of life while in the very process of maturing your ideas about life.

To get the most out of a college like Vassar it is important to orient yourself to the most significant aspects of its environment and not become engulfed by the baser influences that often prevail on a campus.

I do not know whether the Vassar faculty ever heard of experiential education, but now *you* have. So, good learning!

GRANDFATHER

February 3, 1980

Dear Alex,

As you progress in college, you should give thought to the philosophy that underlies the educative process in various institutions. Most of what I say will reflect the educational philosophy developed at Antioch. Colleges do vary. Most liberal arts colleges, for example, believe their most important mission to be to pass down the cultural heritage. Many professors limit their teaching to lectures *about* art, literature, history, mathematics, and other disciplines. An opposite view is that you should not lecture *at* students, but rather teach them to think, how to explore for knowledge, how to search for truth.

In a simplistic way, these approaches can be described as being on the one hand, a reliance on authoritarian sources of ideas, and on the other, as an exploratory method of seeking wisdom. The first method is based heavily on memory; the second, while utilizing memory, is based on the scientific method of inquiry. In the extreme sense, the first provides a cultural veneer and beliefs based upon doctrine; the second, while recognizing the value of gaining wisdom from man's past experiences, assumes that man has not necessarily as yet produced the best of which he is capable in art, literature, technology, and ethical principles. Hence, the educated person should become creative. History does not repeat itself, nature is still evolving, man continues to develop his intellectual and creative abilities.

At Antioch College we were clearly in the second category. We were a liberal arts college, although with some modifications. We required all students to take a distribution of subjects that would enlarge and enhance their cultural knowledge. The basic concepts that we emphasized included such things as facility in communication, a grasp of history, an appreciation of art, music, and literature, and comprehensions of the theories and discoveries in the social and natural sciences. In other words, we did not neglect the acquisition of factual knowledge, emotion-arousing creations, or achieving insights into new knowledge discovered through investigations involving both inductive and deductive reasoning.

However, we did not consider these educational objectives sufficient. The most genuine education is one that influences the nature and quality of life that the individual leads. Cultural knowledge should not be a veneer even though it adds to the pleasure of living and enables one to be erudite in discussions. The meaningful attainment is to learn to utilize cultural knowledge in being creative oneself, and in developing one's power to think and act.

An aspect of this is to have the knowledge, skills, and attitudes acquired in college permeate one's daily life. This includes the occupation or profession in which the person engages. As Horace Kallen, the eminent philosopher, said: "The root of culture is vocation; the fruit of vocation is culture, alike in the institutions of society and the personal life."

Charles F. Kettering, a highly successful business enterpriser, put it succinctly: "Antioch uses a lap-weld type of education, not the butt-weld type." By this he meant that Antioch interrelated firsthand experience with the study of past human experience. This contrasts with the more common method of providing the student with a "foundation" upon which it is supposed that he will subsequently build his life.

Another way to make clear this meaning is to cite the contrasting examples of Antioch's plan with that of Robert Hutchin's idea of studying the 100 greatest books. The latter idea is appealing—to learn what the distinguished men and women of the past thought, and in some cases how they arrived at their convictions. However, the discovery of knowledge has not stood still over the centuries. Many ideas and some of the information in these books are now obsolete, and the plan has no provision for adding great books of the more recent past. Much of the underlying philosophy was derived from reasoning deductively; inductive reasoning, the scientific method, had not yet become the basis for the development of concepts and principles. The study of the great books, taken alone, would lead to reliance upon authority, and would not sufficiently develop the student's own skills in acquiring and analyzing facts, in problem solving, and in testing solutions by application to novel situations.

At Antioch we made some effort to broaden the concept of the cultural heritage. For example, one of our most effective teachers was Manmatha Chatterjee, who, because of his own Eastern background, was able to challenge students' provincialisms. One trouble with professors of humanities is that they have become so steeped in Judeo-Christian, Grecian, Roman, and Reformation thought, they think this IS the cultural heritage. Whereas, the Chinese were thinking about the meaning of life at a time when Westerners were still living in shacks on stilts on a water front where they could conveniently shuck their oysters and clams without having to think much about why they were there or why they were doing what they were doing.

One of the deficiencies in liberal education is that it is overwhelmingly oriented to Western thought. But in today's world, all human beings are interdependent, communication is almost instantaneous through the space satellites, and isolation of cultures is a thing of the past.

To discuss further the Antioch philosophy of education would consume more pages than should go into a letter. If your interest has been aroused you might dip into two books I wrote about it, *Vitalizing Liberal Education* (1944) and *Antioch College: Its Design for Liberal Education* (with Dorothy Hall) 1946, both by Harper.

Antioch was fortunate in having wealthy friends who supported its philosophy both with their interest and their money. Charles Kettering, a member of the board of trustees, was a most interesting, original type of person. He was one of the great inventors of our time. As a result, he became wealthy and was most generous to Antioch, including the donation of funds for five buildings. One of his projects at Antioch was research in chorophyll and photosynthesis. As he explained it, if we could learn how plants, through their chlorophyll and the process of photosynthesis convert energy from the sun into starches and sugars, hence usable energy, we wouldn't have to wait 100 million years for fossilization to provide us with coal and oil. We could tap the sun direct for energy. He was ahead of his time. I wish he were here now to help us tap the energy of the sun, for that seems the best, maybe the only long-term solution to the need of our industrialized society for energy.

On one visit to Kettering's office in Detroit, he told me about his newly invented two-cycle diesel motor, and his need for an oil with which to operate it. He had defined the problem and then submitted it to six of the large oil companies. After a lapse of time he invited them to send research men to discuss the problem with him. He told me he asked them to explain how they might solve his problem. Each went into a complex presentation and in effect said: "If you will give us $5,000,000 we will get busy with research and development." He just let them talk until they had finished. Then he announced that during the interval since he had written to them he had arrived at a solution. Would they like to see it? He stepped into his laboratory and came out holding an ordinary dishpan with some glass and tube structures sitting in it. Then he explained how he could produce the oil needed with this simple laboratory equipment. He really got a big laugh out of putting the oil men in their place.

Kettering was making a highly important point. If you define a problem fully, the solution may become apparent, or derived by simple procedures.

Another good friend of the College was Samuel Fels, the Fels Naptha soap man. He provided the funds to establish the Fels Research Institute, for the purpose of conducting longitudinal studies in child development. He thought we should know more about how to discover and enlarge the potentialities in each individual. I recall one long conversation with him in his home in Philadelphia on keeping an open mind. He thought that if people learned how to keep their minds open to fresh ideas and information, they would be more flexible, find adjustments more easily, and be willing to search out better solutions to problems. An open mind rather than a closed one.

These two projects, investigations into how human beings develop and into the way in which matter and energy are created, helped the College in providing a climate and environment for critical inquiry by faculty and students.

Well, Alex, keep your mind open, look at things critically, develop your reasoning powers, and keep searching for the good life.

GRANDFATHER

March 21, 1975

Dear Matthew,

I want to tell you about how we at Antioch College used our creative thinking and our scientific know-how to create a better community in which to live and work. This is important because most people accept the mores and habits of a community of people just as they are. Indeed, there is always a community set of mind in favor of things as they are. It makes people uncomfortable to change their ways of looking at things and their habits of living. The mores of people are like dogma in religion, they keep people in a vice, in a rut.

The village of Yellow Springs was surely in such a rut when I first arrived there in 1925. Anne and I came by train from New York where I had been working in Wall Street. Dean Philip Nash met us and took us immediately to a house he had selected for us. After we had walked through it, he said he would show us the pump at the street corner which was used by the four families that lived nearby. We could get water for our teakettle there. For some reason he did not show us the little building on the rear of the lot where we could read the Montgomery Ward catalog before tearing out some pages.

We were shocked—we had come to THIS instead of the position as teaching assistant at Harvard that we had turned down. We asked to be shown something else. He said: "This is it!" Poor Anne, a bride of two years, had never had to use an outdoor toilet. We found refuge with the Magruders. Presently we were able to move into an apartment on the second floor of an old house in which a bathroom was being built.

The village had a population of 1500. It was rural-oriented, terribly provincial and self-centered. As long as nothing changed from

147

day to day, the people felt secure. In addition to being located in a provincial section of Ohio, Yellow Springs had been the victim of hard luck. During the 19th Century the village had become the site of a spa/health resort; but this activity had died out, a victim of changing knowledge about health, and the invention of the automobile.

The college in the town, Antioch, had had a great beginning, with the distinguished Horace Mann as its president. But as of 1920 it was down to 50 students, 6 teachers, and dormitories with round brick structures attached to the rear in which there were a dozen or so holes around the wall. The student rooms were still being heated with stoves.

The head of the village was an elderly man, in office for some 16 years, and who lived largely on "fees." The health of the residents was cared for by two octogenarians. The soil of the region, however, was excellent, and the farms had kept the village alive.

Arthur Morgan, an engineer, had become president of the college in 1920. He said it had attracted him because it was so badly run down that he could do whatever he wanted to with it. By the time I arrived in 1925, he had hooked some pipes to the yellow spring, put a tank in the towers of the main building, and extended mains to the buildings and to a few houses in town. The water had a miserable iron deposit in it, but at least it would flush toilets and provide water for a bath. The tubs and bowls became indelibly colored with the yellow pigment which the janitors and house wives scrubbed assiduously without end, and also without results. Morgan also had installed a central furnace in the basement of the main building to heat it and the two dormitories.

As one part of his plan for the college, he envisioned establishing some small business enterprises that would employ students. He believed in work experience as one means of securing an effective education. Before I arrived, a handful of student projects had been started, only one of which survived—the Antioch Bookplate Company. Although some colleges do use local industries to train students and to help them earn their way in college—Berea is the outstanding example—the objective is difficult to implement. In our competitive society the product manufactured becomes too expensive and often lacks refinement. The projects at Antioch supported a few students, but they could hardly be justified for this purpose alone.

The plan would have failed had it not been for another idea. This was to use them to nourish the community. The development of the Antioch Art Foundry was one such project. It began in a small horse barn with one man who made his own brick kiln, and grew into a company with two fair-sized plants and over 500 employees. It has had a great impact on the economy of the community.

My goodness! Look at the rain coming down. It's good for my lawn, I having put fertilizer on it the day before yesterday. The drops patter on the roof above my head. Don't you like the sound of rain on a shingle roof. You see, when I was your age, I used to climb up the ladder into our hayloft and lie on the hay and listen to the rain on the roof. And build aircastles. Do you ever dream about what you are going to do and be when you get older? Patter, patter, patter. . . . If you think about things while the rain is pattering over your head, you can't possibly become neurotic. It is too soothing, refreshing, reliable, realistic.

A project in some ways as interesting as the bronze one was the making of a new type of thermostat. One of our professors, Sergius Vernet, thought it up one day. And so we started a project with the idea.

Thermostats had been in use for a long time and they were reasonably good, but our idea was better. And that is what it takes to become successful—"a better mouse trap." But you have to keep improving on your idea or the other fellow will jump ahead of you. That is why research is so important. The existing thermostats were being made of bimetallic strips so designed that they would expand with heat and contract with cold. We had a different idea.

Do you know about glaciers? How they move, scooping up millions of tons of earth as they move, carving out deep valleys in the mountains? They move because the ice expands. Well, some crystals expand and contract with changes in heat and cold. We took a small bunch of crystals, put them in a capsule, and then harnessed the capsule to a lever. So we now had a little machine that could do a lot of work, such as opening and closing valves. A simple tool setup enabled us to make the capsules, and we employed the Detroit Lubricator Company to make the rest of the gadget. Presently we were selling thermostats to use in washing machines, Ford automobiles, and many other things.

We started the project in the basement of the science building, but as it became successful we moved it to a small building on the edge of the campus. Later the company, which we incorporated separately from the college, expanded still more, and began making plastic items such as valve fittings. Today it has plants in Yellow Springs, Florida, Georgia, and the Netherlands, employs hundreds of persons, and brings a large cash flow into the community. We named the company Vernay Laboratories, Inc., after Serg Vernet.

I confess we had a bit of luck. Or was it really luck? Or perhaps foresight? During the war when the United States invaded North Africa, it had difficulty with the tanks because the thermostats in them would not react properly to the intense heat. Whereupon officers at Wright Field, which was located near Yellow Springs, came to us with the problem. They tried our thermostat and found it to be more powerful and dependable than what they had been using. Immediately we were in big business because they switched to ours.

So this baby project which had required subsidization to get started, now became a big money earner. It also became one of the means of converting a poverty stricken village into one where people could put fresh paint on their houses and eat T-bone steaks. And also do things that put some joy into living.

One of the students we had during the middle thirties was Henry Wallace, Junior, son of Henry Wallace who became Vice President of the United States in 1941. The Wallaces had built one of the major enterprises for producing hybrid corn seed. One of the phenomena of nature is that if you cross-breed two different strains of plants or animals, the product will be larger than either parent. You can also cross-breed to achieve certain objectives; in corn these might be to develop a strain of corn that had hard kernels, or a kernel with certain nutritious qualities, or a stalk and tassel that would resist the heat of the sun, or a plant that would grow best in certain soil. So if you grow hybridized seed, you achieve two results; extra quantity, and corn of the type you wish to produce.

Through Henry Wallace we negotiated with the Wallace organization (the Pioneer Company in Iowa) for the rights for Ohio and the Eastern part of the United States. This meant experimenting to develop corn that would fit well the soil and climate of each of the Eastern states, and the right to produce seed for sale to farmers. As a result we set up a company with the ownership shared between The Pioneer Company and Antioch.

Then we began experiments to develop the desired types of seed. We also had to educate the farmers because they were very skeptical about trying something that sounded so different. Among other things they would have to pay us a premium for seed. Not until we had demonstrated to them, through experimental plots, that our seed would produce 50%, and sometimes 100% more corn to the acre than the seed they had been using, did they really join in the hybridization program. Then they nearly all did so. So we not only had a paying business, but we had helped the farmers to improve greatly their farming and their incomes.

I make it sound too simple. In order to produce hybridized seed, it is necessary to inbreed a particular strain of corn for seven years. Presently we found that we could grow the corn in Mexico where we could get two crops a year, thus reducing by half the time required to inbreed.

Some day when you go on a vacation trip to Yucatan, be sure to read up on how the Mayans raised corn. They would cut the shrubs and trees in a patch of the jungle, then burn the cut materials. This produced ashes which fertilized the soil. In this patch they grew corn. When one patch declined in productivity, they just cut another patch. You can see these patches in the jungle from a plane.

The years of inbreeding resulted in nubbins. If you were not aware of the scientific principles involved, you would just throw the nubbins away. No, don't do that, for the purpose was to make certain that the characteristics you wanted were implanted in the seed. Now take some seed of a local variety of corn, plant one row of it, then a row of the inbred seed, then two rows of the local seed, then one row of the inbred seed, and so on. When the corn begins to tassel you must be very careful, because you must cut off all of the tassels on the stalks of the local corn and leave the tassels of the inbred corn. This results in the fertilization of all of the silks by the pollen from the inbred corn. The two rows of local corn will thus produce the hybrid seed you want.

On the farm we used to put our corn ears in cribs so that the wind could blow through and dry them. But in producing seed at Antioch we put the ears in bins, and then sent steam from our power plant through the bins until the moisture content was lowered sufficiently so there would be no mildewing or spoilage. Now the ears could be shelled and the seed sacked and labeled. On the farm we had a hand sheller, and little Algo often had to turn the crank.

Matthew, when your father buys seeds to plant in his garden, you grab the seed packet and read what it says, whether it is hybrid or not. If it is not hybrid seed, ask him why not get the *best* seed. Then say to him: "My grandfather was one of the earliest people who began to produce hybrid seed for farmers, and he helped the farmers all over the Eastern states to learn how to grow a lot more corn per acre than they had been doing."

The bronze, thermostat, and hybrid seed projects in time all became big successes, and other projects such as the Antioch Press and the Antioch Bookplate Company each employed people in the village. Shortly after I became president of the college, we worked out the idea that the projects should become community projects, developed in a way to nourish the community and help it to prosper. They were separately incorporated; I wrote out the incorporation papers myself. Individuals like the Beans, Mazzolini, J. L. Snook (of the Antioch Shoe project), and Vernet, were given substantial interests because they had contributed heavily to getting the projects well established, and employees and persons in the village were given opportunity to purchase stock in the corporations. The Antioch Bookplate Company had always been a separate project; in others the college continued a stock interest and held royalty rights.

Also it must be admitted projects such as the foundry and Vernay Laboratories had begun to grow so much as commercial operations, it was not advisable for the college to continue to dominate them. The hybrid corn project expanded beyond the ability of our power plant to service it, so our interest was sold to the Pioneer Company and the business moved away.

One interesting consequence of the development of these several industries was that other small industries became attracted to the village. A couple of graduates began to make fine instruments; another graduate developed an engineering products laboratory; a man found a market for table tops made of granite and smoothed to perfection—for use in laboratories; a professor operated a stained glass studio and did work all over the Eastern United States; a graduate established a landscape design service, and her husband an advertising agency; and several other business activities were launched or moved to the community. It seems that when a town is dead nothing can bestir it from its sleepy ways. But if an energizing influence is brought into play, everything begins to stir in a creative way. Antioch College had done this in Yellow Springs.

We did a lot of other things in the community—at times the villagers thought we were doing things *to* them, and of course resented it. When I first began to know the people, some of them were still discussing, after 70 years, how Horace Mann, first president of the college, when invited to join the local Christian Church, had stood in the congregation and announced that he was accepting the invitation but that he was doing so with reservations about the creed! We had our problems in persuading the villagers to change their ways of looking at and doing things, but in each case we usually won after patient effort.

One of our efforts was to change the character of the village government. Some of us had been attracted to the city manager form of government, then a relatively new idea. A committee was formed to look into the subject. Anne was a member. They came up with a recommendation for the change and it was voted in. So the affairs of the village were put on a more efficient basis. In the meantime we had persuaded the village to create a water and sewage disposal system; Hugh Birch, a friend of the college provided some of the funds.

Mr. Morgan had a great love for the woods and decided that the campus should be expanded. It had consisted of 20 acres, neatly confined within four streets of the village. We began to break these barriers, although when we wanted to vacate a street we had to do so over much opposition. We also acquired about 1000 acres of the limestone gorge that passed the front of the campus. This became a park of great natural beauty; and it adjoined the Bryan State Park, the two tracts making a site for recreation, conservation, and public enjoyment.

I shall mention some additional actions we took, but discuss them only briefly because this letter is getting long. In the meantime I have helped Granny crack open a coconut. Have you ever cracked a coconut? And drunk the juice? Like the boys in the South Sea Islands? Only they shinny up the tree first in order to get one. All we have to do is to shinny down to Safeway, not quite as exciting an adventure!

One of the actions was to create a health service for the entire community by using the college clinic as the nucleus. Sort of like the Mayo Clinic in Minnesota, but on a small scale. The plan appealed and after a bit we had so many patients that we had to employ several additional doctors and rent additional space.

We founded an area theater with both winter and summer programs, and with village people participating. In a sequence of summers the theater ran through the complete cycle of Shakespeare's plays—for the first time in the United States.

We started the first nursery school in Ohio, the thirteenth in the nation; and presently there were three in the village, one of the additional ones being an adjunct to our research in child development. We worked to improve the schools and at one point gave a beautiful tract of land as a village park and site for a new school. We introduced concert/lecture series, resuming where the Chautauqua had left off a quarter century earlier. A journal, the Antioch Review, devoted to economic problems and cultural interests, was launched. We had a play program for boys and girls, letting them use our gymnasium at certain times. After our power plant was built we provided the village with electricity, and reduced the rates considerably.

The college took the lead in working out better relations between whites and blacks, and we caused the discrimination against blacks at the village theater and the Presbyterian Church to be discontinued.

Golly, we did so many things! But we succeeded in making a profound change in the character of the community. Matthew, the next time you stop in Yellow Springs drive around and see what a nice community it has become. And try to imagine the contrast with what it was when your grandmother and I arrived and were told that

College president relaxing

154

the only house available for us to live in had an outdoor toilet and no running water.

GRANDFATHER

March 12, 1980

Dear Ilya,

This very moment I have completed making out the annual reports —on federal and state income tax and for the Attorney General of California—for the Kennedy-King Scholarship Fund. The organization is exempt, but nevertheless it takes two days to fill out the forms. As you know, Jean is treasurer of the foundation.

Recently Antioch College asked me to prepare a tape about the founding of Glen Helen, the 1000-acre campus of the college. It has been fifty years since the deed was given to the college, so they are planning a celebration. And want the benefit of my memory as to how it all happened.

The most interesting and valuable part of the glen lay directly opposite the main buildings of the college. This 60-acre tract had been a famous resort during much of the 19th century, a spa of the type so common during the horse and buggy days. It surrounded the yellow spring which flowed 80 gallons a minute and was laden with a yellow iron deposit. Lots of people thought that this water would cure all their ills. This was before we had pills that will cure anything.

The spa at one point included three hotels. One of them was called the "Glen Forest Water Cure Sanitarium." A dance pavilion was still there when I first knew the tract in 1925. We had lots of parties there. Also there was a small lake which provided us with a skating rink during the icy winters. Joanne, Philip, their mother, and I often went to the glen for ice skating and sled riding and for picnics. The college students and faculty made lots of use of the glen.

It is amusing that at one time the college had a rule that boys might go into the glen on certain days and girls on opposite days. Times have changed, haven't they? Horace Mann, when president during the 1850s wrote an interesting letter, now on file in the archives of the University of Michigan, saying that coeducation had been a real success at Antioch; as yet there had been none of those incidents commonly called accidents because of the night-and-day vigilance of the faculty. Now colleges even have coed dorms. Without any faculty snooping around.

Also, in 1825 Robert Owen established one of his Utopian communities on this tract but it lasted only a year. People are always searching for Utopia. I wonder what is happening to the many communes set up by the disillusioned, but idealistic students in the 1960s. It would be interesting to evaluate them now to see what happened to each of them and to the people.

Still earlier the Indians used the area. One of the 80 Indian mounds in Greene County is near the yellow spring. Supposing it to be a burial mound, we excavated it, but someone else beat us to it. We learned that in an earlier excavation a male of the Adena culture, which existed in Ohio between 1000 to 300 B.C. had been found.

During the early 1900s many Chautauqua programs were given there. Chautauquas were an early form of adult education, and for a time were the rage. I witnessed an interesting event in New York. I was having lunch in a hotel with Oliver Carmichael, head of the Carnegie Foundation and former president of Vanderbilt University. He spotted a man entering the room and said he looked familiar. Who was he? I didn't know. After a few moments he jumped up and went to the table of the other man. When he came back he told me that it was Lieutenant Governor Handley. As young men they had traveled together with a Chautauqua, Handley as orator and Carmichael on the gang that erected the tent.

The college acquired possession of this part of the glen in 1920. Later, about 1928, we got Hugh T. Birch, an Antioch alumnus, interested in the glen which made it possible to buy additional land. The change in campus size and nature was spectacular. As a result of the property buying, the college gained a main campus area of some 50 acres and Glen Helen which composed about 1000 acres. Much of this was achieved while Morgan was president, but as business manager and then dean, I did some of the buying and much of the management. The campus setting is one of the nicest in the United States.

Beginning with the area around the yellow spring, Glen Helen (named in memory of Birch's daughter, Helen) follows the gorge until it reaches the Little Miami River, then down the river to an old covered bridge. It is home for beautiful trees, wildflowers, birds, insects, and little animals, and is a retreat where one can sit beside water falls and springs or hike on the trails that lead endlessly

Glen Helen

through the forest. We had some debate whether to make the glen into some kind of park, but decided, wisely, I think, to let it develop in its natural state.

On the east side of the road that leads to the Grinnell Mill used to stand a small cottage, the site where Moncure Conway freed the slaves that he brought from Virginia. Some of the black people who live in the village are descendents of those slaves. At one point I secured some funds to renovate the cottage. I thought it was a valuable historic site, and also could provide shelter for students who wanted to picnic on a rainy day. Alas, after I left no one cared for it, and the cottage has now disappeared.

Isn't it interesting how we wantonly or neglectfully destroy our history. During my years in New York State 21 historic sites were within the state historical program. We had success in getting the legislature to make restorations and we had funds with which to preserve them.

One building was the one-time home of General Schuyler, a hero of the American Revolution. Alexander Hamilton had married his daughter and the wedding was held in this house. On the staircase there was a deep cut, said to have been made by an Indian tomahawk. We tore off the sheds that had accumulated over the years; also the wall paper which proved to be thirteen layers thick. The original paper was an import from China, hand made, of the type fashionable when the sailing vessels plied between Boston and Shanghai. We found a paper manufacturer on Long Island who duplicated it on condition that he could sell it to others. So now if you visit the Schuyler mansion overlooking the Hudson you will see it as it was when originally built.

In 1935 the National Education Association was thinking of staging a celebration in honor of the beginning of Horace Mann's work in education. Maybe you don't know about Horace Mann. I certainly did not when I first arrived at Antioch. But I soon learned that he had been the first president of the college, and that he is credited with creating the public school system in the United States; also with having founded the first teacher training institution.

After conferring with the officials in Washington, I persuaded them to include Antioch as a major participant, giving the first of a series of events throughout the nation. This took the form of a conference in 1936, the centennial year. Papers given by prominent educators were later published in a book entitled *Education for Democracy*.

A feature of the program was the dedication of a Horace Mann monument. When I told Mr. Birch about our plans he was enthusiastic. Aware of the bronze statue of Mann by Emma Stebbins that stands in front of the state house in Boston, he discovered that a foundry in Munich, Germany, had in its loft the moulds in which the original bronze had been poured. So he ordered another statue to be made and at our conference it was dedicated. It stands at the southeast angle of the campus, the highest point in the county. From this elevated position Mann looks out over the glen and toward the main buildings of the college. Mr. Birch said he wanted the statue to remind the faculty and students continuously of Mann's strength of character and industry.

Having put so much effort into the glen, I still have a strong emotional feeling for the area. Each time I return to Yellow Springs, I take a hike over the trails or hug a huge hackberry or white oak tree, feeling a sense of satisfaction over having a hand in helping to create Glen Helen. Colleges and people may come and go, but the glen will be there for a long, long time.

GRANDFATHER

November 27, 1979

Dear Sabrina,

Now that you are in college do you ever think about how a college finances itself? Most students are oblivious to all the effort that goes on behind the academic scenes to subsidize their education. A private college is like a pauper; it has to pass around its begging bowl to get the money to pay the faculty and running expenses, or at least the portion of this that enables the institution to keep going.

While at Antioch as president I did the usual begging, but at one point the college became involved in a real estate operation that was fabulous—a Cinderella kind of venture. An alumnus, Hugh T. Birch, bequeathed to the college a tract of undeveloped land fronting on the most beautiful beach in Florida at Ft. Lauderdale.

Seeing that we were faced with a major real estate problem, I hastened to New York to get advice from Joseph P. Day, the biggest real estate wheeler-dealer in New York and perhaps in the world. His son, Joe, had been a student at the college. Day was quite taken with the prospects and on his own made a trip to Ft. Lauderdale to inspect the property. He conceived a plan under which we would develop 80 acres on the ocean front with apartment houses. The construction would be financed by a huge loan, $30,000,000 from the Metropolitan Life Insurance Company—Day was on their board and claimed he had cleared the matter with the compny. We needed only to put our land in the hopper. The income from the leased properties, according to Day, would easily pay all expenses, including interest, payments on principal, and operating expenses. At the end of 30 years we would have the whole property free and clear; and each year we would have a handsome income. What more could you want?

I had a lot of confidence in Day and knew he had the college's interest in mind. Earlier he had given us the money to buy a house and property, the one in which your mother and your Uncle Philip attended nursery school. So we were all set to get on with the deal.

Mr. Day made another trip to Florida. Arriving at Penn Station in New York on his return he dropped dead. That was the end of that air castle!

After feeling out the possibilities of selling the land, we decided we would get the most money by developing the land and selling the lots. So the college attorney, Homer Corry, and I employed a staff in Ft. Lauderdale consisting of a local attorney, an engineer, an architect, and a sales manager.

First it was necessary to build a seawall along the intercoastal canal. We decided to make it six feet above normal tide level and to make it out of concrete slabs. Most of the developers in this area used a 4 1/2- or 5-foot wall made out of wood. This was much cheaper, but would not retain the water at its highest levels and would not last long. Furthermore, the wood would be a breeding ground for the little black flies, no-see-ums, that bite so viciously.

Then the mangrove had to be removed from the swamp. Mangrove is hard as iron and had to be dug by the roots to prevent future growth and also permit the laying of utility lines. Next we negotiated an agreement with the federal government to pump seashell and mud out of the canal and the adjacent river. This was mutually advantageous because it deepened the waterway—used by boats along the eastern coast of the U. S.—and provided us with fill. We pumped the stuff by hydraulic means. Presently we had a nice level piece of property, 80 acres, six feet above mean tide level.

We put all utility lines, including sewers underground. This was tricky because of the new fill and water-logged earth. Some of it required special bedding underneath. Interestingly, much of Miami was not served by sewers but by septic tanks. I wonder why they haven't had a major epidemic. Perhaps the Cuban and South American immigrants are immune to the germs. Finally we built a system of streets and paved them. For most of this work we were able to employ a Baltimore firm that had had war contracts in the area and still had their equipment available. Fortunately we got a firm price, which came to about $700,000; shortly thereafter a rapid inflation of prices occurred.

One hears a lot about people buying lots in Florida while they are still under water. This was the case with our property. For we had to begin to sell lots before the work was done in order to get money, down payments, to pay our expenses.

Selling lots for small fortunes was a strange experience for me, accustomed as I was to paying $500 for a lot. All of a sudden I had become a "big shot" in real estate. Well, we collected over $3,000,000 from this 80 acres and made a profit of about $2,000,000. And we still had a large tract on the west side of the canal. Of course, these figures do not seem so big in 1979. Sabrina, when is a dollar a dollar?

The lots sold like hot cakes. I guess they should have, for the beach was one of the most beautiful in the world and the closest Florida beach to the Gulf Stream. I tried to persuade the trustees of the college to authorize leasing the lots on long term leases. This was on the theory that since a college has perpetual life, the college would have this valuable property in perpetuity, all the while collecting a handsome income from it. But Corry, influenced by the real estate agents, disagreed and the conservative-minded trustees voted with him. I later discovered that the real estate interests were afraid that with leases, the Jews would move in and "spoil" Ft. Lauderdale in the way Miami Beach had been "spoiled."

I also learned from Corry that one agent had sold a lot to a Jew not knowing he was a Jew; and upon finding this out had voided the transaction. I suspect they bought the man out giving him a nice profit. All of which was revolting. But the real estate operators were an essential part of the team in getting the maximum results from the sales and getting them quickly so we could pay our bills. Just think how the college would have gained, considering today's values, if it still had the propety under those long-term leases. Perhaps also the endowment would not have been lost, as have the securities realized from the sale of the land, during the recent wild expansion of the college.

We did one thing of which I am very proud. We donated the beach itself to the City of Ft. Lauderdale. Part of the bargain was in getting the cooperation of the city in building our sewer and connecting it with the city's disposal plant. But the beach is now a public beach, and not a series of private domains as is the case in Miami Beach and Palm Beach. Furthermore all of the people who live on the interior lots have a perfect right to use the beach even though a hotel may be on the lot fronting the ocean. Jean and I spent our honeymoon on this beach.

Antiochians who visit this part of Ft. Lauderdale can recognize it readily because we named the streets after former Antioch presidents and distinguished graduates.

GRANDFATHER

February 28, 1975

Dear Matthew,

I would like to be younger. Not that I don't enjoy the Golden Years, but because I would like to do something that I could have done if I were younger. Thursday evening a man called me from New York and asked me if I would resume the presidency of Antioch College while the trustees were searching for a new man. He was Stan Thea and said he was speaking for the Executive Committee of the Board of Trustees. I didn't give him an answer offhand because an offer of this kind is given only after matured consideration. But I am not young enough to undertake major and strenuous responsibilities of the kind I formerly carried.

The problem is that the college is in a jam, financially and in morale, and so the president would be in the middle of controversy and divisions of opinion as to what actions to take. He would make decisions but then would have to spend an inordinate amount of time trying to make them stick. When a person is past seventy, he loses some of the intestinal fortitude to contend with emergencies and controversies.

When I was in the army I got my first experience in trying to lift an organization out of a crisis situation. Our company, housed in some old national guard tents in Georgia, was short of clothing, arms, and almost everything in the early stages of our involvement in World War I. We didn't have much budget allowance for food, and the mess sergeant had run the company far into debt.

As Ordnance Sergeant, I was senior in rank so the company commander asked me to take over the operation and pull the company out of debt. I did so by standing over the cook and supervising the amount of meat that the men could have. I can still remember the looks on some of their faces when they saw how little they were getting to eat.

The college had faced a somewhat similar crisis in the 1930's. The immediate incident was the sudden departure of Arthur Morgan, the president, to become chairman of the Tennessee Valley Authority in May 1933. But the crisis that existed was deeper in causes and longer in duration than is implied by the loss of a president.

In a way, the situation confronting the college came up suddenly. President Morgan had gone to Washington in March to see if he could persuade President Roosevelt to give federal backing to a conservancy project for the Muskingum River in Ohio. Morgan was a flood control engineer of large reputation, and was serving as consultant to the conservancy district. When Morgan entered the Oval room for the interview, Roosevelt immediately began to talk about the TVA. Congress had authorized its establishment, and now the President was searching for a chairman. On the spot he invited Morgan to the position. (James M. Cox, former Governor of Ohio, and the Democratic candidate for president in 1920, had recommended Morgan.) Morgan asked for a few days and consulted with Clarence Pickett and me and undoubtedly others. But within ten days from his visit to the White House, he told the President he would accept. He was instructed to go to Tennessee immediately and begin to make the dirt fly. I was dean of the college and was left the responsibility for administering the college. It was not quite that simple, though. Morgan asked me to go with him to the TVA as its chief financial officer. That was tempting especially since the college had such slender finances and its future was in question. But how could both the president and the dean leave? I was committed to Antioch and so I remained. Moreover, dozens of the faculty wrote me letters asking me to stay. They said in effect: "You are now our leader." The letters are in my files since one doesn't throw these kinds of tributes away.

There had been a previous crisis. During 1931-32 President Morgan had taken a sabbatical leave and spent several months in Europe. Vice-President Patterson and I were left in charge. While staying in Portugal, Morgan wrote a several-page letter to the faculty, sent it to his son, Ernest, with instructions to print and make it public. The letter, later called by the faculty, "The Epistle from Portugal," was essentially a diatribe against the faculty for not sufficiently comprehending Morgan's ideas about education and following his direction.

The dean and family, 1932

An orchid to the president from the faculty, 1943

Unfortunately he chose to cite as a principal example, the case of his son, Griscom. The college at that time was using comprehensive examinations as an additional check on the seniors' ability to integrate their knowledge. The previous spring Morgan had asked that his son, who was only finishing his freshman year, be permitted to take the exams. This he did. In the examination, all papers were always typed in standard form and graded anonymously. Three faculty read each paper. Griscom came out lowest in the group and fell materially below all the others. This was not his fault since he was just ending his first year of college and the examination covered four years of college. Morgan, however, had gone over the paper himself and in his letter to the faculty contended that the faculty had completely misjudged the paper. Naturally this provoked consternation.

To quiet the emotions and keep them somewhat under control, I called an assembly of the students and faculty. I read the Morgan letter to the audience and commented on the need to give its contents careful attention, saying that we would set up a faculty committee for the purpose.

The faculty elected a committee, a rather large and representative one and chose me as chairman. We had a number of sessions pouring over the charges and discussing strategy—Morgan had created an issue between himself and the faculty where most of us thought none had really existed. Presently we decided to summon him home and he did come. Thereafter we met with Morgan several times but I continued to preside. We talked the matter out but without resolving the problem in Morgan's mind. I think it became clear that Morgan had written the letter when he was in a depressed mood. This experience, together with my work on the budgets of the college, doubtless was what caused the faculty to ask me to stay with them.

When Morgan departed in May, I reexamined the budget of the college. The year 1933 was the beginning of the deepest period of the great depression of the thirties. All of the banks of the country had been closed temporarily the preceding March by presidential order. The nation was obviously in a bad way economically. This was beginning to affect Antioch because students could not pay tuitions, employers were letting off student employees under the work-study plan, gifts to the college were falling off. On top of that the man who had been so much the college itself, and its chief money raiser, was suddenly departing. The best I could see in the budget picture was a deficit of 40% of the money needed to pay faculty salaries the coming year.

Herman Schnurer, professor of French, came up with an intriguing idea. It called for putting the faculty on a drawing allowance month to month, the amount being based upon the individual's salary but modified by his responsibility for dependents. One man with seven children got a larger monthly payment than the acting president. Need was the determining factor. The difference between the allowance and the basic salary was paid at the end of the half year and year, respectively, but only to the extent that cash was available for the purpose. The rest was cancelled. This plan was adopted by the faculty and also approved by the trustees. It presented a viable mode of operation. It kept the faculty intact instead of throwing some of them onto the breadlines; and it avoided putting the college further into debt. We already had a substantial debt, a hangover from the reorganization of the college in 1920 on which we had to pay interest each year. After I was confirmed as president we put on a financial drive and paid off this debt, but that was later when the economy of the nation was improving.

Financing Antioch during the ensuing four or five years was like turning the hose on a series of fires. Student enrollment dropped, students out of work had to be subsidized, our friends had to cut their gifts, the alumni were not yet in positions of affluence and hence, in spite of unusual loyalty, were unable to help much. The endowment of the college at this point was $160,000 (compare with Harvard's present billion) and the income only $10,000 a year—important but not much help.

The college survived. I suppose that is why alumni of the period, like Stan Thea, tend to think that I have some magical powers to deal with crises. It isn't magic that does the trick. The settlement of a crisis takes much work, constant conferring with the people involved, careful thought about possible courses of action, and a resolution to succeed once decisions are made. It is essential to level with people, giving them the facts that form the bases for your own decisions and helping them to express opinions that are constructive rather than hostile.

Jean and I are sending you a little present. We hope that you like it because it was bought from the Hopi Indians in Arizona.

GRANDFATHER

VI

Having been in on the founding of the TVA, the establishment of the State University of New York, the creation of the first Center for the Study of Higher Education, and other innovations in the public service, I not only want to brag to you grandchildren about my experiences, but hopefully to stimulate your thinking about participation in civic affairs in creative ways.

February 9, 1976

Dear Peter and Matthew,

   Did you ever hear of a river that flows through seven states and drains all 50 states? That was the way the people who opposed the Tennessee Valley Authority (known as the TVA) categorized the Tennessee River. I want to tell you some things about the TVA. I have been reminded of my experiences with it by the death of Arthur E. Morgan, first chairman of the TVA, at age 97. Incidentally, when I was first at Antioch in 1925 there was great apprehension among the faculty that Morgan, then president of the college, might die. At that time the college was almost wholly dependent on him. He seemed to the faculty to be frail, of doubtful health, and working too hard. If he had passed away probably the college would also have done so. Little did we realize that he was to outlive most of the other persons then engaged with him in restoring the college to its one-time greatness.
   The TVA, founded in 1933, has been one of the great innovations in public enterprise. However, Morgan's book, *The Making of the TVA* (Prometheus, 1974), is heavily a recount of his experiences in trying to work with the other two members of the Board. I was amazed to see how Morgan's frustrations had hung on over the many years. It would have been a stronger book, and much more favorable to Morgan, had he related the objectives of the TVA and then spelled out how fully they had been achieved. Many of the programs that Morgan originated were subsequently implemented.
   I made frequent trips to Norris and Knoxville during 1933-36, both as consultant to TVA and concerning Antioch business. Thus I saw the Tennessee landscape and became quite familiar with the conditions in the valley that brought the TVA into existence. To

some degree it was a "make work" venture because 1933 was a year of terrible unemployment and adverse financial conditions. This accounts for one of the troubles within the TVA board—President Roosevelt had instructed Morgan to make the dirt fly. Morgan, in characteristic fashion did so, starting the Norris Dam before the other two members of the board were chosen. When David Lilienthal and Harcourt Morgan, the other board members, came on the job they found that Morgan had made some major decisions. Morgan's character would have led him to do so anyhow; he was self-reliant and impatient with delays caused by consultations. So the other two directors found it convenient to gang together and could thus outvote him. At one point they also relieved him as chief engineer, a move that hurt his pride deeply as is evident by the stress he put upon the incident in his book.

In 1952, some twenty years later, Anne and I drove through the Tennessee valley to observe the changes that had been effected. They were really tremendous. The erosion had been stopped, the barren hillsides were green once again, the new forests were thriving, the huge reservoirs of water were surrounded by parks for recreation and were active with boats and water skiing. There wre barges on the river carrying goods cheaply compared with truck and rail transportation. Power lines led to villages and the countryside, and of course, the people now had power for appliances, light, and heat. The rates for utilities were not high, the TVA having produced electricity at low cost and the rate schedules, modeled after those of the Ontario Hydroelectric Company, were a new departure in rate making taking into account the needs of the householder, the small business man, and the farmer in buying power. Some industries in the TVA area, such as chemicals and fertilizers, had grown in size, and of course, the TVA became the first home for the production of atomic energy. We were impressed by the evidences that the TVA dream had come true.

When Morgan was ousted by Rossevelt in 1938, Lilienthal was made chairman. Under him, the emphasis shifted from land and water development to the production of power. This proved to be a valuable addition to the scope of activities because the demands for power became great during and following World War II. But it was also too bad that the Morgan plans for the development of small industries to be operated by the people—ceramics, furniture, forest products, and so forth, were not carried through as fully as they deserved. Bigness and concentration prevailed over distribution among the many.

Morgan gives me credit for assisting him in evaluating the qualifications of David Lilienthal as a prospective board member. I did this, interviewing some 20 persons in Chicago and Madison and also Dave himself. Governor Philip LaFollette of Wisconsin tried to persuade me simply to accept his endorsement; but how could I do that—regardless of how eminent the man expressing the opinion. The opinions, with one exception, were very favorable. Contrary to these high opinions of the man and his qualifications, I ran into one man in Chicago, a former employer of Lilienthal, who told me a totally different story. This was not Mr. Cassels, as described by Morgan in his book, but George McKibben.

This man described Lilienthal as ego-centered, ruthless, and determined to ride over anyone who stood in his way. These are, of course, the qualities of personality that Morgan encountered as they tried to work together at TVA. Of course, I had reported this to Morgan, but the evidence in favor of the appointment was so overwhelming—in spite of the one adverse opinion (I had gone back to this man three times to quiz him about his story, but he stuck to it)—that I recommended favorably. Whereupon Morgan arranged with President Roosevelt to appoint Lilienthal to the board.

In a recent editorial article in *Newsweek*, Lilienthal speaks of the human element—the land planning, the efforts to overcome poverty and to raise the cultural and economic tone of the TVA region as an example of action in accord with the best recent thinking. I wrote him a friendly note, pointing out that these were the very things that Morgan had tried to get the TVA to do that he, Lilienthal, had opposed at the time. A footnote to the article identified Lilienthal as "the father of the TVA." I wrote to *Newsweek* reminding them that Senator Norris was the father, that Morgan was the first chairman, and that it was Morgan who developed most of the ideas. I sent Dave a copy; but I got no answer from him nor from *Newsweek*. Floyd Reeves had told me years ago that Dave believed that I had recommended against his appointment to the board.

Morgan speaks of Reeves in his book. I had suggested his name to Morgan for appointment as the chief personnel officer. It was because in the earliest days time was so precious and there was so much organizing to do, that I helped Morgan recruit top personnel. Another of these was Harlan Bartholomew, who became the chief land planning officer.

I was drawn in again by Morgan when he was at the height of his difficulties with Lilienthal and was appealing his dismissal to the Supreme Court. This was an effort to bolster Morgan's case, rather than to decide what should be done. Morgan, as usual, had made that decision. But we did thrash through some of the situations where there had been differences of policy.

The chief of these was in the Berry marble deal. Berry was a Tennessee politician and an interim United States senator. When he saw where the Norris Dam was going to be built, he got options on the "mineral rights" on hundreds of acres of land that he knew would be flooded. After the reservoir was full of water, he submitted a claim for millions of dollars of damages claiming that the water had covered his valuable marble. The rock was not marble but a low-quality dolomite of little value. But Berry's claim did not rest upon the marble, but upon his power as a senator. Roosevelt did not want to oppose him because he needed his political support.

Lilienthal and Harcourt Morgan came up on Berry's side, proposing to compromise the claim and thus settle it quietly. This pleased the President and the Senator's buddies in the Senate.

Arthur Morgan strongly opposed doing this because it was perfectly clear what Berry had done. The whole thing was a fraud and to compromise it violated Morgan's code of morals. So they had a big battle, not so much with Berry, but within the TVA board. Morgan was of course outvoted. But this was the kind of action that he could not easily forget.

The President fired Morgan for contumacy. Morgan contended in the Supreme Court hearing that the TVA law vested in the board and the chairman all powers relating to personnel, hence the dismissal by the President was illegal. The Court ruled otherwise. This is one of the rulings of the Court frequently cited to define the powers of the President of the United States over personnel. Roosevelt could not have taken any other action than to correct the situation in the TVA Board; but he should have fired Lilienthal rather than Morgan.

Morgan was unable to see that the personality clashes at the TVA were partly his own fault. At the outset of his chairmanship, before Harcourt Morgan and Lilienthal were appointed, there was reason for his plunging ahead with decisions and actions. His ability to do this was one of his strengths. However, his habit was to bring decisions to a board for discussion expecting them always to be approved. This was why we at Antioch thought of him as "authoritarian."

An illustration will reveal this trait. At the TVA, shortly after the board was assembled, Morgan brought to it a full code of ethics that was meant to govern the behavior of all TVA personnel. This caught H. Morgan and Lilienthal completely by surprise. They had had no opportunity to discuss even the need for such a code. They were a bit astonished by some of the provisions. Naturally they refused to adopt it. This approach to his role as chairman of a board where all members have equal responsibility for their votes, in my opinion was a primary reason why his fellow members united against him. He subscribed to an outmoded entrepreneur-based school of thought, not applicable to government, and not consistent with behavioral theory in organization and administration.

The TVA is one of the most significant developments that has taken place in the United States. The renovation and the development of the resources, human and natural, of this large region could not possibly have been done by the private sector. Neither the money nor the motivation would have been adequate. Furthermore, this was not a profit-making situation. The TVA as a public, semi-autonomous organization was the answer. It is an example that can and will be used in many future situations. At the moment, the nation needs this type of organization to solve the problems of energy, transportation, pollution, and conservation.

The TVA has been a great success. The concept and the achievements are universally admired in other parts of the world. It is too bad that we have not developed more TVAs, but the war intervened, private industry has lobbied powerfully against the concept, and much of the post-war period has been dominated by the activities of conglomerates.

In general, the people are afraid to expand the role of the government. They accept government as the agency to prepare for and prosecute war but not to conserve resources and promote human welfare.

It was tremendously interesting to have been on the scene of the TVA when the egg was being hatched.

GRANDFATHER

January 21, 1980

Dear Ilya,

I've just come in from trimming and digging out blackberry vines. Blackberries have the ability to send out a long stem and whenever it touches the ground, it takes root and starts another vine. So the vine keeps hopping, hopping all over my orchard unless I control it by slaughtering it. It does no good just to cut it off. In a few weeks the vine will again have stems several feet long that take root and begin hopping forward. I wonder why they are so persistent when they can see that I don't like this. And I murder them. But we do like *some* blackberries; they are delicious. We eat them with cream, make jellies, put them on ice cream, and make liqueur. But I don't like them to run over me the way they do. Well, tough life for those that do. Me with my grub axe.

Guess who is going to be the next President of the Rossmoor Schoolmasters Club? The members are mostly retirees, but include many individuals of high distinction. However, the club has been limited to males and has had rather hum-drum meetings. I am helping to open the gates to women and introduce some social features, and I shall put some sparks into the programs. Do you think I will land on my fanny?

Speaking of education, I had some experiences right after World War II that broadened my own horizons considerably. The most important one was as a member of the President's Commission on Higher Education. It met during 1946-47 and upon conclusion issued a five-volume report entitled *Higher Education for American Democracy*. I have a personal copy with the gold embossed seal of the United States and also my name in gold on the hardback cover. Maybe you would like to have it some day.

On a visit to Washington in the winter of 1945, Donald Kingsley, Assistant to President Harry Truman, asked to see me. Don had been a professor of political science at Antioch College, one of the young men I had hired for the staff. When he came for the interview he appeared very immature, and had I not been on the point of leaving for Manitoulin, I might not have employed him. However, he did have stellar recommendations. He turned out to be one of the ablest teachers, and scholars, we ever had. Much later he was the civilian who teamed with General McArthur in Korea. After that he became a vice-president of the Ford Foundation.

Don said that the President was going to establish two commissions, one in science and one in education, to survey post-war needs. I suspect this was Don's idea, but the President had made the decision. He asked me for suggestions and for recommendations for the commission on education.

I thought the appointees should be persons of imagination and experience and whose concerns would be with public policy and not merely with the welfare of their own institutions. I suggested three men: T. R. McConnell, Earl McGrath, and Alvin Eurich. All three were appointed. And to my surprise, because Don had said nothing, I was also named. The Commission had 28 members, all a bit unusual —among them Milton Eisenhower, Agnes Meyer, Horace Kallen, Ordway Tead, Oliver Carmichael. Apparently political affiliations had nothing to do with the appointments.

We met frequently in Washington. We had a sizable staff to do the research. The Chairman was George Zook, the president of the American Council on Education, the most prestigious organization involving all of the post high school institutions of learning. One staff member remarked that I always sat at the table with a little black notebook in front of me—I still use the notebook, a looseleaf binder, so it is always current with whatever I am working on. It is really very convenient, so I recommend the idea to you.

Our task was a sweeping one—to examine all of post-high school education and recommend public policy relating to it. The need to do this can be understood when one appreciates the situation of the colleges and universities just after the war. Men and women of college age who had been in military service were returning to the campuses in huge numbers; a larger percentage of women were becoming interested in going to college; and black students were beginning to ask for more education. There were also emotional charges of discrimination by colleges and professional schools, especially the medical schools.

The colleges, moreover, had been starved for funds during the long depression and war years, a span of about 15 years. This meant that additions to plant had been delayed and so the facilities were totally inadequate to accomodate the postwar bulges in enrollment. Furthermore, the maintenance of buildings had been kept at a minimum and much repair and renovation were needed. During the war, because of the needs of the war machine for technically trained men and scarce materials, it had not been possible for the colleges to purchase equipment or to take advantage of improved equipment and newly designed products. For these various reasons the institutions required huge sums of money and, as often happens, the Federal Government was the logical and perhaps the only source of large funds.

Congress had already put into action a scholarship program for returning veterans, the "GI Bill," indicating that the government was encouraging veterans to go to college. Great numbers of them did so. Now the question arose, would not a federally supported scholarship/loan fund assist economically disadvantaged youth to get to college? What talent was the nation losing because so many youth could not afford to go to college?

The Commission quickly agreed that equality of opportunity to go to college was a primary issue. Hence we proceeded to make an inventory of talent among young people. For this purpose the Army General Classification Test, which during the war had been given to some 10,000,000 young people of approximately college age was used. A really large sample and covering all social, economic and ethnic groups in the population. From the results of the tests we concluded that 49% of youth had the intellectual competence to attend college for 2 years and 32% for 4 years.

The total post-high school enrollment in 1939, the last normal prewar year, had been 1,494,000 students. We decided that the nation should establish a goal of 4,600,000 post-high school students. This was a huge increase, but looking back on subsequent developments the recommendation proved to have been a modest one. We were of course concerned with the interest of the nation rather than merely those of young people who took the initiative in applying to go to college. That is, we thought that a nation should seek out its talented young people and help them to get an education thereby adding to the nation's human resources.

Catholic members of the Commission were determined to recommend financial aid from government to private colleges. Other members were equally opposed. One day there was a really terrific debate. The principal participants were Monsignor Frederick Hochwalt, then the top priest in charge of Catholic education in the United States; Bishop Bromley Oxnam, a leading bishop of the Methodist Church; and Rabbi Stephen Wise, probably the greatest Jewish leader of his time.

Such extemporaneous, emotional orating I had never heard. These giants in religion literally left their seats and paced the floor arguing their respective views, the Catholic on one side and the Protestant and Jew on the other. They were concerned with many facets of the problem, but mainly these two: the destruction of the freedom of private institutions through the seductive influence of public funds; and the probable deterioration of the public school system if some of its funds were diverted and if people were pitched into controversy over public and private education. The Commission voted overwhelmingly not to grant public funds to private institutions.

Another emotional issue was that of segregation. Here there was a north-south split. The recommendation was to end segregation. Four members entered a reservation. I have never understood one of these votes. Lewis Jones had been president of Bennington College in Vermont and later became president of the National Conference of Christians and Jews. But at this time he was president of the University of Arkansas. I suspect he voted to keep segregation because he was afraid of criticism in his state. May his conscience rest in peace!

One recommendation was that as the number of veterans eligible for the GI Bill declined, the government should transfer the funds to make them available to youth who needed financial aid. We advocated establishing a large scholarship fund as a continuing federal policy. In retrospect, it can be seen that it took years for this fund to be established; but as of today, the federal government does make available to students in need really generous funds. It also provides or subsidizes substantial loan programs.

Certain of the private universities were shocked by these recommendations. They got two foundations to finance another survey covering substantially the same ground. Their commission recommended that a much smaller segment of the population be educated —essentially the intellectually elite. They barely mentioned the public community college whereas our commission made this type of college a key element in the future of post-high school education. We strongly advocated changing the name from "junior college" to "community college," thus shifting the emphasis from merely offering the first two years of a senior college to a program that would give both general and vocational education, also courses of interest to adults and that would promote the cultural activities in the community.

About five years later, President Eisenhower set up still another commission to survey these problems. Although Republican oriented, it made recommendations similar to those of the Truman Commission.

I think the Truman Commission made a profound impact on higher education. Nearly all of the recommendations have been implemented. The community college movement grew by leaps and bounds. For a time the recommendations about general education and vocational education were followed. Vocational education, especially in the 2-year colleges has grown tremendously. General education, although taking a back seat during the '60s, is again receiving much backing from educational leaders. This ingredient in higher education continues to be typical of higher education in the United States, much more so than in European countries. In some ways, the liberal arts college is unique to America.

Also the federal government has come to the aid of the institutions of higher education in a significant way. This is especially notable in medical education, and in scientific research. One of the effects of the support of research has been the bolstering of graduate level education.

In 1956 I wrote to Harry Truman describing the achievements of the President's Commisssion. In his response he said: "I certainly got a kick out of your last paragraph."

The President's Commission not only influenced national public policy relating to higher education; it also influenced the future actions of the several states. For example, immediately following this, New York established a Commission on the Need for a State University. I was invited to become Associate Director of the New York Commission; the Vice Chairman of the Commission was Oliver Carmichael; and when the State University of New York was authorized by the legislature, Alvin Eurich became the head of it.

In 1949 I was asked to direct a study of higher education for the State of Connecticut. Connecticut had some distinguished private colleges of which Yale, Wesleyan, and the Hartford Seminary are examples. But its public university and teachers colleges were minimal and relatively unknown. Yet the private institutions were serving mostly out of state youth and ignoring those in Connecticut. For example, the children of the recently immigrated Italian farmers of the Connecticut Valley had virtually no opportunity to go to college. Actually they had not been going, but now in this postwar period they wanted to go and Connecticut had made no provision for them. We strongly recommended an egalitarian policy, which meant large scale development of public institutions. This has happened.

Later, the Surgeon General's Commission studying medical education and aid to medical students, of which I was a member, recommended that the federal government take greater responsibility for financing medical education, medical research, and students in the health fields.

So you can see some of the consequences of the work of the President's Commission on Higher Education. Among them we now have 11 or 12 million students in post-high school programs, a huge increase in the number of adults who are taking college level courses, and the universal adoption of the community college idea—the most recent addition being the campus in Dallas for which your father and Uncle Philip designed the plant and campus. It is fair to say that the President's Commission defined the issues, pointed the way, and mapped a model program for post high school education in the United States.

GRANDFATHER

November 11, 1976

Dear Sabrina,

One day in January 1947, while sitting at my desk in the president's office at Antioch College, I received a call from Albany, New York. Dr. Floyd Reeves was on the phone. Floyd and I were well acquainted; he had been on the Board of Trustees of Antioch College. He was one of the most experienced educational survey specialists in the United States.

Floyd said, "Do you know what we are about to do in New York state?" I said, "no." "We're starting to make the most significant study of higher education that has ever been made. I have agreed to direct it, but can be here only half time. We want you to come on as Associate Director to conduct the study under my general supervision."

The study as outlined by him was exceedingly interesting. As it happens, I had been wondering about my future at Antioch. I had been there 22 years, president or acting president for about 15 and I had reached 50 years of age. If I stayed at Antioch I should commit myself for several additional years. But the constant problem of money raising was disheartening. Temperamentally I was not too suited to money raising. It took only a portion of my time, but a lot of my nervous energy. The strain was persistent. Antioch had just secured the Birch endowment which would amount to $5,000,000 or more, and I thought the income from that would put us on easy street. The post-war inflation with its increased costs and salaries, however, wiped out any advantage from the new income. This considerably deflated my optimism.

Anne and I discussed the subject carefully; she was involved in community affairs and emotionally rooted in Yellow Springs. So was I, but I thought that a brief experience of this sort would be very refreshing. I accepted the New York assignment, but returned to Antioch weekends or at least every two weeks. In this way I continued as president of the college, but with substantial help from Vice President Boyd Alexander in the day to day operations. Reeves agreed to the plan.

So, in February 1947 I began work in Albany with the Temporary Commission on the Need for a State University. The commission, chaired by Owen D. Young, former president of General Electric, and Oliver C. Carmichael, vice chairman, president of the Carnegie Foundation for the Advancement of Education, was composed of 20 prominent citizens, together with 9 ex-officio members. The latter included all of the leaders in the state senate and the assembly, the Commissioner of Education and the Chancellor of the University of the State of New York. Based upon the legislative authorization, the commission had been appointed by Governor Thomas E. Dewey. With this personnel the commission was in position to do a thorough job, and it had enough money appropriated to do it. Moreover, we could employ a couple of dozen expert consultants and an adequate staff.

The reason the state legislature had authorized the Commission lay in the highly emotional situation that had developed in the state, and more especially in New York City, over the policies of the colleges and universities for admitting students. It was alleged that there was extensive discrimination against Jewish students. There were also some charges of discrimination against Catholic students, and to a lesser extent against Negroes. In other words, the private colleges in New York State were being maintained primarily for the benefit of Wasps—the white, protestant elites.

The problem became acute immediately after World War II. Enrollments had been low during the war, because so many college-age men, and also women, had gone into the armed services. Money was not available for building new buildings, and indeed none was needed for the time being. But as soon as the war ended, a huge influx of students took place. On top of the regular flow of students, no longer inhibited by the war, the returning veterans came rushing into the colleges. And with generous scholarships from the federal government.

The private colleges of New York—and they were nearly all private—were unprepared to accomodate this influx of applicants. So they selected applicants they thought "best fitted" their particular campus. Of course, they had had this admission policy all along, but the discriminatory pattern had not showed so clearly as it did after the war. Moreover, the depression and war years had brought changes in the thinking of the American people, one of them being that our historical equal rights policy should really be implemented.

So in New York there was the dual problem of increasing the facilities rapidly—something the private colleges did not have the financial means to do, and of enforcing an equal rights policy in admissions. The commission was to study the problem and make recommendations to the legislature and the governor, especially with respect to the need for a state university in New York.

It may seem strange that this state, which at the time was the largest in population and wealth among the states, did not have a state university. Proposals for one had been advanced from time to time. In 1784 the question arose whether King's College should be taken over by the state and made a state university, but there were strong forces in opposition. A compromise was adopted that resulted in King's College (now Columbia University) being continued as a private institution; and the state would establish the University of the State of New York. The latter, however, was not an operating institution, but instead, an overall planning and regulating agency for all colleges and universities in the state.

At another time, after President Lincoln signed the Land Grant bill encouraging each state to set up a college of agriculture and mechanic arts (engineering), it was proposed to have one in New York. At that moment Ezra Cornell offered to establish what became Cornell University on condition that the state would "farm out" to it the obligation to teach and do research in agriculture and engineering. Hence, the federal lands and money were given to Cornell, a private university, but with some professional schools that would be supervised by the state. When the subject of a state university was again raised in 1912, the same flurry of opposition occurred, and the state instead set up a scholarship program to help students attend a college of their choice.

By 1947 New York State had established 21 state colleges and 9 post-high school institutes; also, the City of New York was operating the City University of New York. The state colleges included 11 teachers colleges, 6 professional schools managed by private universities, and a scattering of others. But it had no state university.

There was strong agitation, especially from New York City, for a state university. The advocates wanted the state to equalize opportunity. On the other hand, the Regents and the existing institutions strongly favored the historical tradition of encouraging private higher education. It was interesting to me to discover that the Board of Regents, which was charged with policy formation and administrative supervision of all education in the state, had only one member, Susan Brandeis, who had attended a public university.

The private institutions were secretive about their admissions data. Being an instrument of the legislature, however, the commission had subpoena power and gained access to all the data. It was an enormous job to collect the admissions figures, categorized to reveal racial and religious status from the more than 100 institutions.

The study of admissions was the largest segment of our total effort, but in addition we made economic analyses, especially an analysis of the ability of the state to help finance higher education. We studied the relative standing of New York among the states in the support of higher education, the trend of births in the state, the trend of increased attendance at colleges and universities, and the extent of student migration out of and into the state.

We made estimates of the needs of the state for educated personnel, especially for doctors, dentists, nurses, and social workers. We compiled data about the available space in the institutions and made estimates of future needs for plant.

Two very interesting hearings on medical education were held. All of the nine deans of medical schools in the state, the deans of the five dental schools, and representatives of the American Medical Association attended. Senator Benjamin Feinberg, majority leader of the State Senate, presided. The several deans obviously had held a skull practice before coming. Dr. Rappleye, Dean of the College of Physicians and Surgeons of Columbia University, was their spokesman. He was a highly distinguished man in the field of medicine and had directed a study of medical education which was published in the bottom of the depression.

In his speech at the hearing, Dean Rappleye recited data to prove that there was a sufficient supply of physicians and hence no need to expand the medical schools. We recognized much of what he said and knew that it was coming from his report of 1933. This was 1947 and the conditions affecting the needs in medicine were profoundly different from what they were when people had little money for doctors' bills. After he concluded, the AMA man got on his feet and with many flourishes declared that not only were there sufficient physicians, but that in New York City there was an oversupply of some 5,000 doctors. He said that if the number of doctors was increased, many of them would have to engage in illegal and shady actions in order to make a living. He predicted that there would be a great increase in the number of abortions, as an example of the extremes to which doctors would have to go. He said nothing about the sections of the state where the ratio of physicians to population was one-fourth what it should have been.

Dr. Rappleye's "facts" and arguments were directly contradictory to what we of the staff had presented to the commission. His conclusions, however, appeared to be similar to those of Governor Dewey; or rather, Dewey seemed to us to oppose action that would require the state to spend more money on education. Senator Feinberg, as the Republican leader in the Senate, was close to the Governor.

It happened, however, that the Senator was suffering from very high blood pressure. He had even made trips to North Carolina where they were testing some new ideas about rice diet and low salt usage. He had spent many hours in doctors' offices cooling his heels awaiting his turn. This was most fortunate for us, because he immediately saw that the position of the deans and the AMA was ridiculous. Feinberg convinced the Governor and the leaders in the legislature of the urgency of the situation and thus facilitated passage of the necessary legislation.

After the new law authorizing the state to finance four new medical schools was enacted, a remarkable thing happened. Four of the deans —Buffalo, Syracuse, Albany, and Brooklyn—who had joined in opposing any extension of medical schools came to see me. Each of the four asked that his school be taken over by the state. They had in hand data and drawings to show how they would be able to enlarge their facilities and their enrollments if only the state would solve their financial problems. Syracuse and Brooklyn shortly thereafter were taken over by the state and considerably enlarged. Presently Buffalo was also made a state school.

A comparison of the facilities available at the colleges and universities with the predictions of future enrollments, showed a wide disparity between needs and facilities. It was decided that the best way to accomodate large numbers of additional students would be to encourage the development of a system of public community colleges throughout the state.

The idea of "community" college was new at the time. The concept was an expansion of the institution called the junior college which dated from about 1906, but no public junior college had been started in New York State (except nine post-high school technical institutes).

There was one fight within the commission over the community college idea. The department of education wanted them to be state institutions in the same manner in which the Board of Regents had already begun the nine technical institutes. Various others, especially the representatives of the Governor, advocated a system of local colleges, the expenses of which would be shared between the community and the state. After a prolonged debate, the Director of the Budget of the state, John Burton, suddenly said, "Why not charge operating expenses one-third to the students, one-third to the local taxpayers, and one-third to the state; and in the case of capital expenditures, split that 50-50 between the local community and the state." Almost immediately everyone agreed and that became the law.

This incident reveals in a striking way how standards are sometimes created. We commonly think of standards as idealistic—for example, the Ten Commandments—but more often they are compromises of differing opinions. Most laws get enacted on this basis. T. V. Smith, the philosopher turned statesman said that it is the essence of politics to find decisions that are generally acceptable but at the same time move forward step by step toward an ideal.

The public community colleges are also one of the solutions to the problem of equality of opportunity. For these institutions must be free from biases as to who should be educated, and since most of the students commute from their homes, the financial barrier is largely removed.

In addition to establishing a system of community colleges, it was decided to enlarge the system of state 4-year colleges. The 11 state teachers colleges were well distributed over the state—by design—on the theory that if local persons were trained locally they would be apt to remain in the locality to teach. The colleges had been held strictly to teacher education in order not to compete with the private liberal arts colleges. But we decided to change that.

The commission recommended that these colleges should be the nuclei for liberal arts programs and, in appropriate instances, such curricula as business administration, social work, engineering, and so forth. Also we proposed to create some new campuses at the 4-year level. This development, too, would help solve the discrimination problem because the public institutions could not discriminate on grounds of race, creed, color, or national origin. They would be near the homes of youth who then could commute to college. Thus the 4-year programs would reach a large number of students previously deprived of the opportunity.

The staff contended that a single state university could not begin to supply the needs in New York State. Instead, the various state institutions should be coordinated in a state-wide system. When the Governor saw that this was the trend of thinking, he tried to pull a fast one. The commission was nearing the end of its work, and had adjourned for Christmas, 1947. During the vacation, Dewey got in touch with Chancellor Tolley of Syracuse University and together they concocted a plan whereby the state would take over Syracuse and thus make it the state university. And, of course, Dewey would get the credit for having established a state university. This would be popular in New York City and in turn would enhance his chances to get New York backing in his race for the Presidency of the United States in 1948. The move would cost little and would add luster to Dewey's reputation as a highly efficient administrator of public affairs.

Irwin Steingut, minority leader in the state assembly, learned of this move in time to throw a red herring into its path. He connived with Ben Fine, the education editor of the New York Times, to print several of the confidential reports of our staff. So on or about January 1, 1948, the Times quoted extensively from our findings, and reported the action by Dewey. Comparing the two proposals it was perfectly clear that the Dewey move would really accomplish nothing, much less contribute to solving the problems of New York. The commission reassembled about January 9. The members were in an uproar about the deceptive ploy of the Governor. Even some of Dewey's friends on the commission turned against him. So the commission rejected his plan by an overwhelming vote.

Governor Dewey, who pretty much controlled the Republican majority in the legislature, was opposed to any move that would cost much money; he seemed also protective of the private institutions. I went to Albany thinking that Dewey was a competent man, but I gradually got an unfavorable impression of him. When I talked with him he lectured me about higher education, although *I* was supposed to be the expert for whose services the state was paying.

One day he called me on the phone—a half-hour conversation—and tried to convince me that any enlargement of the number of graduates from the colleges would result in an oversupply, and these frustrated persons would turn against society. I recognized the source from which he got this idea—Kotschnig's book, *Slaves Need No Leaders* (1943). Kotschnig endeavored to prove that the rise of Nazi Germany could be attributed to the frustrations of college-educated youth in Germany. When, after World War I, the graduates of German universities could not get jobs appropriate to their training, they became Nazis. I did not accept the thesis, and in any event argued that it did not apply to American conditions. Indeed, I thought that if we didn't open up the colleges to more of our youth, those additional to the socially elite, the nation would have a rebellion on its hands.

To get a law through the legislature, however, it was necessary to compromise with the Governor. The compromise plan became the State University of New York. Its board was appointed by the Governor. It took over from the Regents the existing institutions and received statutory authority to develop additional ones. The Regents were left only with a sort of veto over the larger scale plans.

In the course of time, this unvierstiy has become the largest in the United States and now composes undergraduate and graduate institutions, professional schools of all kinds, and several new campuses, some of which have become major universities in themselves—e.g., Stony Brook, Albany, and Buffalo. Certainly this development has been meeting the needs of the state, consistent with the findings of our commission. It became a model for the development of systems of higher education in many of the other states. It also, unfortunately, brought great confusion in the organization of education within the state, and an unbelievable bureaucracy at the capital which, for a time at least, tried to make all the decisions about higher education in the state.

The New York study found much evidence of discriminatory practices by the colleges and the medical schools. The barriers to students led to some interesting subterfuges. For example, one Jewish youth, in his desire to study medicine had applied to 34 medical schools. Some Jews were applying to schools of veterinary medicine—the first two years in both schools were primarily basic sciences—in the hope of later transferring to human medicine. Large numbers of students of Italian extraction were going to schools of medicine in Italy in the expectation of returning to practice in the U. S.

The discriminatory practices by the private institutions were so bad that the staff decided to try to persuade the commission to recommend legislation on the subject. Thereupon Father Gannon, President of both Fordham University, a Jesuit school, and of the New York

Distinguished alumnus award, University of Kansas, 1949

Association of Colleges and Universities, was appointed chairman of a special committee to consider what action to take. The Association was strongly opposed to any action by the state, on the ground of state interference with private institutions. Gannon at first agreed with this view. I think that Owen Young, Chairman of the commission, also agreed. In any event, one day I had a long talk with Young during which I think I persuaded him to support our recommendation. After much consulting, Gannon also decided to support legislation.

A bit earlier, New York had launched the first Fair Employment Practices Act, and it had been a success. So we decided to model a Fair Educational Practices Act after the F.E.P.A. The essence of the law is that it sets up a state official of the ombudsman type, with appropriate staff, who has the duty to hear and investigate complaints about unfairness, and to initiate proceedings to enforce the law if mediation is not successful.

The commission got the state legislature to enact three new laws: the Community College Act, the Fair Educational Practices Act, and one establishing the State University of New York. A major revolution in state policy.

Sabrina, some day if you wish to have it, I will give you my volume of *Reports of Temporary Commission on Need for State University, 1948*, which has my name on the cover. Also, among my records will be found the notes that I made for myself during the meetings of the Commission.

GRANDFATHER

May 10, 1977

Dear Alex,

Did I tell you that we made a trip East during March? The main reason was to attend a couple of affairs in Chicago. For one thing, this was the annual meeting of the American Association of Higher Education, an organization in which formerly I was quite active, and frequently on the program. I was on the Executive Committee for six years, and on one occasion almost became the President. The committee decided to nominate me, then they were unable to locate me. They finally found Anne and me in Montevideo, but by the time I was able to return their call to discuss the subject, they had had to turn to someone else.

The other meeting was a celebration of the 20th anniversary of the founding of the Center for the Study of Higher Education at the University of Michigan. My 80th birthday was also a reason for celebrating, so they said.

The Michigan program has been quite successful in that it has given training for administration to oodles of men and women, both in post-doctoral and doctoral programs. A surprising number of these graduates have become presidents, deans, directors of accrediting agencies, state-wide coordinators, and the like. They call themselves "Algo's Boys," or at least those who graduated while I was there do. I feel proud of this achievement. I think of myself as having discussed in class and in seminars a lot of ideas about higher education, and through these graduates, spread my influence throughout the United States. Maybe that is an optimistic note, but I like to think that I was doing something really worthwhile. I administered a successful program, but that was merely the means toward a larger social end.

During the 19th century and earlier it had been the custom of the colleges to elect religious leaders as president. More recently it was thought that distinguished scholars made the best educational leaders. I agree that a person of scholarly interests and achievements has requisite qualifications, but in the light of present-day complexities of administration and within the social millieu, I think additional preparation is needed, including an understanding of the role of education in society, a perspective relating to the whole institution (as distinguished from specialized interest in one discipline), knowledge of administrative theory and practice, and skills in public relations.

In establishing this program I started something new among the universities. Our program at Michigan was the first one formalized as a "Center for the Study of Higher Education." I conceived the name thinking that it signified the study by advanced students, and also research and writing by faculty. The University of California at Berkeley followed suit, and subsequently a hundred or more other universities initiated such programs. Before our program was begun, a few universities had begun to give some courses on the problems of higher education, notably the University of Chicago, New York University and Ohio State University; but there were no doctoral programs as such. Nor were there many research programs relating to the function, organization and administration of colleges and universities.

My experiences on the President's Commission on Higher Education and with the New York Commission on the Need for a State University had informed me about the crucial problems of the post war period, and made me sensitive to them. Antioch College had given me ideas about the objectives of higher education and acquainted me with teaching methods and program innovations. It was these experiences that led me to conceive of a center for the preparation of administrators and educational leaders.

I discussed the "Center" idea with three universities, Harvard, New York University, and Michigan. At Harvard, Dean Francis Keppel of the School of Education accepted the idea with apparent enthusiasm. It was to combine elements from the Graduate Schools of Business Administration and Public Administration with the new program in education. But then he ran into an obstacle. The faculty in education wouldn't go along unless they had full control. I had favored Harvard in my thinking because I was a graduate of the business school, but at this point I dropped the university from consideration.

New York University, through Dean Melby, took up the idea and offered me a nice job. Indeed, over a period of a few months, Melby offered me my choice of three good jobs. I visited the university and asked to see the available space. It was in a large and terribly crowded room where a dozen or so professors had their desks. I was also told that my courses would have to attract enrollments of 40 people to make them viable financially. On top of that I decided that I could not live in downtown New York. I would have needed to commute to Connecticut or some place where I could find grass, trees, and birds, and this would consume some two hours each day on trains and subway.

The University of Michigan, on the other hand, offered me an opportunity, a relatively free hand, and substantial backing. The salary was less than that at NYU and about half what I had been receiving in Albany, but I decided that there were offsetting compensations. For example, good backing for my project, a nine month's work period, and a beautiful community to live in.

Then there was almost a slip up. The appointment had to be ratified by the Board of Regents, ordinarily a routine matter. But some Regent, according to Dean Edmonson, had raised a question about my "radicalism," pointing to my membership in the American Civil Liberties Union. However, after a delay, they let me by. I understand that President Ruthven strongly advocated my appointment; at my first conference with him he said, "I have not met you before, but I know all about you."

At first I worked alone at the university, having arrived there in September 1950. I have always thought that a college dean or president should be an educational leader, and therefore his outlook on life and his scholarly competence should be formed by the university as a whole and not merely by professors of education. Professors of education are much maligned, but they do tend to get enmeshed in how-to-do-it courses and these become highly fragmented. Many students in education become teachers and administrators without getting sufficient historical and philosophical orientation for their roles. In any event, I asked the university to set up a university-wide committee composed of deans or high officials to which I would report my plans and get advice. This was a device to get the whole university interested in what I was doing, and I succeeded.

Then we launched a "Forum on College Teaching" with some six or eight meetings each year. I worked out a series of topics and organized discussion panels composed of selected deans plus professors whom students had identified as outstanding in some respect. For example, one might be outstanding as a lecturer, another as a discussion leader, another who used case materials, or models, or audio-visual aids, another noted for the care with which he examined students. These men and women would discuss questions that I had prepared and also questions from the audience. The turnouts unexpectedly were quite large, numbering on the average about 150 persons—teachers, teaching assistants, and members of my own class on teaching methods.

I continued the forum for about five years. In the second year, probably because of this visibility, I was elected to membership on the advisory committee to the president, and two years later became its chairman. In the meantime, I had developed four graduate level courses with satisfying enrollments. A few doctoral students emerged so I began to direct their theses.

The Chicago meeting in March was really in celebration of the 20th anniversary of the founding of the "Center" with a substantial grant of funds from the Carnegie Corporation. This took place six years after I had gone to Michigan.

The Harvard Business School had begun a summer institute for student personnel officers, at the suggestion of a student/colleague of mine, Edmund Learned, and I had been on the faculty a couple of times. After a year or so, Harvard received a nice grant from Carnegie. I thought it would be interesting to have the institute held part of the time at Michigan. I called John Gardner, President of Carnegie, and set up an appointment. Dean Harold Dorr, in charge of the summer activities at Michigan, went with me to New York.

We were met not by Gardner, but by James Perkins, Vice-President. He said the grant to Harvard had been unconditional and could not be changed. But he asked me what other ideas I had. It happened that a few months earlier I had prepared a prospectus for a program on training college and university administrators and sent it to the Ford Foundation, but the request was denied. I said to Perkins, "I have tried to interest the Ford Foundation in a program to train college administrators but they turned it down, however, I still think it has merit." He said, "Can we see a copy of the proposal?" I said, "Yes, I have a copy in my briefcase." So I dug the item out and handed it to him and he remarked that they would study it. Within a short time we got a grant of $350,000. The moral is, it pays to have a backup plan in your briefcase.

I learned that Gardner, on his own, had developed an idea to help establish three such programs, and had picked T. R. McConnell at the University of California, Earl McGrath of Teachers College, Columbia, and me, as the possible recipients of the funds. All three of us had experience as college presidents.

The enlarged program was launched in 1957. I had been working out my plans in detail. As one person for the basic staff, I wanted an outstanding man or woman in philosophy/history. I was making an extensive search when Ordway Tead, Vice-President of Harpers, suggested John Brubacher of Yale. Earlier Tead had sent me the galley proofs of the new Brubacher and Rudy book, *Higher Education in Transition,* for an evaluation. I liked it. In Japan, a professor of Nara University had asked me to help him on some interpretations of Brubacher's book on philosophy, which he was translating into Japanese; and in Rio, the Minister of Education had commented that he thought John Brubacher was the most outstanding philosopher of education since Dewey. So Brubacher's qualification appealed to me. Upon contacting him, I discovered that he was ready for a new venture.

A similar search for a man knowledgeable about finance, organization and public policy, turned up a tip that M. M. Chambers wanted to return to higher education. I had worked with him in examining a branch of the University of Massachusetts, and he had been my principal associate in making the state-wide study of higher education in Connecticut in 1949. At that time he was a senior staff man at the American Council on Education, but had retired from that job to become a hog farmer. I knew he was unusually capable and well informed with many publications to his credit. I renewed my acquaintance with him and employed him. Both men proved to be excellent teachers and fine writers, all of which added to the lustre of the department within the university. The three of us, supplemented by some others, became the mainstays of the Center.

A key feature of my plan was to offer substantial fellowships to a few post-doctoral students each year. We looked with favor on applicants who had a doctor's degree in some discipline, and had motivation and the personal qualifications for administrative leadership. They would spend a year with us, free from financial and teaching responsibilities. They could audit courses of their choice, attend a weekly seminar of faculty and fellows, and investigate interesting colleges and universities. On occasion they got some internship experiences. All of this worked out very well.

Along the way we were able to get additional funds, one renewal from Carnegie and grants from the Ford and Kellogg Foundations.

A year or two following the announcement of our program, Jesse Bogue, President of the American Association of Junior Colleges, asked to talk to me. He thought there should be a similar program to train junior college administrators. We worked up an idea for the purpose and the Association arranged a meeting in New York to which Ford and Carnegie Foundation representatives were invited. I gave the principal talk advocating the plan but nothing came of it. After a few more months, Ed Gleazer, successor to Bogue, was able to interest the Kellogg Foundation. As a result it made awards to nine universities situated in various parts of the country. Michigan was one of them.

In the meantime, we kept educating the officials of the University of Michigan about our work and its needs and were able to persuade the university to take over gradually the financing of some of the faculty and to secure improved space. As a result the Michigan

A trilobite tribute at Michigan, 1964

program, as contrasted with many others, is well embedded within the university and is less dependent on outside funds. As of today, this program is clearly the most outstanding one in the United States. Indeed, in a recent evaluation, Michigan not only was ranked number one, but was awarded more points than the combined score of the two universities that ranked second and third.

As an adjunct to the Center, we organized an Institute on College and University Administration. Each year for several years we had about 60 college administrators register. This too helped promote the Center, and was of benefit to the university in establishing ties with many colleges and universities throughout the country. The university became known as a place where administrators could get professional help. It also resulted in a larger flow of applications for our doctoral and post-doctoral programs.

When I was about to leave because of having reached the age of retirement, the faculty of the School of Education asked me to give them a talk. At the conclusion they gave me a standing ovation. Which made me feel good. The university also gave me its Sesquicentennial award for distinguished service. On the back of the bronze medal is engraved, "Knowledge, Wisdom, and the Courage to Serve."

Let me tell you about the presentation of the award. As a part of its planning for the Sesquicentennial celebration the president of the university appointed a committee to plan and stage an international conference on higher education. I was made its chairman. In thinking up the program, I interviewed foundation, association, and government officials, and consulted with educators to get ideas for topics and suggestions for speakers. As a result we secured outstanding participants from Europe, Asia, Africa, and both North and South America. Among them were Eric Ashby, Constantine Zurak, Zakir Husain, Jean Capelle, Ingvar Svennilson, Choh-Ming Li, James B. Conant, Eni Njoku, Alexandr Alexandrov, Yoichi Maeda, and several other persons of high distinction. The papers they presented were published in a volume entitled *Higher Education in Tomorrow's World,* edited by me. (University of Michigan, 1967).

A major event was a luncheon presided over by Charles Joiner, now a federal judge. After the food plates were removed, Charlie asked me to come to the podium. Whereupon he conferred the medal on me. I was astounded and managed to stutter a little acceptance speech before this distinquished audience of educators from around the world.

It was thrilling to receive some invitations from other institutions to continue my work. One was an inquiry from Southern Illinois University whether I would join the "distinguished retirees" program there. It would have been a pleasure to be associated with Buckminster Fuller and the other notables. But Carbondale did not appeal to us as a place to retire.

Another invitation was from the Southern Regional Education Board to direct a new program of assisting the Negro colleges of the South in the further development of their institutions. In Atlanta while I was being interviewed the state legislature rejected a Black, Julian Bond, even though he had been elected. This action put a damper on my thinking about dealing with officials and the legislatures of the South. As a consequence I declined the offer.

The invitation that I accepted was at the Center for Research and Development in Higher Education at the University of California, Berkeley. Here I could plan my own work, and with considerable freedom do what I wanted to do. A beautiful way to retire. Moreover, an opportunity to write several books and additional journal articles.

Soon you will be going to college. As you do so, meditate upon the words, Knowledge, Wisdom, and the Courage to Serve.

GRANDFATHER

PS: The World Affairs Council, which is dedicating a building, has asked me to write a brief essay on what the world will be like in 2027 when the time capsule will be opened. Do you have any ideas?

October 27, 1979

Dear Ilya,

After all that effort Jean and I made to show you the wonderful colleges in California—you know, don't you, that California has the biggest and best of everything—now you go flying around the East to see some more. Well, some people are never satisfied!

I must admit that the colleges you plan to visit in November are really outstanding. In my day, we used to rely on two Knapp studies that rated the colleges and universities by the percentage of their graduates who became scholars or scientists. On this rating Reed, Swarthmore, Oberlin, and Antioch, in that order, were at the top. So in visiting Swarthmore and Oberlin you are getting near the top.

Swarthmore is a very interesting college. It was sort of a mediocre place until about 1920 when a new president came in with a new idea, that of giving students the option of enrolling in honors courses. This was independent study, but was also aimed at shifting from the lecture-recitation-regurgitation teaching process to the seminar-Socratic method, putting the emphasis upon student learning rather than on professorial spouting off. The plan attracted much attention, one result of which was that Swarthmore got lots of money to hire excellent faculty and build up its plant and library.

Oberlin has always been an excellent college and probably has not changed. One thing that has made it so is the substantial endowment the college received from Hall, the inventor of the aluminum process. But also it was the pioneer in giving women an opportunity in education equal to that of men; and it was one of the intellectual centers of opposition to slavery. These things happened a long time ago, but the Oberlin spirit seems still to be there.

Once when I was making comparisons for the benefit of Antioch

College, I spent three days on the Oberlin campus. I came away very impressed with the overall quality of the place. I was not so impressed with the food, as I got a terrific belly ache. Indeed one morning I got the "runs" so badly I had to discard my shorts.

It seems to take some kind of stimulus to cause a college suddenly to have a surge of vitality. Oberlin because of its activities in civil liberties; Swarthmore with its honors curriculum; Reed due to its plans for providing a cultural influence in the Portland community; Antioch with its use of experience as a factor in education.

But Ilya, there are over 2,000 colleges and universities and dozens of them are high grade institutions. Working as a member of a committee for several years with the Exxon Foundation to select meritorious colleges for grants, we identified 300 private colleges for recommendation to the Foundation. At another time, examining the private colleges in Iowa for the Gardner Cowles Foundation for the same purpose, three institutions were recommended as quite good academically and some others as satisfactory.

Some funny things happen when a college is being examined. In preparing for my visit the president of Buena Vista College in Iowa had lined the walls of his office with charts to prove what a great institution it was. After explaining the statistical curves, he asked what I wanted to see. I said the library. As we descended a flight of stairs leading to the stacks, reaching a platform, there staring me in the face so that I couldn't possibly miss it, was one of my own books. I thought the college was very marginal. However, this little college has recently received on of the largest single gifts of money ever given to a college.

The size and quality of the library services is of singular importance to a college. Arriving in the evening at Iowa Wesleyan College, I was directed to the gymnasium to meet the president. There he was, at a women's basketball game, all dolled up in a blazer that the students had given him for promoting the team. Directly across the street from the gym was the library. Walking in, I found a woman in charge whose desk was planted in front of the entrance to the book area as though to say, "Just try to get a book!" The rest of the help were part-time students. So the library had one professional of faculty rank. In athletics, the college had nine coaches.

At another liberal arts college the library was well stacked with books that on close inspection turned out to be about one third law books, bequeathed by an attorney to the college. They had almost no relevance to the educational program.

One of the colleges in Iowa is Upper Iowa University. Formerly a Methodist college, it had been dropped by the church because the church felt that it did not need four colleges in the state, nor did it have the resources to support so many. People in the community and alumni got together and kept the institution alive. When I visited it, the enrollment was about 200, composed largely of freshmen and sophomores. This "university" was virtually a junior college. Recently I saw an ad in a San Francisco paper offering students an opportunity to earn a degree without attending the institution. The ad was by Upper Iowa University.

At one college, the trustees had taken money from the endowment to help pay current bills, and replaced the securities with a note signed by the officers for the board. In legal effect, the college had promised itself to repay itself!

Of course a college can't educate you. Your education is up to you. You get out about as much as you put into the effort. What a college can do is to provide good facilities, library and laboratories, a congenial atmosphere—one conducive to study and learning—a faculty to guide you in your learning and to give you knowledge and ideas that supplement, complement, and explain the books, also steer your thinking into fresh channels and inspire you with fresh insights. So it is important to size up the appearance of the campus, the campus tone, the quality of the facilities and the library, and the qualifications and interests of the faculty members.

This may be merely a grandfather's prejudice, but I think you are a particularly nice person, with many talents. You have such clear skin and gorgeous hair, and there is always a gleam of mischief or something in your eyes. You really have an unusually fine personality. Also you seem to have good intellectual competence.

Furthermore, you have a multitude of talents. In this respect you go beyond the usual college applicant who thinks the only thing that counts is the ranking on academic achievement tests. From observing many students, I am not at all sure that the top student in grades is the one most likely to make a social contribution in life, or live the happiest life. Other qualities, such as imagination, creativeness, empathy, manual dexterity, physical endurance, emotional stability, are of great importance. In many occupations, for instance, creativeness is more valuable than the ability to verbalize is.

Don't judge me too harshly by the extent of my verbalization in these letters!

GRANDFATHER

November 23, 1968

Dear Grandchildren,

On November 17 and 18 I was involved in a most interesting meeting with several Indian Chiefs of the New Mexico, Colorado, and Arizona tribes and pueblos. Among those present were Domingo Montoya, Chairman of the All Indian Pueblo Council, Charlie Vigil of the Jacarilla Apache tribe, Leonard Burch of the Southern Utes, Robert Lewis of Zuñi Pueblo, Juan Chevarria of Santa Clara Pueblo, James Hena who is Director of the Indian Community Action Program for the eight northern pueblos in New Mexico, and Wendell Chino, Chief of the Mescaleros. We met at the Mescalero Reservation near Alamogordo, New Mexico.

The occasion was to review the progress being made in the Indian Community Action Program. This is an effort by the various Indian communities, with guidance and a bit of subsidy from the Federal Government, to become self-sufficient economically, and to improve the status of their education, health, and culture. One of the aims is to make these communities attractive for young Indians who become educated or enticed by the big cities to return to the tribe, enjoy a reasonable standard of living, and live happy lives. At the time I was consultant to the University of New Mexico and the president invited me to accompany him to the meeting.

The Mescaleros sent two small planes to Albuquerque to pick us up. After a bouncy ride we arrived at the reservation. We drove first to the Community House for a preliminary meeting at which Chief Chino briefed us about the Mescalero reservation. The land area is large and mountainous, with one peak rising 12,003 feet high. It is heavily timbered, but includes nice valleys. Fifteen hundred pure blood Apaches live here, as do 1800 others who have tribal membership. Some of the latter are part Indian, and others are Whites who have married Indians, often to get the benefits of free land and housing. The people are related by language and culture to the several other Apache tribes of the Southwest. It was from here that

Chief Geronimo launched the last effort to push the White man out of the territory.

The Indians drove us around the reservation, showing us much new housing, a new hospital, a school, a new community center costing $1,300,000, with swimming pool, recreation, craft, and office rooms; also part of the herd of 5000 Herefords, the fish hatchery, and the sawmill. The tribe has 40 buses and trucks, each equipped with a walkie-talkie. Tourism is one thing to which they are catering, with a beautiful ski resort, and fishing and hunting.

We drove up the peak 9700 feet to a beautiful lodge, where we had a banquet of roast beef and all the trimmings. The setting was delightful, with magnificent views. President Ferrel Heady and I shared one of the cottages, which was spacious, had two double beds, also good heat which we needed as it had been down to near zero the night before. At the dinner the Assistant Chief of the Mescaleros made a speech and we all got acquainted. The Chiefs were impressive, several of them being college educated. But it was disappointing to see them in conservative business suits rather than in the regalia to which they are entitled. They spoke good English, and excepting in size, color, and facial features, they could have been Caucasians.

The setting was the ski resort. It has two runs, one at 9700 feet and the other above 11,000. When the snow is on, the resort employs 125 people. Apparently the planes, not owned by the tribe, are sent all over Texas and elsewhere to bring people to the resort and a nearby race track.

While eating the delicious roast, I thought of another occasion when my grandfather, Lewis Donmyer, on a trip to Oklahoma stayed overnight with some Indians. He joined them in a camp-fire meal. The central dish was a big kettle from which everyone dug out chunks of meat. After a long day's horseback ride, he was famished and so helped himself generously to the meat. As he dipped in for another helping, the Chief said, "Dig down deep, there's more puppy in the bottom."

Lewis Donmyer's wife, my grandmother, was a Custer. My mother said she was a cousin of the General George Custer, the Indian fighter. In the famous massacre, the only survivor on the White side was the horse, Commanche. After Commanche died he was stuffed and now is in the museum at the University of Kansas. When I was a boy I thought that Custer was a colorful hero but now I am repelled at the thought of how the Whites tried to decimate the Indians. On several occasions I have gone to the museum and as I look at Commanche I wonder about the behavior of supposedly civilized men.

The Mescaleros had sued the government for land that had been taken from them and won $8,000,000. The Utes told me they had won $7,000,000. A portion of these funds was being used in the development programs. Did I mention the Chief of the Cochitas? He told me they are taking advantage of a big dam being built on the river near Santa Fe to create a tourist center. The Utes are using an old narrow gauge railroad that runs into the mountains near Durango, Colorado to attract tourists.

I played only a minor role, but was a fascinated spectator. The Indians have been pushed around badly by greedy, bigoted Whites. Perhaps the Indian Community Action Program, with leadership from within the tribes, will at last enable this distinctive group, the indigenous people of the Americas, to regain pride of race and heritage, and develop in a socio-economic manner to sustain themselves and live in harmony with the White-based culture that has engulfed them.

GRANDFATHER

Jean and Algo at Wupatki, 1974

VII

When I was the age of Ilya and Peter I began to think about religion, politics, the economy, and social problems. Later I had some unique experiences relating to ethnic discriminations, the military, medical education and services, business operations, and community development. I relate these to show you grandchildren how I changed my views about human problems as I became more aware of the consequences of social action.

August 17, 1979

Dear Peter,

Jean and I do a lot of reading these days about nutrition, diet, exercise, meditation, and other things relating to health. It makes me think about the fascinating changes that have taken place during my lifetime in foods, medical services, and our knowledge of health. Also for some years I have been involved with problems relating to health and the distribution of health services in the nation. I mean the availability of health services to everyone, their escalating costs, the education of physicians and dentists, the chaotic elements in our health insurance plans, the adulteration of our foods, and the pill habits fostered by the pharmaceutical industry.

February, 1905, was an exceedingly cold month. As a 7 year old, walking home from country school, I was excited by the snow drifts piled as high as the hedge along the road. Brrrrrrrrr—On the morning of the 16th, we 3 kids, Bertie, Merle, and I, arriving at the foot of the stairs that descended from our unheated bedrooms, were met by Dad, all excited, who asked if we wanted to see our new sister. NEW SISTER!! My goodness, where would a new sister have come from in the middle of the night while we all were sound asleep. We had no idea that anything like that was in the offing. Whereupon we were escorted into the guest bedroom, where there was a red hot stove, and saw Mother lying in one bed and this tiny girl, little Beulah, all swathed in blankets asleep in the other.

It seems that during the night Dad had run down to the neighbors and asked one of them to drive his horse to town, 3 miles away, and get the doctor. Evidently the doctor had come, but we had not heard the commotion. Very strangely, about 10 that morning Grandmother Donmyer came driving into the yard. Perfect timing. We ran out to tell her the big news, but she didn't seem too surprised.

I have learned in later years that Grandmother was a "healer." Charles Kenison, Beulah's husband, told me that when he was a baby and had an illness, his mother had taken him to see Mrs. Donmyer and he had been cured. Maybe he was about to get well anyway, but don't be too skeptical about the psychological aspects of illnesses and their cure.

Although it was the most important event in my life, I do not remember being born. Do you? But it must have been by natural birth and in the spare bedroom where there was a stove. Since Beulah was breast fed—I watched this with much interest, and also how Mother would rub some stuff on her nipples to wean the baby—I am sure that I must have been. I think all babies at that time were breast fed, the natural way.

A year or so after her birth, Beulah developed an ominous looking infection on one of the labia majora. Our parents watched it with much anxiety. It seems it never occurred to them to take her to a doctor. Instead they waited until it became well festered, and then operated on her themselves. They laid her on blankets near the door of the sitting room where they would get good light. Dad got out his razor, boiled it, and then gave the infection a swift slice. A huge amount of puss shot out which they cleaned up with cloths—I hope boiled ones. At first the folks said we couldn't watch, but we insisted; so there was the whole family engaged in a delicate operation. Somehow the baby survived.

Just think what that operation would cost today: attendance by a pediatrician, consultation with a surgeon, admission to a hospital, physical examination and blood tests, use of the operating room and equipment, anesthetists, nurses, use of the recovery room, an additional day or two in the hospital, and finally a discharge, after much paper work for insurance. That size of bill would have been catastrophic—with no insurance available in those days—for our family.

One day I was helping drive a hog that didn't want to be driven. Hogs can be so stubborn. While chasing it, I ran into a rusty barbed wire fence and got a long rip in my left thigh. Dad kept a big tin of salve with which he treated all wounds, of which there were many on the farm, and this is the treatment I got. I didn't get lockjaw, but I still have a long white scar on my leg.

The only time I remember that a doctor came to the house was an occasion when Mother had an excruciating abdominal pain. The doctor examined her, but gave no treatment. I suspect that she had a gall stone that was passing. She recovered quickly.

Mother was always concerned about her health. Instead of consulting with local physicians, she would go to health resorts. After my birth she went to Excelsior Springs, Missouri, a noted spa. Spas were "in" during the 1800s. Another place she visited was the Temple of Health in Kansas City. This was a place devoted to psychological therapy, massaging and other non-medical treatments. Dr. Francis Donmyer, a great uncle of mine, was on the staff. He did the massaging. Mother complained continuously about her back; she attributed her trouble to having fallen off a horse. In later years I had some x-rays taken of her back, but the doctor could find no injury.

Grandfather Donmyer's last illness made quite an impression on me because he suffered such pain. His wife's skills as a healer did no good. They had Dr. Gaines to see him and he advised an operation, but Grandfather was adamant in refusing. I was curious and asked Dad some questions. He explained that Grandfather had some cement-like blockage in his urinary tract. I am sure he had an enlarged prostate, and very probably cancer. He died ten years before his time.

I seem to be dwelling on the Donmyers, but the Hendersons never seemed to have illnesses.

As a boy I had lots of trouble with my teeth. They were crooked, with one tooth obtruding a bit—a continuing embarrassment to me—but either the art of straightening teeth was not yet developed, or my family was ignorant of the possibilities. Probably we could not afford it. In any event, crooked teeth were accepted as normal, so nobody, except me, was much concerned.

I also had lots of caries. They were let go until the tooth began to ache. And because it ached, the dentists would kill the nerve. I lost four teeth from this and now wear a bridge that is a great nuisance—food keeps getting under it and this annoys me. In a fifth tooth I had an abscess, and later a costly root canal operation. Isn't it wonderful today to have well trained dentists, regular examinations of the teeth in school or otherwise, and treatment before the teeth are destroyed?

Our water was from our cistern, rain water collected from the roof of the house. It was real soft and great for washing. Dad and I cleaned the cistern at intervals. Once we found a mouse but didn't tell anyone. We were shaken one day when we learned that the entire Scott family north of Solomon had been wiped out by typhoid fever, attributed to their cistern. Probably they never cleaned it.

We were clean ourselves, but the men in the family didn't like to use the privy. It stank. No lime was used. Flies everywhere, although our house was screened. I wonder how people lived before screens were invented. On a safari trip to Kenya, passing through the Maasai tribal area, I saw this Maasai, sticking his head in the window of our station wagon, with two dozen flies just sitting on his face. I suppose because of the ocher with which he smeared himself. Funny, he didn't seem to notice them.

Of course, people were not too aware of germ carriers. Bacteria were discovered by van Leeuwenhoek in the 17th Century, but their relationship to disease was not well known until the time of Pasteur who did his research only a few years before my birth. In 1860, within one month, 3 Henderson children died of diptheria. Isn't it too bad that inoculations were not available to them.

People had such short lives. While composing at my typewriter, I have Donizetti's La Favorita playing, a tape I made a few weeks ago. I make my own tapes from FM music. Have you tried doing that? It is a great hobby because you can then play the tapes over and over. Poor Donizetti, a brilliant composer, born exactly 100 years before me, died at age 51. Just think of the additional creative composing he might have done if he had had the benefit of modern medicine.

Dad and I were careless with our milking. The cow barn was filthy. It never occurred to us to wash the udder before milking. If dirt fell into the milk we just fished it out. But that was the way things were done before rudimentary hygiene was practiced.

During my first year at Antioch College, I accompanied our bacteriologist to the farm where we got our milk. It was one of the best farms of the region. And we had had no trouble with the milk, but we did want the men to be clean. In the midst of a long discussion about sanitation, which was lacking in the barn, the men's mother came out and informed us in no uncertain terms that the milk was OK. She had "raised her children on that milk and there was nothing wrong with it." Period. After a tactful wait, we switched our business to a dairy that used good sanitary practices, and also knew how to process their hay to preserve the vitamins. On the farm we had always let the hay lie until it was well bleached of its chlorophyll, thus losing much of the nutrients in the hay.

My education about health matters came gradually, but I made the most progress after I joined the faculty at Antioch College. At Antioch we had an outstanding physician, trained in both medicine and public health, Dr. Perino Wingfield. Perry and I became good friends, and when I became an administrator we found it easy to work together in getting a modern clinic, with good diagnostic equipment and services set up.

During World War II our village lost to the armed services the only young doctor it had. We were left with two octogenarians whose medical ideas were formed in the 19th Century. Early in my days in the village I went to one of them with an occasional complaint. He practiced in a bedroom of his home, using the closet for his pills and stethoscope. He made many of his pills right there. It reminds me of the elderly man on the Board of Regents in New York whose father had built up the pharmacy business he owned. He told me with much amusement how his father always put several different ingredients in a pill in the hope that at least one of them would do the work. On the farm we used to get our pills, the few we needed, from the Watkins Company. Its horse-drawn wagon came through the countryside at regular intervals, supplying the people with pills, cough syrup, vanilla extract and sewing machine oil.

During the war Perry conceived the idea of making the college clinic available to people in the village as well. I thought this a good idea, and we proceeded to create a regional medical service. In a surprisingly short time we had on the staff 9 physicians of varying competencies, all housed together, with nurses, laboratory assistants, and the most modern equipment. We were attracting a large number of patients from surrounding cities.

In 1930 the college had launched a longitudinal study of child development, beginning with the foetus. Philip, one of the first guinea pigs, is still going for occasional examinations, and I understand that you and Matthew are—nicht wahr? This study, still under way, has important implications for health, and also the study of nutrition, the environment, psychology, and medicine.

I have been very proud of establishing the medical services; yet in retrospect I would make one important change. Our college students paid a flat fee that entitled them to comprehensive medical benefits. But we put the village people on a fee-for-service basis. We should have introduced the insurance feature also. However, our model was the Mayo Clinic, then a highly popular institution. I once was a guest of Dr. William Mayo, son of the founder. He showed me all through the facility, and also arranged an overall health checkup—at no cost!—for me.

It was a bit later that Henry Kaiser told me of the plan he had started at Grand Coulee and Oakland, He introduced me to Dr. Sidney Garfield who had conceived the idea. Garfield showed me all around the Oakland building, the labs and operating equipment. He told me of the working conditions for doctors, and the annual costs to patients. He said the California Medical Association had tried to undercut his efforts, but he had had no trouble in getting the services of highly competent physicians and surgeons.

Henry Kaiser fascinated me. One weekend when in Washington, I called Eugene Meyer, publisher of the Washington Post, and asked if I could bring the Antioch students who were working in the city to his home on Sunday to talk with him and Agnes. He said: "Fine. Come to dinner, and have the students arrive at 8.00." At the dinner, there was Henry Kaiser. After the meal, Meyer invited Kaiser to come with us, and then asked *him* to talk with the students. Kaiser grabbed a straight back chair, reversed it, straddled the seat, and with his huge eyes glowing above his Humpty-Dumpty like body, regaled us with the story of the Kaiser Permanente Health Plan. Meyer, in an aside to me, said it was he, when head of the Reconstruction Finance Corporation, who had picked Kaiser to build the Liberty ships.

I now belong to the Kaiser Health Plan. It is a health maintenance plan and a good one. It is a comfort to have right at hand such good diagnostic, laboratory services. Emergency services are available night and day. I might still have my right eye had not all the doctors in Rio been at their country homes for the weekend when I needed urgent help. I did reach by phone the medical officer of the American Embassy, but he refused to see me. The skunk.

While still at Antioch I helped conduct the state-wide survey of higher education in New York, an important aspect of which was to study medical, dental, and nurse education. At that time the state had 9 medical schools and 5 dental schools, all private. The issue was their adequacy in dealing with post-war needs and demands in the health area. Also there was a highly emotional issue caused by discriminations against Jews and applicants of Italian and Polish descent. The medical schools had a strong bias in favor of Wasps. For our study we secured such outstanding specialists as Dr. O'Rourke,

Dean of Tufts Graduate Program in Dentistry; Lucile Petry, nurse and Assistant Surgeon General; and Dr. George Perrott of the U. S. Public Health Service.

Through this study I learned a lot about medical education and about the practices of the American Medical Association. Our data and projections showed the need for much stronger institutions and for large increases in the number of doctors, dentists, and nurses. Fortunately the Legislature and Governor Dewey accepted our recommendations, so New York State now has much more adequate medical education.

The AMA seemed to us to foster a policy of restricting the number of physicians. This was an understandable stance because the shortage enabled the doctors to increase their incomes fast; faster than the plumbers, whose union also was effective. The AMA lobby, especially in Washington, is really terrific. They have repeatedly blocked the way to a national health program.

A few years ago I prepared a carefully researched paper on the costs of medical education and sent it to the journal of the AMA. Back it came with a letter saying that they would publish it if I would temper my views about the costs. Since my facts were soundly based and I didn't like being censored, I sent it to the journal of the American Council on Education which immediately accepted it. This was actually a better medium of publication because this journal is widely read by university administrators who have the responsibility of controlling budgets. At least they are supposed to have this power; actually medical schools get so much grant money that they refuse much control by the university over their affairs.

Presently I was invited to chair one of the sections of the National Health Assembly, the one on education. Each section discussed the problems for 2 days, then the chairman made a report to the Assembly. In my report I presented the idea that if physicians and dentists would use adequately prepared assistants, they could treat more patients and at less cost. I was followed by the chairman of the section on dentistry, who was then dean of the School of Dentistry at the University of California at San Francisco (and later chancellor). Instead of reading his report, he took his allotted time to jump all over me for having suggested such a ridiculous idea that anyone other than a dentist could work in the mouth of a patient. The mouth belonged to the dentist.

I had encountered a similar situation in New York. Psychologists had approached the Regents with a desire to be licensed. I worked with them to produce draft legislation, but before putting it in the legislative hopper, I sent it to various interested parties for comment. The medical group came back with a strong objection. We had used the words "diagnosis" and "therapy," and the doctors said these terms belonged to their profession. No one else should be permitted to use them. I took issue, believing that the only justification for licensing psychologists was to assure public protection in diagnosis and therapy. So we were stalemated.

Well, I got the idea for assistants from Dr. O'Rourke, an authority on dental practice, who said that trained dental technologists could clean out caries and do simple fillings, thus enabling many more patients to get treatment at lower cost. This idea isn't really so new. The Russians have had Feldshers for a long time, and in China there are the "barefoot doctors." In the cities these assistants work with the physicians, but in the less populated areas, where physicians prefer not to go, they are of great help in making preliminary diagnoses and in giving elementary treatment. When medical referrals are needed they make them. In China they carry contraceptives and educate about family planning. What a great relief this can be for rural people. It is interesting that 25 years after the Washington conference, doctors have begun to use physicians' assistants and nurse practitioners. Several medical schools, originally at Duke and Colorado respectively, are now training them.

In 1949 I was appointed by the Surgeon General of the United States to a commission that evaluated the government's program of financial assistance to medical schools and medical students. We issued a three-volume report that cited the need of recognizing health problems as national in scope, and hence the responsibility of the federal government in extending and improving medical education. During the years subsequent to the White House Conference and the Surgeon General's report there was a surge of governmental support for medical education and the provision of health services.

For several years I conducted a seminar in the School of Dentistry at Michigan on curriculum and teaching problems; and I had been a consultant to the faculty in the School of Public Health. The latter had a very difficult problem of constructing a core curriculum out of such diverse specialties as bacteriology, statistics, sanitary engineering and administrative skills. I assisted them with procedures for defining the educational objectives and coordinating them with relevant subject matter. In dentistry the teaching was very stereotyped, and the dean was trying to effect some changes in the outlook of his faculty.

My experiences relating to medical education led to being involved with the founding of four medical schools. Two of these were launched in New York State while I was organizing and administering the newly created State University System. Another was at the University of Mew Mexico while I was consultant to the president of the university. This was an interesting case. The people of the state suffered from deficient medical services, being unable to compete for the services of physicians. So the university started a school. Unfortunately they selected a dean who had the usual medical school model in mind. As a result the school was geared to turn out specialists who, excepting for a few who would practice in Albuquerque and Santa Fe, would flee the state. So here the people were taxing themselves in support of a dream which had no chance to become reality. Fortunately, this dean soon left for greener pastures.

The fourth school was at the Davis campus of the University of California. The new dean asked me to help on some curriculum and teaching problems. One of the problems was to get the veterinary faculty and the faculty in human medicine to collaborate on basic science courses. It is strange how difficult this is. In New York for a while we were unable to license graduates of the School of Dentistry of Columbia University because the Schools of Dentistry and Medicine had a joint program the first year. After all, dentistry is a branch of medical science—although you can't tell dentists that! But the Association of Dental Schools would not approve the Columbia plan. And under the state law this prevented our licensing the graduates.

Most medical educators are very rigid in their thinking. But not all. For example, the University of Michigan, with an imaginative young dean—recently he has become president of the Upjohn pharmaceutical company, whereupon I bought some stock in the company—decided to introduce instruction in nutrition. To do so it was necessary to curtail some other subjects because the medical curriculum is very crowded. For example, by rethinking the course work in anatomy usually taught as though the students were to become anatomists, they found content that could be eliminated. So nutrition was introduced. At last the medical students were getting insights into nutrition as a factor in maintaining good health.

Speaking of anatomy, when the medical school at Michigan was started in 1849, a professor of anatomy was employed. He arrived at the Ann Arbor railroad station accompanied by a 6-foot box which he took to a loft over a store in town. There students could dissect the cadaver in secret, for Michigan law prohibited such use of cadavers. The study of dead bodies is essential; but it is of fundamental importance that the medical student gain a full understanding of the development of human beings, as living people, from foetus to old age. The medical school at Case Western Reserve introduced an innovative program of this type. Instead of beginning with a cadaver, the student begins his study with a pregnant woman. Makes sense.

In 1971 my research assistant and I published a monograph on "Admitting Black Students to Medical and Dental Schools." Our data showed that in 1969, excluding the 2 Negro schools, only $9/10$ of 1 percent of the students in medical schools were black. We analyzed the need, especially in urban centers, of having more Black physicians. One can travel literally for miles through the black districts of Oakland without finding a physician. We recommended an increase in the admission of qualified black applicants. Subsequently there has been a significant increase. One of the schools that did so was Davis where the famous Bakke case of reverse discrimination arose.

Although progress has been made in educating a sufficient number of physicians, and Jews, Blacks, Italian, and Polish Catholics, and also women are no longer discriminated against as heavily as when we made the New York study, not too much progress is being made in making health care available to the whole population and on a basis that people can afford. Of course, we do have numerous insurance plans and these assist those lucky enough to come within them. They have done much to make hospital services more available to people. They have also unintentionally been the cause of increased costs to the patients. Furthermore, they are duplicative in coverage. I have four different insurance plans, highly duplicative. I can't afford to drop any because former employers pay the costs. But the costs are there. Somebody pays.

In this county there has been a strong drive on the part of a consortium of private hospitals, encouraged by people who want to save taxes, to "take over" the County Hospital patients. But when the proposal is examined carefully, it can be seen that the private hospitals want only the paying patients; they carefully exclude mental patients, drug addicts, alcoholics, migrants, the poor, and patients requiring long care. They also propose to operate on the usual fee-for-service basis, open ended, with the privilege of billing the County for overruns. This certainly would not solve the health problems of the disadvantaged people, nor would it reduce the costs to taxpayers. In her capacity as cochairman of the committee on the County Hospital, while on the Grand Jury, Jean was instrumental in preventing this change—for the time being at least!

I own stock in three pharmaceutical companies and enjoy receiving the large cash and stock dividends. But I must say that the ardor with which they try to squeeze out more and more profits rather appalls me. The rivals that produce Anacin and Tylenol respectively try to outdo one another by making extravagant claims for their product to induce a gullible public to buy. "Doctors recommend most!" An unlabelled pill with the same content would cost much less and be just as effective in relieving pain, real or imaginary. Peter, don't get addicted to pills. We swallow them by the billions when a few million would do the trick, and would be better for us.

There is nothing more important than the health of people. We have the best trained doctors and the best specialized medical services in the world. We have lots of patient-oriented doctors who take great pains to render good service. Not all of them are money mad; in many cases, considering the liability insurance and office costs, and uncollected bills, their charges are not unreasonable. But the health statistics show that the distribution of the health services is badly skewed. We are much below some other countries in the way in which all of our people have access to medical services. We badly need a comprehensive health policy and plan. Can we afford it? When people think of the cost they consider only the addition to the federal budget. They overlook the costs at present, which are both duplicative and exorbitant. Of course we can afford a unified plan. It is all a matter of priorities.

Proper nutrition is highly important. Peter, don't eat cereal that is more sugar than grains. Don't add salt to food that has been properly salted when being cooked. Study the contents on packages you buy to see what the additives are. Foods are produced and marketed today with two objectives in view: to maximize profits, and to avoid spoilage. The health of people is of small concern. Don't get habituated to the fast food places; a lot of this stuff is full of junk—the increase of fibre in one well-known cereal is wood pulp. Remember these materials become a part of your body. Don't take up smoking;

the data are quite clear that smoking is a major cause of cancer, and this is a terrible disease. Eat lots of greens, grains, nuts, and less red meat.

Let me tell you about my breakfast food. I grind up several grains, mix them, and then cook for ten minutes. That way I don't have to buy the boxed cereals at high prices and low food value. I grow lots of green vegetables and we go out to Brentwood where we can pick fruit off the trees. Thus we eat things that are ripe, juicy, and full of vitamins. Some of the time I bake my own bread. Although I always order whole wheat bread at the store, some that is sold with that label looks pretty pale.

My latest venture is to grow sprouts, an indoor sort of gardening. It is easy. Just take a few seeds—beans, lentils, triticale, alfalfa—put in a small jar, water them three times a day but drain off the water, and in four to six days, presto, you have an excellent food. The point about seeds and grain is that they are life producing and sustaining. And when you sprout them, their fats and starches are converted into vitamins, sugars, and proteins. The value of sprouts as food was known in China as early as 2939 BC. So this is not just a fad.

Genes are also a factor in health, and on your father's side at least you have inherited good genes for health. Your Great-Great-Great-Grandmother Henderson lived to age 90, and your Great-Great-Great-Grandfather Donmyer lived to 87—at a time when nearly all people died at half that age. Your father once told me I should live to 87 to emulate my Great-Grandfather; however, I think into the 90s would be better. Well, we shall see.

When you are past 80, as I am, you will see the wisdom of much of what I have been saying in this letter. Here's to your health and a long and happy life.

GRANDFATHER

November 7, 1978

Dear Alex,

At the moment I am on a national panel that is trying to synthesize our ideas about trends that will affect our lives during the 1980-2000 year period. The objective is to anticipate the educational needs of this period. One of the questions asked in this week's survey was:

"What will be the spiritual-religious trends that will have impact during the period?" An easy question, you will say—just look at the Jesus freaks, those who are rabid against abortions and want to suppress homosexuals, the born-again Christians, and the Bible-waving preachers on TV.

I could answer the question hastily by saying that we should countereducate against these trends. However, I cannot define religion so narrowly, nor do I think we should be defensive. Christianity is only one of several major religions. Furthermore, religion is not just a set of dogma, even dogma from the Bible or the Koran, but rather a guide to the good life in the good society. Religion in my view should not be authoritarian, but exploratory.

When I was your age I was sort of betwixt and between in my attitudes toward religion. I was developing a strong social motivation, but I also felt ties to the religious outlook of my family and my community. I really was quite ignorant, having little knowledge about the origins of life, the existence of Jews, Mohammedans, and Buddhists, the history of ritualism—golly, was I ignorant. You, of course, have had the advantages of much superior cultural environment, and of the best available education. You may know more than I do about the discoveries of the Leakeys that reveal the age of man, but I have visited the site of their excavations, so there! Because of my interest in fossils, I'll bet I know more than you about amoeba in the Precambrian formations. Life has existed for more than a billion years; indeed there is fresh evidence from Australia that bacteria-like organisms existed some $3\frac{1}{2}$ billion years ago. And australopithecus and hominid skeletal remains predating 3,000,000 years are being found in several places in Africa.

So how can the fundamentalists adhere to the Biblical stories of the age of man, or that woman was created from one of Adam's ribs? I suspect that you were created by a sperm from your father entering an egg of your mother. But knowing that doesn't explain how all of the genes of both parents function to determine your characteristics. You have a strong resemblance to your Grandmother Anne, so perhaps her genes were predominant in your case. In any event, how can that many DNA particles possibly be compressed in a microscopic sperm and egg? But we know that they are.

Although I grew up in an environment that had many advantages —for instance, it was much more attuned to nature than is life in urban America—one of my regrets is that it was so limited intellectually. My parents were intelligent and had normal school educations; but they did not have the advantages of liberal learning, good books and literary journals to read. As kids our source of books was a small collection at the Presbyterian Church. But these books were mostly popular novels and were not mind developing.

My Dad who for many years was the dominant member of the school board, on one occasion got the board to buy a set of books for the school. A few weeks later I was prowling through the school house—I used to like to raise an unlocked window, crawl in, and nose around—missed the book collection, looked in the round-bellied stove and saw the ashes of the books. We never knew whether this was a malicious book burning, or merely the thoughtless act of some tramp, who, as in La Bohème, found a convenient way to keep warm at night. That was the end of our modest little library. How I wish now that at your age I had been informed about and able to read what some of the great thinkers had to say about living the good life.

People who live in an environment of intellectual poverty feel more secure if they adhere to traditional beliefs and the words of the Bible.

Alex, be serious with me. Do you think that God created woman from man's rib? Of course, we know that he must have created man first, otherwise how could there be any seeds from which to create other men and women? Maybe you don't buy that? Wouldn't it be funny if we found out some day that God is a woman, maybe a Chinese woman? Do you think that Jesus was created through immaculate conception? Having been raised on a farm where I saw all kinds of copulations going on—chickens, hogs, cattle, dogs, and what have you, I somehow questioned some of the church doctrine that I heard on Sundays.

On one occasion my folks and we kids went to church to hear an evangelist. He showed some slides to make his points and I can still see one that depicted hell, or so he said. There was this vast cauldron much like what you see when looking down into the Kilauea Crater; and sticking out of this fiery surface were countless legs and feet as though all of the sinners of the world had been cast into the fire head first. I couldn't buy that. I doubt whether my father did. I never heard him mention hell.

Another time the family attended a revival meeting that all of the churches in town sponsored. The Woodmen's Hall was filled to capacity. At a point during his shouting at us, the evangelist suddenly said: "Will all the women now cross their legs." I suppose they all dutifully did so. He waited a dramatic moment then announced happily: "Now the gates to hell are closed." Here I was, a growing boy, beginning to feel the sexual appetites welling in my system, being told in vivid terms that sex was evil! These strange religious men were trying desperately to save me and others from a terrifying experience after death. I was just beginning to live *now*. Well, I was skeptical about these ideas. I was still groping for the meaning of life, but didn't find much help in the Presbyterian Church of my day.

Occasionally I observed Mother quietly reading the Bible. The Bible is full of folk lore, and the King James edition is a classic in English literature. But I'm sure that Mother got some kind of inner reassurance from its messages.

Mother expressed strong opinion only on one or two things, one being liquor. She probably regarded drinking as a sin, but she may have been an admirer of Carrie Nation whose little hatchet had been smashing the saloons of Kansas. In my boyhood the state was dry. Mom displayed her wrath one time when her three brothers staged a party with beer brought from Kansas City. And she left me with a prejudice against liquor. Although I now think that a bit of alcohol is good for a person who is getting older, I am dismayed and concerned at the prevalence of drinking today, especially among young kids; and also the waste of human abilities and the sorrow caused others by alcoholism.

Mother was disturbed when Bertie and I began to go to card parties in our Irish card-playing neighborhood; but she never forbade us to go. We did not dance. I learned to dance in college, but at the cost of stepping on quite a few toes.

Drinking, gambling, dance, sex, these were the sins on which the church sermons were based. These strictures on habits undoubtedly became embedded in the preachings because they had caused so much human suffering. Sex? Sex was a no-no. Sex was never, I mean NEVER mentioned. In the family circle, that is. Of course, the boys talked sex a lot. I suppose the girls did too, but if so they never told us. Maybe they were sexless. But I would have been a better male companion on my honeymoon if I had had a bit of sex education. At the university I did join a group at the YMCA that had a woman from Kansas City tell us all about sex. Well, not quite all. A lot of what she did tell us was wrong, as I later discovered.

Dad was a long-time trustee, and later an elder of the church. But in our home we had almost no religious expression—no family prayers, no grace at the table, indeed almost no discussion of religion. However, there were attitudes about work on Sundays. The Berrigan's wheat field was opposite our house and they would cut wheat on Sunday. The Donmyers once said that they would let the wheat rot before they would violate the Sabbath. Once Becky Ruch, a cousin, and her husband came to dinner. Becky decided to take some eggs home with her. There ensued a long discussion with Mother whether she should pay for them, it being Sunday. Would she be violating the Sabbath by buying something? Sounds strange, doesn't it, being so accustomed to see the supermarkets doing a rousing business on Sundays.

This reminds me of having dinner with other threshers at the Mike Tim Sullivan house. It was a real feast, as the threshing meals were, with beef as the main dish. Mrs. Sullivan was busily passing dishes when one man asked: "It being Friday, why are we eating meat?" Mrs. Sullivan, a good Catholic, laughed and replied: "Well, I guess it really won't hurt you." It didn't hurt me, a good Protestant. But poor Mrs. Sullivan ended her days in the Insane Asylum at Topeka. Do you suppose the good Lord was punishing her? The Catholics couldn't eat meat on Friday, and the Protestants couldn't sell eggs on Sunday.

For some years I was in a Sunday School class taught by Bert Ramsey. He had a gift for leading us in discussion of moral concepts. He did a fine job and I feel grateful to him. I think there is something in the idea of indoctrination such as through the Sunday School or the old McGuffey Readers. Indoctrination, however, can be dangerous when in the control of authoritarians.

In my book, *Vitalizing Liberal Education,* I described the effort to discover moral values as being a matter of posing opposites such as honesty and dishonesty, justice and injustice, temperance and intemperance, beautiful and ugly, and evaluating the consequences of adhering to one or the other of the two courses of action. Man's experience in following the respective courses of action should reveal which is best for humanity in the long run. Bert Ramsey had the ability to cause us to reflect on these meanings. Poor Bert, they found him one day in his hog pen where he had fallen dead and the hogs had eaten part of his body.

It makes one think about the significance of the body. I was always skeptical about the claim that Jesus had emerged from his tomb and ascended bodily into Heaven. When a horse died, we would drag the body to a remote corner of the farm and let the maggots and the scavengers devour the flesh. Thus the shell that had been the animal became sustenance for other life. On the Via Veneto in Rome there is a monastery where one may enter caverns with walls that are decorated with bones taken from the bodies of deceased monks. There is a similar room in a cathedral in Evora, Portugal. Imagine being in a dark, dank cavern decorated with human bones. Not bats, people. It makes one shiver. But the monks believed that it is only the soul that has significance. After the soul has departed to heaven, it doesn't matter what happens to the body. Indeed, the mere dissection of the body shows the strength of their belief.

I am convinced that the most sanitary method of removing a body is by cremation. It can also be a quick way of enabling the chemical substances to become useful in creating new life.

Cremation in India is a religious ceremony. I once rode along the banks of the Ganges where I could see three cremations in progress. But one body was being rowed to the middle of the river. I asked my companion, Henry Azariah, Principal of the Allahabad Agricultural Institute, why? He said the body was unclean; perhaps the victim had had smallpox and it wouldn't be right to cremate the body.

Alex, I have been discussing a doleful subject, especially when writing to a 17 year old young woman. Shall we pause and sing one stanza of "Marching Through Georgia?" Oh dear, that is doleful too, concerned with laying Georgia waste in order to make the people submissive to the aims of the North. OK, how about a Negro spiritual? Isn't it strange how easily the black slaves took up the Christian religion? Or the Indians became converted to the Catholicism of their captors and decimators? Perhaps this shows the power of mysticism in the presence of ignorance and superstition.

But don't scorn my idea of singing because songs have a major role in religious experience. One of my contributions to the church was singing in the choir. In college I was a member of the Ochino Male Quartet. We sang regularly at the Presbyterian Church in Lawrence, and on occasion at outlying churches. We enjoyed doing so, but also we got paid which helped with our meager finances. My sister, Bertie, played for the church services in Solomon.

Somehow all of these religious practices kept going through my mind when I was your age. Just what should one believe?

Two days later: a hike around the lake, the antique clock class, a visit to a horticulture garden (I'm trying to find the right shrub for a spot), and other things that keep me busy, I realize that what I was writing above was on the negative side of religion. From another view, the Jewish/Christian ideology has been highly influential in determining the course of Western civilization. In the East, the Gurus have brought peace and contentment to many people. Confessions to a priest help to relieve guilt feelings. The Church stands ready to help in time of personal need. Some churches, such as the Unitarian, which I now support, play active roles in social causes.

In high school I began to enlarge my horizons and got much interested in social issues. Not so much from the courses, which were college preparatory, but rather from debate and discovering a more intellectual environment.

Being high school valedictorian I had to give an address at commencement. On the way home Dad asked: "Where did you get all those ideas?" I guess I was growing out of my environment.

Have you ever thought about how one's environment encompasses you and shapes you? An obvious instance is language. Why is it that as a child you didn't speak Singhalese or Eskimo? Lots of kids do. One's environment also includes religious beliefs and rituals, and you become socialized by them.

Don't get me wrong; social customs need to be passed down to each new generation. That is mostly what liberal education is all about. By accumulating wisdom the human race advances. But we don't need to accept all of the prevailing mores. It is the business of education to evaluate and select what is best for man and society. So as I passed through high school and college I became aware of a vast storehouse of fresh ideas. I was really hungry for them.

In college I helped to organize a group called Ochino. I was its second president. It was based on Christian ideals and excellence in scholarship. We invariably ranked first among all of the fraternities in scholarship standing. We were very conscious of the social problems of the day. Some members were active in their respective churches. I feel that I got a lot from that fellowship. But I now feel that we were too narrowly focussed on the Christian religion. The intellectual turmoil of the 60s made us conscious of the erroneous beliefs about Christian infallibility, White supremacy. We really were possessed of racism. Is it too much to expect that some day people of differing religious beliefs, supposedly idealistic, will collaborate for the common good? Or will we continue to harass and fight one another, as for example in Northern Ireland, the home of our ancestors?

I have often regretted that I did not have more and better science in high school and college. My biology consisted of classifying plants and memorizing the names of the bones of the body. My geology teacher talked about the beauty of the Garden of the Gods, which I had already seen, and she made us memorize the names of minerals. As a result of this remarkable education I can still recognize shepherd's purse, and I know that we have a tibia; sometimes I can recognize quartz. We learned nothing about geologic ages, the way plants convert the sun's energy into starches and sugars, or the way cells divide.

In college a group of us, out of class, invited a mathematician to meet with us and explain Einstein's theory of the relation of matter and energy. I asked him how one could conceive of the fourth dimension, there didn't seem to be any really. He said: "Time." That helped me to jump out of one pool of ignorance.

My interest in the geologic ages began, not in courses, but in conversations with a famous paleontologist, Charles Sternberg. Through him I got some perspective about time, about the origins and evolution of life, and about how to uncover history that is buried not in the printed page but in sedimentary deposits and volcanic ash.

I feel sure that life is a continuum, with me only a part of it. When I cease to exist life will nevertheless go on, at least until the earth itself dies. Even then there will be high orders of life on planets in other solar systems, or so I believe. In the meantime my genes will have passed into my descendents, and even though quickly diffused some of the DNA characteristics will be identifying me for the indefinite future. And my ashes will help form bodies in which fresh life will recur.

Time? Will it ever stop? Start counting 1, 2, 3, 4, and on and on to infinity. In San Francisco Jean and I have eaten at a restaurant above a health food store where both sides of the narrow room are solidly covered with mirrors. One looks at a wall and there is a reflection, and another reflection, and another reflection, seemingly without end. Maybe that is the way with time and space.

There are, however, some things that I cannot fathom. I understand the Big Bang theory of the origin of the universe. The proof seems to be in the manner in which the galaxies are speeding outward in space. OK. But where did the mass of gas or whatever it was that caused the Big Bang come from? And is there an end to space, or do the galaxies just keep going?

GRANDFATHER

PS: Jean and I have arranged with the East Bay Regional Park District to plant a small grove of Sequoia Redwoods in our memory with a bronze marker which says: "Symbols of Life's Continuity."

June 12, 1979

Dear Sabrina,

Back from college and busy trying to make some dinero with which to return for your third year? You lucky stick, being able to go to such a fine college as Vassar. And shortly graduating.

I'm sure you will be concerned about what you are going to do, about marriage, and a whole lot of things. Incidentally you need not worry about your asthma any more. All you need to do, according to *Foxfire* volume 2, page 31, where it discusses sourwood honey, supposedly the best honey according to the mountaineers, is cut a sourwood limb to the exact height of yourself and put it under the doorstep. When you get taller than the stick, your asthma will be cured.

One of the things I thought about a lot at your age was politics. Maybe because I was quite successful in debate. I have just read a clipping from the Solomon Tribune of 1913 extolling our debate team, and it said "Algo Henderson was the outstanding speaker." Mother had clipped and saved the item. As mothers do.

Another reason I was interested in politics was that I actually thought I might be president some day. When I was in school, the way to achieve everlasting glory was to become President of the United States. The history books gave us romantic ideas about Washington, Lincoln, and other famous politicians. We became dedicated loyalists; the United States was clearly the home of the free and the brave. Anyway if you were born in a log cabin or on a farm, you were a natural for the presidency.

I have often wondered what the girls of the day thought. Women couldn't even vote, although an occasional one ran for office—witness Belva Lockwood who ran for president on the Equal Rights ticket in 1884. Just think it wasn't until I was about 21 that women were given the vote, nationally that is. Wyoming had started the trend earlier in 1869; and Wyoming was also the first state to elect a woman as governor.

You could never guess for whom I voted for president in my first election. The two big parties had nominated Harding-Coolidge, and Cox-Roosevelt, respectively. My economics professor at K. U. said, "they were like a sedate team of grey mares." I was not attracted to Harding in spite of his charismatic face; I underestimated Cox, and also Roosevelt for whom I later voted for president, but didn't think much of either of them at the time.

So I voted for the Socialist candidate, Eugene Debs. At the time he was in prison in Atlanta. But I thought he was being persecuted for being a Socialist. Also I was attracted by some of the concepts of Socialism, such as the public ownership of natural resources. If I had my way, the big oil companies wouldn't be getting so rich, because we the people would own the oil, a natural resource. Just look at the multimillionaires we made through giving away so much land to the railroads; and now we are having to pick up the pieces by spending billions to get the railroads back onto a workable basis.

Today we are paying through the nose because of our chaotic oil policy. I ask you, how can profit-making companies, even huge conglomerates, in their self-interest which prevails over the public interest, afford to do the research and pilot operations really necessary to find new sources of energy? Even if they made huge profits, as they are being permitted to do, how can they take the large risks involved in some aspects of the search for energy? Could the Tennessee Valley job have been done by the private utilities; of course not. So now the oil companies are buying up the primary sources of coal and uranium in order to get a stranglehold on energy. Hurrah for Senators Metzenbaum and Kennedy for trying to do something about this.

But I didn't intend to discuss political issues. I had the good fortune to know a few of the presidents. Hoover: I visited him in his home in Palo Alto and he took me to dinner at Stanford. While sitting on the terrace of his home overlooking the city he told me stories about his life. He had had a hard time sleeping at night thinking about problems. So he formed the practice of keeping a note book on a stand by his bedside, and when he began to worry about an urgent problem he would record his thoughts. Then he could go back to sleep.

Hoover was an able man of excellent character, but his idea of the dominance of individualism in society was too archaic for our complex, modern society. Government should protect or advance neither the individual nor the social interest to the exclusion of the other. Its role is to find a viable means of reconciling the individual and social interests; and this relationship changes as society becomes more complex and interdependent. Hoover's failure to recognize this principle when he was president caused him to be retired after one term.

I have a tape of Cavalleria Rusticana playing—one I made a year ago. Don't you think this opera is gorgeous? In the meantime I had lunch, Jean being in San Francisco, and ate some of the steamed rhubarb that I prepared a bit earlier in the morning. Out of my garden. It is easily made and delicious. Try it. Also I had a bit of ham that I smoked last week when we had thirteen people here for dinner.

Franklin Roosevelt visited Antioch once, when I was in charge of the college. The only time I met him. But of course during the days when I was going back and forth to the TVA I had a lot of second hand contact through Arthur Morgan. FDR had asked Morgan to get the Norris Dam going immediately in order to provide employment. So maybe he was more interested in getting us out of the depression than he was in the ideology of the TVA. But I admit that he became social minded as evidenced by the many reforms begun in his administration. On the whole he became one of our best presidents.

I came to know Truman the best of any of the presidents. Partly because one of our Antioch faculty, Donald Kingsley, became one of his top assistants. It was Don who got the idea for the President's Commission on Higher Education to which the President appointed me. We had one very enjoyable meeting with Truman in the Oval Office. In speaking about our work, he did an excellent job. He seemed very knowledgeable about higher education. The amazing thing is that he had not gone to college.

Truman was much better informed than was Thomas Dewey who tried so hard to become president. I got well acquainted with Dewey when I was helping direct the New York Commission on the Need for a State University. One trouble with Dewey was that he thought he already knew the answers, whereas we were there to find answers to the problems arising after World War II. While in the region I directed a state-wide study for Chester Bowles, Governor of Connecticut. He would listen to what I had to say before expressing opinions; and when he talked it became clear that he had good information and had reflected on the problems.

After I had gone to Michigan and Truman had retired to Independence, Missouri, I wrote to him a brief evaluation of what the Truman Commission had accomplished. He wrote back to the effect that we did a good job, didn't we.

I knew Eisenhower from the time he became President of Columbia University. Each year the Board of Regents in New York has a convocation with a noted speaker. One year they chose Eisenhower. They also decided to award him an honorary degree. Now at this convocation the new presidents of the colleges in the state are given special recognition. I had had the presidents in my office to brief them on what was to happen, except Eisenhower who had been cornered by the Regents. I had gone into the Regents' room to meet him but it didn't seem appropriate or necessary to tell him that I was going to introduce him.

My act was the first on the program, and the head of the oldest institution had to be first on the list. So I introduced Eisenhower and asked him to stand. Whereupon he turned to Regent Moot beside whom he was sitting, and in a loud whisper, said: "Now what the hell do I do?" I think that characterizes Eisenhower well. He was no good as a university president, and didn't do much as president of the United States. On one occasion I was in a group who were received by Ike and Mamie at the White House, but if you get an invitation to shake hands with the President and First Lady, don't feel too bad if your pet squirrel has tularemia and you don't dare leave it alone.

You know, don't you, that you are related to Eisenhower? It goes something like this: One of your great-great-uncles, Jacob Henderson, was married to Hattie Dorflinger, his first wife, whose older sister was married to an Eisenhower, whose father was a brother to Ike's grandfather. Treasure that.

Come to think of it, if you have four grandparents, eight great-grandparents, sixteen great-great-grandparents, and so on, doesn't that mean you may be related to Caesar and King Tut, and goodness knows whom all? Just imagine having so many ancestors. Going back more than 3,000,000 years. And how do you figure this all out as you trace backwards and find that the population becomes smaller and smaller? Horrors, maybe you have a tiny drop of black blood in you, since the oldest known skulls have been found in Africa!

My contact with presidents has become less as I become less active in things with political ramifications. I didn't know Johnson but I was on a task force that evaluated his political views and actions as compared with those of Goldwater. I emerged strongly on the side of Johnson. Too bad he chose to stop Communists in Vietnam. Or try to.

I never met Nixon but I was acquainted with Jerry Vorhees and Helen Gahagan (Douglas) who were respectively his congressional and senate opponents when he first sought public office. Nixon began his ugly career at that point by trying to smear these excellent people with his vicious charges, which unfortunately the gullible public believed.

The smearing that any politician faces is one of the reasons why good people avoid running for office. You have to be willing to take big doses of it. During the Red-hunting period, I was publicly attacked by a judge in Xenia for "permitting Antioch to house Communists." I gave him a lecture on the principles of freedom of speech guaranteed by the Constitution. Whereupon he challenged me to a public debate. But friends advised me strongly not to accept. I confess I was a bit tempted, since I was skilled in debate. And I also saw that if I won, it would set me up as a bright young political star in Ohio. But better sense prevailed.

Incidentally, when the Freedom of Information Act was passed, Antioch got a copy of its record from the FBI. It revealed that the Cincinnati office of the FBI had planted some persons in Yellow Springs to pose as Communists in order to smear the college. I got a copy of my record from the FBI and it was very disappointing, being so mild, but goodness the money the government spent on compiling information about me! Such a silly business, and so disgusting in the light of American idealism.

I once had tea with Mrs. William Howard Taft, a stuffy occasion. I did enjoy hearing her husband speak because he had such a wonderful belly laugh.

Eleanor Roosevelt was the person I came to know best. We had her as a guest at Antioch a couple of times, and I always entertained her and presided at the meetings. She understood the need to discipline herself to overcome her deficiencies, as when she took public speaking in order to change her voice from a high pitched whine to a pleasing conversational tone. Her effectiveness, however, was not in her appearance but rather in her ability to articulate her thoughts. Harding had charisma but Doheny and Fall raided the Teapot Dome right under his nose. Eleanor was a person of integrity and a keen observer of her environment. She rose to greatness because she devoted herself to the public good.

I was in the civil service twice. Once in the World War I period, in Washington, where I was for a while in a statistical section that prepared information for the Secretary of War; and the second time in Albany, where at first I worked for the State Legislature and later as Associate Commissioner of Education. Both experiences were worthwhile. However in New York I found it difficult because the decision-making process was so different from the situation in a private enterprise. One can't make decisions with the same ease and decisiveness. He must go through innumerable consultations and get all kinds of approvals.

For example, when I was getting the State University of New York organized and off the ground, I asked for an executive assistant to assist me in my contacts with the college and university presidents. I got approval for the budgeted item and Regents' authorization quickly. But then I had to clear with the Civil Service Commission. They approved a staff addition, but with the title of "school inspector" or something as banal as that. I fired the request back saying that that title was impossible when working with college presidents. How would the President of Cornell react if I sent as my representative a "school inspector?" The Commission reconsidered but this was the title that was on their list where the duties were as I had described them. So I requested a hearing, which they granted. After I had made my case they deliberated further and then asked the State Budget Director for advice. He said: "Why not call it "Executive Assistant?" That was precisely the title I had requested! But a whole year had passed and this was the period in which I needed the help most badly. The experience taught me a lot about government procedures.

Bureaucracy, however, is a phenomenon of size and not merely of government. The worst case that I have encountered was with General Motors. In May 1940, President Roosevelt declared a national emergency relating to the war situation in Europe. Among other actions he requested General Motors to step up the development of their two-cycle diesel engine for possible use in trucks and tanks.

GM about August 1 came to Antioch proposing a research and pilot project in finding light weight metals for the motor. I and staff from our foundry, together with Vice President Evans and staff of GM met intensively for 6 days at the end of which we had an agreement. We at Antioch were ready to sign and go to work. GM, however, referred the agreement to various of their experts for review and opinion—the general counsel, real estate staff, patent attorneys, and others. Each officer proposed amendments. Each time I rejected them as changing the agreement. This went on for weeks. Finally I sat down and wrote a final wording myself and sent it to Evans. He responded that my wording was indeed the agreement that we had reached. He suggested one minor amendment which I immediately accepted. This was now March 15, more than a half year's delay on a matter that needed urgent action.

Delays are sometimes beneficial. In California we have had since 1976 a Coastal Commission that must pass on all developments within 1000 feet of the ocean. Developers and business companies had been using up the coast line so rapidly that shortly there would have been nothing left of its beauty for the public to enjoy. The Commisssion acts as a zoning agency. This seems to be the only way the public interest can be protected from the despoilers who merely want to make money. Developers need to be restrained, otherwise a gorgeous treasure such as the Pacific Coast would become a glut of factories, plastic matchboxes, and dump heaps. But variances require hearings, investigations, and Commission consideration. This causes delays. Often the delays are good in that it gives time for the public to react.

We have had Civil Service since 1883. It was a much needed reform because of the manner in which politicians were staffing the public offices with henchmen, wheeler-dealers, and crooks. Today the Civil Service once again needs reform. It has become a device for keeping dead wood in the service. Double-dipping is rampant, nepotism is common, pensions have got out of hand. A good administrator has his hands tied in being unable to select competent assistants. The Public Employees Union seems more interested in protecting the vested interests of its members than in promoting the public welfare.

Sabrina, I am beginning to have doubts whether our much revered Republic with its balance of power structure is adequate for our nation today. The President and the Congress have great difficulty in agreeing upon needed actions, Congressmen are too much pawns of the lobbyists, getting elected is a traumatic experience and so costly that it is counterproductive in getting able candidates, and the system fails to fix responsibility and demand accountability for actions taken. I am not sure what is the best solution but I think the parliamentary plan has more to recommend it than does ours. Under the plan a political party has to assume responsibility, choose the leader in government, and resign when they lose the confidence of the public. Whoever is Prime Minister is also the leader in getting legislative action.

I hope I don't sound too negative about politics and public service. You know, of course, that I was recently president of the local Democratic Club. Government is essential; we shall need more rather than less as time goes on. Our social structure requires it.

So don't become one of those reactionaries who are "agin" all government! And if you want to run for President some day, it's OK with me. Why not?

GRANDFATHER

March 28, 1975

Dear Alex,

Your school, whenever you describe what you do, always sounds terrific. I understand that all three of you girls were up to your necks in the opera that you just gave. That is great fun, isn't it? And one learns a lot about music, acting, and working together to bring a performance to perfection. I used to sing in Gilbert and Sullivan, but I also remember especially Dido and Aeneas. Antioch helped rescue from Germany a man who was part Jewish, William Fiedler. Bill was an orchestra/chorus director of considerable talent; and the first musical event at Antioch that he staged was Dido and Aeneas.

Do you know that when Hitler first came to power and was shouting racist slogans at the people, a great many of the most talented scholars and artists of both Germany and Austria fled to other countries? Their contributions to art, music, science, and medicine, after arrival in the United States were tremendous. Some universities, such as NYU and the New School for Social Research greatly enhanced the quality and creativity of their faculties by employing these refugees.

We got two couples at Antioch—the Fiedlers, and Fred and Marianne Littman, both of the latter being fine sculptors, students of Maillol. As an expression of gratitude to me, Fred made a head of me, now in the Antiochiana collection at Yellow Springs, and one of

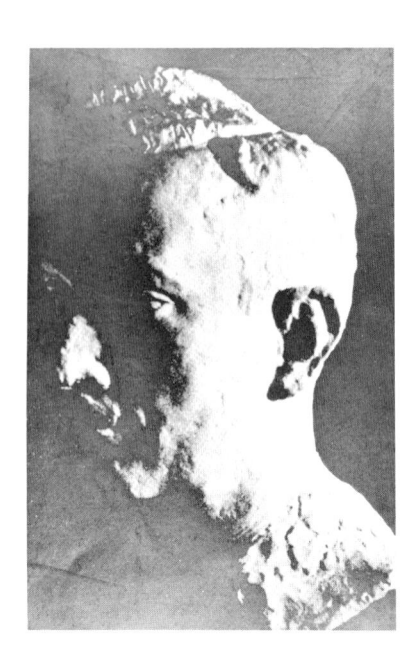

Bronze by Fred Littman

Philip which Jerry has. I discovered at one point that some students had taken my head to a dormitory, put an old slouch hat on it, and a cigarette in its mouth. What a blasphemy!

In your school do you have Blacks and Chicanos? And courses on human relations? Do you learn to know some Blacks or Chicanos individually, so that you think of each as a person and not as part of a group? Our cultural heritage is such that we have the habit of thinking about people who differ from us, if only in skin pigments, in stereotypes. As though all black people were like sheep, all just alike.

On a visit to Dallas in the 1950s I was attending a national conference on education at one of its leading hotels. Dr. Caesar Toles, who had received his doctor's degree at the University of Michigan, was principal of a high school in Dallas, and also director of a branch of Bishop College. I invited him to come to see me at the hotel. When we met in the lobby he told me they wouldn't let him enter the front door. He had to go around to a kitchen door where a friend let him in. He said the hotel was afraid that if he came in the front door, it would give the place a bad image. Dallas was not yet ready for that sort of thing.

One morning at Antioch, Jessie Treichler, my assistant, came in my office and pulled up a chair to the desk. I could see from her manner that she had something important on her mind. She said: "I want to tell you about a happening last night." A group of students from Antioch College, accompanied by a similar group from nearby Wilberforce University, had gone to the motion picture theater. A rope penned off a small section of seats at the left-hand rear of the room and all Negroes had to sit behind it. When the Wilberforce group entered the theater, they sat behind the rope. The white students arrayed themselves in aisle seats and each one saved the seat next to him or her.

After the picture had been started (this was in the days when there was only one show and it started at a set time) the Blacks came forward and seated themselves in the places beside the Whites. The proprietor stopped the show and ordered the Blacks behind the rope. Each in turn handed him a typed statement of the law in Ohio, which made discrimination in theaters illegal. The proprietor then sent for Mayor Lowell Fess. The mayor came, took one look at the slips of paper and beat a hasty retreat. After several minutes of pleading that his theater would be ruined, the proprietor started the show again. The rope was down for good. The theater did not lose business; indeed, it gained some because Negroes could now go there with self-respect, as could also people at the college who had objected to the segregation.

Would you believe what happened the next day? I was astonished. The Minister of the Presbyterian Church asked to see me. Now the Presbyterian Church was the most elite one in the village. It had the nicest building, and the most prominent of the villagers and farmers belonged to it. This minister wanted to tell me that the college should stop "meddling in the affairs of the village." He said that things had been peaceful and happy at the theater; he was well acquainted throughout the community, and he knew that both Blacks and Whites were contented with the rope; so why did the college "want to stir things up?" I smiled at him, said we had no intention of stopping our efforts to make the community a good place in which to live, and gave him the heave-ho as soon as I politely could.

The same church caused another ruckus later. Let me give you the background and then the incident. We were looking for a person to head our music department and came upon a graduate of the Oberlin Conservatory who seemed to have the best qualifications—Walter

Anderson. He could play several instruments, and was excellent as director of chorus and orchestra. His specialty was pipe organ. After we had employed him, he arranged with the Presbyterian Church to play their organ. Presently they were calling on him to substitute for the regular organist. Seated at his bench he was obscured from most of the audience, and inconspicuous to the rest. And he played beautifully.

After a time the pastor—a different man from the one mentioned above—asked him if he and his wife would like to join the church. They said: "Yes." The elders met and voted them in. Then the word got around that they were Blacks; members of the congregation raised hell. "We will not stand for having a Negro in our church; there are two Negro churches in the village, let them go there." In spite of the commotion and the pressures on them, the elders and the minister held their ground. As a consequence some dozen families moved over to the Methodist Church which was still lily-white. Subsequently, the minister resigned. But some people at the college who had not been going to church, now joined it. In the course of time, at least some of the families that had got so hot under the collar, moved back. Times were changing.

Isn't it interesting how the "best" people in the most elite church, professed Christians, can be so bigoted. Do they think that God is a white, male, Presbyterian? What does the Christian way of living really mean?

But it wasn't only the Presbyterians. A lot of people in the community didn't like our efforts to rouse them from their provincialism. They called us Communists. Because Jessie Treichler was blamed for the picture show incident, groups of teenage boys drove past her house and threw rocks in the windows. At the heart of the trouble was the deepseated prejudice against black people.

I think that I grew up relatively unprejudiced. We had only one Negro in the Solomon community—Negro Ped, as he was called. He belonged to the same church as my family did, although he was the janitor. My father took me to him one day and he greeted me in a most friendly way. I admit his color seemed queer, although we all got badly sun-burned in the fields. Certainly our skin was anything but pure white. I don't know if there were any Jews in Solomon. We did shopping at Jewish merchants in Salina. I observed that my mother would always pull a thread from a suit she was buying for me, unravel it and study the threads, and sometimes touch a match to it. When I asked her what she was doing, she said she didn't want to buy shoddy. Do you know what shoddy is? Bits of yarn so short they might pull apart. I think she didn't trust the Jewish merchants, but I'm sure she tested the threads at any store. This was before the government introduced standards into merchandising.

As a boy I was much impressed one day when a group of harvest hands were discussing the hard times and one man, a Negro, asked: "How would you all like to be both poor and black?" His conversation made me realize for the first time that Blacks do have difficulty in getting good houses and enough to eat. Because of discriminations against them. In employment and other ways.

It was in the army when I first became really conscious of the feelings many people have about Jews. As a senior sergeant I was asked by the company commander to recommend men as possible candidates for officer's training. I mentioned a man in my tent who seemed to me to have good potential. "But isn't he Jewish?" I really didn't know. And I hadn't realized that it would make a difference.

Discrimination against Jews was the principal issue in the New York legislative inquiry in 1946—48. The issue was whether the colleges, especially the medical schools and the liberal arts colleges, were discriminating against Jews in their admission practices. This was a very emotional issue in New York City where so many Jews lived.

Our commission uncovered many interesting facts: clearly 5 of the 9 medical schools did discriminate; 14 of the liberal arts colleges had quotas for Jews, usually 10 percent. On the other hand we found that about twice as many Jews as non-Jews, relative to the numbers graduating from New York City high schools, were actually going to college.

This last fact raised an intersting controversy as to what was really discrimination. A son-in-law of the famous Rabbi, Stephen S. Wise, invited me to lunch and asked me to suppress the New York City finding. He contended that discrimination occurred whenever a person didn't get into the college of his choice. Although I agreed that this was discrimination, I refused to suppress data that showed that Jews did get to college.

Well, anyway, our findings were clear, and so the question became what to do about it. A proposed state university was the answer many people wanted—and the State University of New York was created. The state had relied heavily upon private institutions, and these were said to have the "right" to admit anyone they chose; or refuse to admit. Some of us got the idea for an antidiscrimination law, with an ombudsman to enforce it. This became the Fair Educational Practices Act.

When a person gets all hot and bothered about something, he needs a way to get relief. One way is to talk with someone about it. Yell and scream if need be, but talk. Well, an ombudsman is a person to whom you can go with a problem and tell him about it and get his help in finding a solution. Do you have one at school? If not, why not?

The Fair Educational Practices Act, when passed by the Legislature, provided for a person to hear the complaints of students who had been refused admission to a college. I selected as this person, Fred Hoeing, who had been employed as a counsellor in the Fair Employment Act office. Fred then became available to anyone who wanted to complain to him. When he decided there was merit to a case, he would talk with the college officials to get their side of the story. If he still thought the complaint had merit, he would order the admission of the student. If the college refused, he would bring the case before the Regents for a hearing. If need be, the case would be taken to court for action.

The very first case was at a well known secretarial school which had denied admission to a young woman because she was black. When Fred talked with the officers they changed their minds and admitted her. President Case of Colgate University, who had opposed the legislation, later told me he was glad to have the law. He said before that time, he had to cater to alumni and townspeople whereas now he could merely say to them: "This is the law in New York." New York's law was the first of its kind; now other states have such laws.

There is a question as to whether people should be compelled by law to behave in this way. But on the other side is the ideal that we have in the United States that everyone should be able to get an education in relation to his interests and abilities. Law often follows the development of mores, but it can also lead toward establishing better ones. The New York law seems to have done that.

In 1957 Anne and I visited the Union of South Africa. Principal S. Pauw of the University of South Africa, Pretoria, held a reception for us. When I asked about the South African policy of apartheid, he gave a fascinating explanation. He said: "We Vortrekkers (people of

Dutch descent who had migrated from the Capetown area to the Johannesburg/Pretoria region) were for a long time suppressed by the English. They wouldn't let us keep our customs, and they wanted to do away with our language and religion. They dominated us politically. Now we are in power. But having been through the experience of suppression, we don't want others to suffer the same thing. So we have created separate enclaves where the natives (blacks), the coloreds (people of black and white admixtures), and the Indians, can live in their own communities, have their own schools and customs, and live as they wish. Of course, we shall have to maintain the police power and foreign relations." A strange rationalization for keeping people suppressed.

Nevertheless, although the colleges for the various ethnic groups were wholly separate institutions, the Vice-Chancellor of the University of Natal, E. G. Malherbe, told me that he employed some natives in parts of the university where they could be kept hidden. He introduced me to some of them. The reason he got away with it, he had been head of the secret intelligence during the war and he had files on several national leaders. If they gave him trouble about the race problem, he could pull out the files and make them public. The point was they had been collaborators with the Nazis during the war.

It was only 8 years ago that we happened to be in Atlanta the day the Legislature excluded Julian Bond, a Negro, from taking his seat. How times have changed in this short space of time. Atlanta electing a Negro as Mayor. In Dallas, Dr. Toles could now enter the hotel through the front door. We are making progress, aren't we?

While in New York I was invited to membership on two national commissions dealing with race relations. One was as Chairman of the Committee on Equality of Opportunity of the American Council on Education. The Council is a prestigious organization but our committee was not terribly effective—partly because the President, Arthur Adams, would smile and nod favorably as we presented ideas for action but did not follow up with action. We did, however, hold some conferences of educators and issue a few publications. I wrote one that I called "Balm for a Troubled Conscience." In it I analyzed the progress of Negroes, especially in the South, in getting the benefit of higher education. By coincidence my pamphlet was published just before the Brown vs. Topeka 1954 historic decision of the U. S. Supreme Court. It reversed the "separate but equal" earlier decision by the Court, and now declared segregation to be unconstitutional.

The other commission was the one on Educational Organizations of the National Conference of Christians and Jews. Later I became chairman of this committee, and by virtue thereof a member of the Executive Committee of NCCJ. This organization was originally concerned with the relations of Catholics, Protestants, and Jews. It promoted discussions of the frictions among these groups. Protestants and Catholics are both Christians; and Jesus had been a Jew. So why get uptight about differences in creed? Why do people become so prejudiced against Jews? Just think what the Nazis did—put 6,000,000 Jews into the furnace.

We were trying to keep anything like that from happening here, or for that matter anywhere. During my service as chairman I went on a nation-wide speaking tour to talk about the problems of race relations. In New Orleans Jews attended the public meetings and fancy receptions, but Blacks could not. I asked to meet with some Blacks, then found the meeting had been arranged within the seclusion of a lawyer's office. So it was time to devote our attention to the problems of the Blacks.

We arranged workshops, published materials, made speeches, and

NCCJ conference, St. Louis, 1954

gave awards for distinguished service. It is hard to evaluate the results, but one thing is clear—during these years considerable progress in deriving better interracial understandings, and securing for the disadvantaged better educational opportunity was made.

I want to mention three friends of mine in Yellow Springs. One was an elderly man who owned the house next door to my garden. He was especially proud of the fact that his father had been a plantation owner in Kentucky. He knew who his father was, but his father didn't recognize him. So he was half white and half black. But by our mores a Negro. Reminds one of how the Nazis identified Jews.

Do you remember our spool-legged table? One day another black friend, Mr. Coleman, had an auction. I spotted on his back porch a decrepit-looking table that I recognized as an antique wash stand. I examined it and found it to be walnut. So when it came up I bid $2.50 and got it. I scraped, cleaned, and polished it, and now it is the first article of furniture you see as you enter our front door.

Another friend of mine was Joe Curl after whom we named our new gymnasium at Antioch College. He had not attended the college but he had played on the baseball team. When he died I attended his funeral at one of the Negro churches. I was late so they ushered me and some others to the front platform where extra chairs had been placed. It was a long service with two preachers. I sat there busily daydreaming when I suddenly heard the chief minister say: "President Henderson will now address us."

So Alex, let's role play a bit. You are sitting at a funeral thinking about some nice boys, when all of a sudden the preacher says: "Alexandra Pratt will now address us." Just what do you do now?

GRANDFATHER

June 4, 1975

Dear Ilya,

Well, we are at last out of Vietnam. The college-age kids helped to get us out by fiercely opposing the venture, some by saying: "We won't go!" But what do 12-year olds think about it? Do you talk about war at school? Do you discuss alternatives to war in reconciling disputes between nations? Do you study the rise of militarism in this country? Do you feel apprehensive that the military gets stronger and stronger? And is this good or bad?

When I was your age, people thought that the United States was a country to which those who were oppressed could come and enjoy freedom. One of the freedoms was to avoid compulsory military service. I used to think how wonderful it was to have a country where you didn't have to engage in petty fights such as recurred so often among the nations of Europe.

The people of Europe inherited their feelings about security, and maintaining it by force, from the Middle Ages when each Lord of a castle constructed a moat with drawbridge, and maintained his own armored staff. Later the dukedoms were consolidated into nations, and each in turn drew a line around their territory and built forts and trenches, and trained armies to protect the borders (or to go on raids across them.)

Some people argue that this is human nature; and they point to animals that circumscribe their individual territories by leaving their scent on the bushes, or to birds that stake out a territory which they defend vigorously. We have one foolish towhee that keeps flying against our bedroom window because he thinks his own reflection is an enemy bird. Only I wish he didn't start defending his territory at 5 AM. People build fortresses, tanks, and planes to defend their territory, following their animal instincts, or so it is contended. Do you think war is "natural?" Or do you think maybe there is some better way to settle disputes? Among intelligent beings.

The slogan that got us all excited about World War I was that we would "save the world for democracy." I was idealistic, and naïve about international affairs, so the slogan really grabbed me. First, the day I finished summer school at the University of Kansas, 1917, I headed for Topeka where the Kansas National Guard was being mobilized. I talked with the Kentucky Colonel who was in charge of inducting the Guard into the Federal service, and he persuaded me to become his personal secretary. I did, and this lasted about a month. Then I was notified of openings in the War Department in Washington, so I went there. Immediatley I was assigned to a charting department (logistics). Our job was to prepare charts for the office of the Secretary of War to show him the correlations between the recruitment of men for the army and the procurement of equipment.

Presently I was told by the head of the department that if I would enlist I would be given the highest ranking sergeancy in the army, Ordnance Sergeant. Enlistment appealed to me because everyone in

Washington was thrilled by the progress we were making in saving the world for democracy; and I thought it my duty to get in the army. I was inducted as a private on November 21, 1917, and within 10 days my warrant as noncommissioned officer came. So there I was all dolled up in my country's uniform. Occasionally we drilled, and always did so in the oval in front of the White House. I learned to salute and to do squads right, and that was about all.

Every now and then we would see Woodrow Wilson whizz past in his car, with top down (no bullet proof glass, no array of secret service agents), and we got a big thrill. It was he who was always talking about saving the world for democracy. We believed him, and I still think that he thought he was doing just that. The political struggle that ensued in the United States when he advocated the League of Nations, killed him. But the idea of forming a world government has been bungled even worse since he died.

In March of 1918 I was sent to the University of Pittsburgh for more intensive training in logistics. My chevrons caught the eye of the commander of our contingent there, who rightly singled me out as the senior in rank. This led to embarrassing consequences. I marched a platoon of soldiers onto the drill ground, did a few squad rights, and thought to myself that I was pretty good. To give the troops a brief rest, I lined them up at attention and set out to teach them a few elementary positions. One thing I did was to give the command "Hands salute!" Up went all the hands to the foreheads. Then an awful thing happened; the hands stayed at salute, and I didn't know how to get them back down!

I thought to myself surely there must be a way to do this. There always is. My Dad used to say: "Give me a piece of barbed wire and I can make anything." So while they were all standing at attention I walked up and down the ranks correcting some inaccuracies or instances of improper dress. All the while desperately thinking, how am I ever to get those hands back down. Presently I got an inspiration. I got out in front where a commanding officer stands and saluted. It worked like a charm; the hands came down. Just shows that you can solve your problems if you concentrate on doing so.

One of the courses that I took was Taylor Shop Management. Frederick Taylor is known for his advocacy of efficiency in the operation of manufacturing plants—the use of time and motion studies, for example. So we were studying how to run army supply depots efficiently. After we were married, I happened to mention in front of my wife, Anne, that I had taken a course in Taylor Shop Management. Several years later I discovered that she thought I had been learning how to run a tailor shop.

Some time in May we moved to Camp Hancock in Georgia near Augusta. The camp commander was Colonel James Benét, the father of Stephen, William Rose, and Laura Benét, each of whom became a distinguished poet and writer. We inherited some old Pennsylvania Guard tents. They leaked. We drilled in three inches of sand and the sun was hot as blazes. We were not furnished with light uniforms until August. At certain functions we had to wear our woolen jackets. These buttoned up to the neck, having a collar that fastened with hooks.

On Memorial Day some 10,000 troops were herded into a large pit, made for the purpose of practicing secret tactics such as bayonet drill and kicking an enemy in the balls. The heat in this confined space was blistering. We stood in close ranks, which meant half of the usual 30 inches apart, at attention while a Southern Baptist preacher gave the invocation. He prayed interminably, not only to save democracy, but also to save us all from our sins. Men began to drop in their tracks and I got a most uncomfortable feeling. I might be the next one to drop. Shortly men were being carried over the banks as thick as fleas, to be revived with fresh air. And there stood the army officers and the preacher on top of the bank under a canopy, with the breeze blowing across them completely insensitive to the problem the men had.

I do not recommend army life. Enlisted men have to do all the dirty work and some of them have to act as servants to the officers. As a ranking sergeant one of my duties was to select men for details, such as serving the officers, or carrying out the kitchen swill. One day I was walking down the company street when I heard a voice in one of the tents call out: "Duck! Here comes Old Monument Face."

One of the less pleasant things was to answer short-arm inspection. This meant lining up with one's penis hanging out and passing in front of a medical officer. As we passed we gave it a squeeze to see if any pus emerged. I never had VD so was never yanked out of line for treatment.

In the army one learns how to get around the rules without getting caught. For example, I've seen men walk over to a pile of blankets, lift one up, look at it curiously, and then walk away with it. They were stealing, but after all it was army property, and of course no one would tell. I acquired eleven wool blankets but in a "legitimate" way. When troops were sent overseas, I would search their tents for discarded blankets and then exchange them for new ones. Sleeping in a tent as I did all through the winter meant freezing unless you made a sleeping bag of lots of blankets.

People say that army discipline is good for young men. For many of them it is the reverse of that. While under discipline one is being taught by his peers how to "get by" the regulations—witness the widespread scandals at West Point about cheating in the exams. The armed services teach you to obey a command, true, but of course *any* command. You can teach a dog to respond to a command. So you substitute someone else's thinking about what is right and wrong for your own convictions. This may be acceptable in a dictatorship, but is hardly the kind of moral and intellectual training that should be given to future citizens in a democracy. People mistake army manners for moral fibre.

But to return to the events of World War I, I was in Camp Hancock until November, having in the interval gone through an ordnance supply school and the officer's training camp. When I got my commission as Second Lieutenant, I was directed to go to Camp Penniman, Virginia, on the James River near Williamsburg. I went by way of Washington and happened to be there the day the armistice was signed. A girl friend and I got into such a crowded jam on the street beside the White House I thought we were going to be trampled to death. Of course there was great jubilation, for had we not kept the world safe for democracy?

I discovered that my mission at Camp Penniman, which was really a DuPont shell loading plant, was to keep civilians and enlisted men from fighting. They fought because the enlisted men were getting $1 a day, and the civilians, mostly women, were getting $8 a day, for doing exactly the same work. It was a case of impressed labor. Here I was on guard duty after having been trained in logistics in Washington, at the University of Pittsburgh, in the supply school, and in officer's training camp. Well, that's the army for you.

My most disillusioning experience with the army came years later during World War II. At Antioch College we got caught up in the fervor of stopping the Nazis, and among many attempts to help the nation, took an army unit to train. We went to much effort and expense to recruit the necessary teachers and rearrange our facilities. After a few months the contingent was suddenly removed. Without notice and before the end of the term. We were stuck with commitments on their behalf and asked to know why the sudden action. The explanation was that our water supply was polluted. This sounded fishy, but we discovered there was one 3-unit apartment house on the black list of the State Health Department. So we immediately put in new plumbing, giving the owner a free ride. Then the water was certified as OK.

But the army then contended the men were needed in the battle of the bulge. This was plausible, but not the original explanation. To try to get to the bottom of the matter I took a delegation, including Mayor Fess and former President Morgan, to see the Fifth Corps commander at Columbus. The General repeated the story about the water and wouldn't budge from his decision. So I decided to go on to Washington and the Pentagon. After leaving the General's office I visited the officer's toilet; there I found that they were using an old fashioned roller towel, the kind that had been outlawed in Ohio for many years. I felt like shoving the General's nose in the dirty thing.

In Washington I got the run around everywhere until one Colonel took pity on me. He said: "Come with me." Then led me to another part of the Pentagon and into a large auditorium. There we sat down in the center out of ear shot of anyone, and presumably out of range of bugging devices. As he turned to me he said: "I will tell you what happened, but if you tell anyone, I will have to deny that I told you." This Colonel later became President of Georgia Institute of Technology. Strange how this caliber of man could become so subservient to the West Point officers who controlled everything. But it is part of the system.

It seems that some one in the village of Yellow Springs had written a letter saying that we had a bunch of Communists at the college and that the troops should be removed. The colonel said I would have to "go very high up" if I wanted the troops back. I could have taken my story to Eleanor Roosevelt, and through her to the President, but decided that in view of the crisis in the war caused by the German offensive, we should not bother the President with our small complaint.

Through United States Senator Harold Burton I was able to get a copy of the letter. It was anonymous, but analyzing its language I identified it as having come from a former professor of chemistry with whom we had parted with none too good feelings. I thereupon wrote a letter to the Yellow Springs News giving the full story, and describing the man sufficiently to let people know who he was. This incident with its several facets shows one aspect of military behavior.

When World War II came along and it appeared that we had not really saved the world in WWI, I turned to some efforts to try to find solutions other than war to solve conflicts between nations.

One effort was to educate the surrounding community about international relations and issues. With collaboration from the American Friends Service I helped to organize and direct a series of public meetings held at Antioch College. We called it the North Central Institute of International Relations. Most of the sponsoring members were from Dayton and they included many prominent citizens. At each session we had a principal speaker on the selected theme, and then open discussions.

As one speaker we had Eleanor Roosevelt. She was a most interesting and gracious woman who always spoke off the cuff, but who had thought out carefully what she wanted to say. Following one of these occasions a terrible thing happened. The Chicago Tribune, that great newssheet of the Midwest, came out with a front page feature, including a cartoon in color showing Eleanor dragging the American flag in the dirt. They quoted, completely out of context, a sentence from her extemporaneous talk at Antioch, something to the effect that the United States should sometimes subordinate its policies to accommodate other nations in fulfilling their needs. I immediately got in touch with the Editor, vigorously protesting such an unfair attack. He responded: "Well, she said it, didn't she?" What a way to present the news!

During a question period a man asked an involved question, so I asked him to repeat it. I still couldn't make out what he wanted to say and said: "Let's go on." Mrs. Roosevelt jumped up from her seat and said: "Let me try." She kept after the man until he was able to communicate with her. We always entertained her for lunch and these glimpses of her personality were fascinating. On one occasion I took her by the arm and escorted her into the kitchen of the tearoom so that the cooks and dish washers would have the opportunity to see and speak with her. She seemed to enjoy it.

In 1943 our neighbor university, Wilberforce, invited me to preside over their annual International Day, which I did. This was really a program on race relations and more domestic than international, but at that time it was needed. The experience gave me some information and insights where I had been rather naïve. For exam-

Eleanor Roosevelt at Antioch

ple, at the very first meeting the first item on the program was to sing the national anthem. What was my astonishment when we sang an anthem that Negroes called *their* national anthem—based on a poem by Langston Hughes. A better choice actually since our "bombs bursting in air" anthem is very militaristic in theme. Also I learned that they had their own equivalent of Phi Beta Kappa—because up to that time Negroes had been barred from the "white" one. I was in a new culture, and discovering how ignorant I was about Black people in the United States.

The most ambitious effort in which I joined was the World Confederation of International Groupments, also known as the Free World Association. This was essentially a "think" group that came into being as World War II was deepening in intensity, and which had as its aim to help set directions for the development of the post-war period.

Before this organization was originated, Don Kingsley and I had organized a conference of world intellectual leaders at Antioch. Don worked up the list of participants and I chaired the conference. The members included several of the persons who a bit later became organized as the Free World Association. So Don and I felt that we had provided the initial stimulus.

The Free World group included such persons as Li Yu Ying, President of the National Academy of Peking, and also one of the 7 founders with Sun Yat Sen of the Chinese Republic; Alvarez del Vayo, who had been Minister of Foreign Affairs in the Republic of Spain (before the Franco period); J. P. Warbasse, President of the Cooperative League of the U. S.; Rabbi Stephen Wise, President of the World Jewish Congress; Henri Bonnet, later French Ambassador to the U. S.; Pierre Cot, former cabinet minister in France, and subsequently head of Air France; Alexander Meiklejohn, former President of Amherst College; Wou Saofong, former member of the League of Nations Secretariat; Henri Laugier, Professor, University of Montreal; Luis Quintanilla, Minister of the Republic of Mexico; Michael Straight, Editor of the New Republic; Hugo Fernandes Artucio, Professor, University of Montevideo; Anup Singh, Director, Research Bureau, India League of America; Milos Safranek, Czechoslovak Foreign Office; Hu Shih, Chinese Philosopher; Feliks Gross of Poland; Louis Dolivet, later Editor of the Free World Magazine which was launched as part of the effort; and quite a few others. One sidelight that I visualize readily is of Hugh Shih coaching me on how to pronounce his name.

I must tell you more about Dr. Li. He and his German wife stayed in our house at Yellow Springs and we staged a dinner party in his honor. Just as we were preparing to enter the dining room, Mrs. Li said to Anne: "You know Dr. Li is a Buddhist and does not eat meat...." Anne was flabbergasted and quite put out because she'd used all her ration stamps on a beautiful roast beef. Fortunately the cook had prepared generous dishes of vegetables. So everything went smoothly. But we were to have mince pie for dessert. Anne decided to serve it and say nothing. Li ate it with much gusto and pronounced it very good.

Li's vegetarianism came to the fore at a later meeting in Los

Angeles. He was to give an address at a large public gathering about the Free World ideas, but since he spoke French better than English, he decided to use French and have an interpreter. Li launched into a long monologue, the interpreter nervously trying to get him to pause. A break finally came whereupon the interpreter said: "Dr. Li says it is good to eat vegetables."

On a visit to Taiwan in 1956 I asked the Ministry of Finance and Economics, which had sent Dr. Ma, Undersecretary, to greet us at the airport, to see if they could find Dr. Li. They did so, and we arranged an appointment. You must appreciate that he was a very short Chinese with a wispy goatee. So I towered over him. But when he opened his mouth I got a pungent blast of garlic that nearly knocked me over.

I have no way of knowing whether all the effort we put into the World Confederation of International Groupments ever did much good. But quite a few of the persons went on to become influential in world affairs.

One of the organizations that I had expected to work through was the National Council on American-Soviet Friendship, Inc. For a brief time I was vice president of the committee on education. But the organization was taken over by a clique of Communists who ignored the rest of us. So I and many others resigned. My membership later got me into some trouble. In 1950, friends of mine in Yellow Springs and elsewhere began to tell me that the FBI had been around prying into my affairs; that I must be under consideration for a high post in the Federal Government. This went on for about 6 months, when finally the FBI contacted me. They asked me to explain my association with the American-Soviet Friendship. I asked them why? The response was that I had been appointed a member of the Surgeon General's Committee on Medical Grants.

The exasperating thing about this was that in this unpaid position I had been functioning already for 2 years, the commission had made its studies and had prepared a 3-volume report. My work for the government was finished. Furthermore I am confident that the FBI already had a fat dossier on me, for the garbage cans of Atnioch had been pawed over by 3 agencies: the House UnAmerican Activities, the Army Intelligence, and the FBI. This miserable business may have reached its height under President Nixon, but it certainly did not begin there. As I can testify from personal experience.

Where was I, Ilya? Oh yes, I was telling my grandchildren not to rely on brute force to settle disputes. To use rational approaches. To organize people so you will not be alone, but will have some umph, strength of that kind rather than rifles and missiles. Don't permit the innocuous outcomes of some of my efforts—for world peace, for instance—dishearten you. It took centuries to get rid of the moats that surrounded the castles of Europe. Each drop of water helps to erode the rock.

Confrontation with bombs and warships will not lead to world order and peace. The true role of the United States should be to assist the developing countries, and those that are casting off the bonds of colonialism, maldistribution of resources and various forms of oppression, to lift their people out of poverty, ignorance, superstition, and disease.

GRANDFATHER

P.S.: Tell Peter and Matthew, it is good to eat vegetables. And tell Sabrina and Alexandra *not* to eat garlic just before talking with boy friend.

Addendum, 1981: Now the United States is arming itself to the teeth as the road to peace. Peace? This is really the route to a nuclear holocaust and the devastation of the earth.

January 11, 1980

Dear Matthew,

Thank you very much for that beautiful "Flower Still Life" by Van Huysum. It is an especially nice Christmas present. Granny and I are lucky to have a grandson who has an eye for fine art.

We are also lucky that you have saved money for luxuries of this sort. I am always parsimonious about my gifts. This attitude I am sure is one of the lasting results of having had to be so economical during the Depression which struck this country when your Dad and your Aunt Joanne were small children. It was very severe and lasted for several years. In this day of affluence it is hard for anyone to realize how bad our economic condition was at that time. An insight can be seen by comparing the Gross National Product in 1933, which was $55 billion, with the present nearly 3 trillion dollars. Gross National Product, simply stated, is the sum total of productive activity in the nation, measured in dollars.

At Harvard I had taken some courses in the graduate division of the Department of Economics, one of which was devoted to the fluctuations of the business cycle. Since the beginning of the Industrial Revolution in the early part of the 19th Century, business activity has fluctuated from low to high and the reverse on the average of every 7 years. Ordinarily the dips in activity are called recessions, but when they are severe they become panics.

I remember the panic of 1907, but it was not nearly as severe as the one of the 1930s. The causes of the cycle from prosperity to recession are complicated, but business behavior resembles the actions of sheep. They all run in the same direction at once. In prosperity everyone manufactures lots of things and merchants sell lots of things. But then inventories get overstocked, and credits get overextended, people borrow money or run up charge accounts beyond their current ability to repay, so then everyone curtails activity. Consumers have less money and credit with which to buy things. So it is like a snow ball, the depression rolls on until something stops it.

When I left Harvard I thought I knew all about the subject. But in 1929 I had bought a few shares of Curtis-Wright airplane stock being under the delusion that the air industry was "going to town." All of a sudden, in October, the stock market crashed. My stock dropped precipitously. The holders of business stocks lost billions of dollars, so my tiny loss was peanuts; but it made me realize that I didn't know as much as I thought I knew. The moral is, never become overconfident in thinking you know everything about everything. Even a Harvard degree doesn't insure that.

Another signal was received when the Florida land boom crashed. Florida has limited acreage of land, everyone's ambition in the East is to vacation or live in Florida, so everyone wanted to grab a bit of land there while the getting was good and before the prices got too high. The result was tremendous speculation in land. The bottom suddenly dropped out of the market. People clamored to sell before they lost too much money or went bankrupt from being too far in debt. The losses were huge. But of course the land itself was still there, and eventually again became valuable in dollars. Land doesn't go away; it's only the dollar value that fluctuates.

In the midst of the growing panic of the 1930s I received two phone calls that were interesting. One was from Wesley Sternberg who had bought a lot of bonds on margin but now his loans were being called. He pleaded for me to help him, partly because he said Lucile's money was at stake. When Wesley and Lucile were divorced, I gave Lucile a job at Antioch. It was difficult for me to say "no" to Wesley. But not knowing when the market would stabilize I decided I could not afford to risk my money for his gain. In any event, I really didn't have any money to loan to him. He had taken unwise risks in his desire to make a fast buck and now was suffering the consequences.

The other call was from Case, Pomeroy & Company in Wall Street, New York. Walter Case had given the college some $200,000 with which to start what became The Antioch Industrial Research Institute. As of the time of this call, probably in 1931, we still had on deposit at the Miami Deposit Bank in Yellow Springs about $180,000. A vice president of the company told me to get that money out of that dinky little bank right away and put it in a Dayton bank. He said the bank would go under and we would lose all of our funds. I said I would do no such thing; that if the college withdrew a large deposit from the local bank, everyone would learn of it and immediately create a run on the bank. This action would be the very thing that *would* wreck the bank.

The epilogue is instructive. During the subsequent bank panic, our little bank came through in good shape, whereas one of the two large banks in Dayton went bankrupt. Stability and security are sometimes best in a small situation.

One hears occasionally of men in Wall Street who jumped out of windows when they lost a lot of money in the stock market. One of them was Walter Case.

I am reminded of the tragedy that befell my college buddy. We had been close friends at K. U. Later he named his son Algo, one of the four Algos that I know to have existed. During the Depression Carl (Simon) had difficulty in finding secure employment and became depressed. In 1935, I think, he became an insurance agent and took out a large policy on his own life. After the policy had run long enough so that suicide would not bar payment to his wife and family, he shot himself.

By coincidence I am playing Otello, a tape I made from a Met Opera. Music while I compose helps lift my spirit and penetrates the inner recesses of my brain when I am recalling events from the past.

Otello had a top command in the service of Venice, but his life ended tragically. I like the opera not only for its music, but because I once heard Paul Robeson play the role. Robeson, a Black, fitted the role of the Black Moor beautifully. And he had a golden voice. Once we had him come to Antioch for a recital and assembly talk. He said that to be a great artist one had to be devoted to and excited about a cause. This depth of feeling enabled the artist to rise to great heights. Robeson probably enjoyed Otello because of the tragedies in his own life.

Although he was a concert artist of the highest reputation, and a graduate of Cornell, Robeson experienced all kinds of humiliations—people willing to listen to his golden voice, but unwilling to eat with him or permit him to sleep in a comfortable hotel. He went to Russia for a few years hoping to find in Communism a different attitude toward black people. I think he became disillusioned there also.

Herbert Hoover became President in March, 1929, and was President for about 3 1/2 years following the stock market crash. When he was Secretary of Commerce under Coolidge he advocated the preparation of plans for huge public works that would be kept in reserve until a depression began, then put into action by the Federal Government. An excellent idea. But during the crisis he seemed unable or unwilling to take steps to counter the cyclical movement. The Depression got deeper and deeper.

A new feeling swept the nation when Franklin Roosevelt was elected in 1932. The worst was yet to come, but Roosevelt talked about dispelling fear, and started with a bang to put into action a number of corrective plans. Not that he knew too well how to deal with the problem, but at least he was willing to try things. One of his first acts, the National Recovery Act, was a distinct failure. It was authoritarian, and declared unconstitutional by the Supreme Court.

Roosevelt was inaugurated on March 4. On the 6th he ordered all banks closed. Knowing the hostility in business circles about government interference, Roosevelt was afraid that the business men and bankers would panic further as he announced some of his plans. To prevent a bank panic, he closed the banks.

At this time I represented the college on the Board of Directors of our local bank. An urgent meeting of regional bank officials was held in Xenia and Russell Stewart, President of the bank, asked me to go with him to the conference. One item on the agenda was a proposal to establish an insurance plan to protect depositors of banks when a bank fails. I spoke in favor of creating a federal agency for this purpose; some of the bankers were opposed to "governmental interference." During that year, 1933, 4004 banks failed and the losses to depositors were nearly $4 billion dollars.

But don't worry, Matthew, because Congress did enact the Federal Deposit Insurance Agency to which nearly all banks and savings and loan associations now belong. Unless you have a deposit in excess of $100,000 you are now protected by this insurance. And the risk of bank failure is much less.

The number of people who were unemployed increased rapidly. The bread and chow lines in the cities—people on the verge of starvation—were terrible to see. Maybe you have seen pictures of them.

One day a man stopped at my office reminding me that he had been a fellow student in the Law School at K.U. Presently he asked me for a small loan. He was trying to get to the East coast but was completely out of money. I gave him what he asked for. That was the last I ever heard of him. Or of my money. Oh well, little as I had, I had more than he did.

Farming was badly depressed. My father was still farming in Kansas and had a really bad time because of the low prices he had to take for his wheat and other products. Among the items of legislation passed by Congress was a national farm act. The theory was that since manufacturers had protection from foreign competition through the tariff (the Hawley-Smoot Tariff Act of 1930 under Hoover was very biased in favor of American business but interfered seriously with international trade, which was a factor in bringing on the Depression), the farmers also needed protection from adverse swings in market prices. The new law provided an "inverse" tariff.

The Act permitted the Federal Government to work out agreements with farmers to control production and give price supports to those farmers who participated. This helped the farmers greatly. In the course of time Congress redressed the evils of the tariff programs, but as so often happens with interest groups, farmers lobbied hard to keep the price support system long after the need had diminished. This is one reason why we have been paying such huge bonuses to large corporations that are engaged in agriculture. Today we still support milk, tobacco, and other farm products—the carry-over of an idealistic plan of the Depression to a rip-off by agribusiness.

But isn't it a sad commentary on the nation's ability to plan its economy when the production of food was curtailed at the very moment when millions of people were upon the verge of starvation?

Edward B. Cristy, my father-in-law architect, was much affected by the Depression because building activity dropped almost to zero. Fortunately, the Roosevelt administration instituted many public works programs, thus giving architects, engineers, and laborers some employment. An architect may dream of creating a Parthenon, but during a depression he may need to design highways in order to buy socks and peanut butter for his children.

Early in May, 1933, Arthur Morgan, the President and chief money raiser for Antioch College, left to become Chairman of the TVA. Thereafter he became absorbed in his new work and gave almost no attention to the college and did not help us raise money. Our enrollment was dropping badly, resulting in less and less tuition income. Philanthropic gifts were going into relief for the unemployed and other social services. We were getting nothing from the Government.

Our "drawing allowance" plan of doling out our available cash to faculty in accordance with *need* saved the day. Not only that, but it enabled us to retain all of our faculty instead of turning many of them into the breadlines. Our neighboring colleges—Wittenberg and Ohio Wesleyan—dismissed a third or more of their faculties. Even so, at one point Wittenberg's top salary for a professor was $1800 for a year. Ours never fell that low.

Our family was not too badly off. I had continuous employment. Our drawing allowances were enough to keep our grocery bills paid and to keep us warm. We had a lovely house, owned by the college, for which we paid $60 a month rent. It had 3 bedrooms, 2 baths, and an especially nice study, with fireplace, for me. At one point we did rent out the upstairs for a while and that helped.

I had a huge vegetable garden, an entire 60 x 150 foot lot. I thought that others might benefit from raising their own vegetables and had some college land plowed as a garden plot. I offered tracts free of charge to any faculty, employee, or student who wanted to have a plot. In addition to myself, 2 persons took advantage of the offer. Golly! People don't realize the economy, and also the recreational value of gardening. It helps mightily to while away the hours and weeks and years of a depression by working at a project. Especially feeding yourself and family. Even when starving, people would rather stand in a food-stamp line than to dig in the soil. A food-stamp, or other welfare program we need, but we also need to retrieve the skill—and the attitudes toward work—of raising carrots and beans.

We had to cut corners and therefore did not indulge in luxuries. Philip wanted a shop, so I made him a work bench and bought him some elementary tools. I was telling a student about having done this and he asked to see it. I proudly showed him my work. Then he asked: "Where are the tools?" Of course he meant a layout of power equipment, which we couldn't afford. But I have always felt bad that during the Depression I couldn't get Joanne and Philip some of the things they would have liked. Matthew, you and Peter have no way to realize the advantages you have had in getting so many things you want and in getting the benefit of excellent educations.

Antioch, in spite of the widespread unemployment of people, had good luck in keeping its students placed in the cooperative work program. We took advantage of much seasonal work, such as in department stores prior to Christmas and Easter. But we also made other placements. We used the argument, both with employers and with the labor chiefs, that giving a job to Antioch students gave employment to *two* persons, because they alternated on the job. It also enabled them to remain in college rather than joining the breadlines. This had a surprising appeal.

However, a student might go to a job and in three weeks or so land back on the campus because the employer could not pay him. In this predicament the Keith Fund of Boston, through an intermediary, Ralph Rounds, gave us funds with which to employ unemployed students. We created what became known as the "Glen Gang," the name being derived from the work they did in Glen Helen in planting trees, making paths, repairing bridges, and opening springs. On a small scale our gang was similar to the Federal work programs, such as the Civilian Conservation Corps.

When Roosevelt was Governor of New York he reforested huge tracts of land in the state through offering this kind of employment to people. If you travel in New York today, you will see vast forests with fully grown trees that were planted during the Depression. When he became President he launched similar programs throughout the nation. Thus our labor resources were not wasted, but instead were used to create national assets of large importance.

Matthew, when you go hiking in national parks, take a look at the paths, stone bridges, stone shelters with fireplaces, and various new-looking stands of trees. They are the results of the government work programs during the Depression. Sometimes you can find a little plaque that gives the date and the unit that did the work. These young men and women not only got employment during a difficult period, but also learned how to work, how to make things like bridges, and how to enjoy life away from the noise, confusion and pollution of our cities.

The Depression had an unexpected, but salutary effect on the curriculum and teaching at the college. We had the alert kind of faculty and students who became concerned with what was happening in the country. Here was this nation where the people had been so imaginative, inventive, industrious, and relatively prosperous, suddenly thrown into a gigantic tailspin, with the people idle, depressed, starving. What was wrong? Why does this reversal of fortunes have to happen? Why does a nation of people, able to produce an abundance of food, have millions of people unable to buy food? Our answer was to pay farmers to produce less food so that the price would be high enough for them to avoid bankruptcy. Is it not possible to design a better socioeconomic system?

The college had been oriented toward solving problems of meaning in our individual lives, toward exploring society while examining its cultural patterns and their impacts on life styles, and toward learning from past human experience how to plan the more perfect society. So here we were up to our necks in a highly realistic laboratory, the Depression. The learning process was greatly accelerated. Everyone was searching for answers. The students, back from their off-campus jobs, had dozens of questions on their minds. Classroom discussions became vigorous and stimulating. The college experience was genuinely educative.

We initiated some projects of significance in improving the well-being of people in the community. For example, Paul Treichler, Professor of Dramatics, evolved an idea for an area theater. I concurred and gave him help from the college. The main purpose was to expand the program in dramatics to include participation by village people and attract audiences from nearby cities. However, we also thought that this collaborative type of activity, artistic and inspirational, would help get people's minds away from the depression-oriented gloom, thus improving the general morale.

We did not have a comprehensive plan or make a concerted effort in attacking the Depression, but obviously we did address the problems of unemployment, income sharing based on need, bank stability, economic activity, food production, health services and morale.

Our family, in spite of lowered income, did engage in a couple of luxuries. One was the camp in Canada. But since we got the land for $250 (our half) and we built the cabins ourselves one at a time and used logs from the trees in the forest, we didn't need much cash. And we had wonderful vacations at very little expense.

Then your Grandmother and I in 1934 took a 5-week trip through Europe—with Connie and Les Sontag, using their car. The reason I did so was because some of my colleagues at Antioch thought I needed more sophistication in world culture, me, the somewhat rustic farm boy from Kansas. So this was a matter of personal importance to me and for which I had saved some pennies. On one such trip I borrowed money on my life insurance policies in order to get enough funds for the trip. These were good years for foreign travel because everything was very cheap. Quite different from 1979.

By 1939 the Great Depression was well on its way out. If one counts from the stock market crash in 1929 it had lasted ten years. The natural forces within the business cycle, stimulated and helped along by the New Deal measures had become effective. But also the outbreak of war in Europe in 1939 gave American industry a sudden lift producing war materials. One of the terrible things about war is that it provides widespread employment and also large profits. Even larger wages for labor. But where does Government get money with which to fight a war? From taxes and borrowed funds of course. War prosperity is artificial, and use of natural resources in war is a tremendous waste of them. Witness the devastating effects of the Vietnam war.

In a free enterprise type of society, how can we smooth out the fluctuations in the business cycle? The fumbling efforts of President Carter and the Congress to control and reduce the effects of the current inflation and accompanying unemployment, remind one of the "do-nothing" program of the Hoover administration. I had a discussion with a neighbor this week who contended that all we need to do is to stop printing money and balance the Federal budget. Granted that the budget should be in balance, the Government isn't just printing a lot of money. The Federal Reserve Board, an autonomous body, controls the supply of money. What the Government does do is to borrow money just as business and individuals do. It is purchasing power, which depends on credit as well as paper money, that can create inflation.

At Harvard I had a graduate course on the Federal Reserve Banking system, taught by O. M. W. Sprague who had conceived the Federal Reserve Bank plan. So I know what the monetarists are talking about when they blame money as the cause of inflations and depressions. This is a simplistic diagnosis.

The problem is immensely complicated. One aspect of our current inflation problem is the enormous increase of credit in the country—the use of credit cards, overgenerous loans on real properties (favored by the tax laws), and the really tremendous increase in international borrowing. Within this context the borrowing by the Federal Government is only one factor in the overexpansion of credit. People and institutions are borrowing against the future and in doing so help create inflation.

Another aspect is the impact of the continuing deficit in our foreign trade which is the main cause of the weakening of the dollar, reducing its purchasing power. In addition to being caught with our pants down in our excessive demand for oil, we are still suffering from carrying on the Vietnam War without paying for it at the time. Inflation is a way of diminishing war debts. Still another factor is the wage-price-wage-price spiral which is extemely difficult to stop, rising or falling, in a free society.

The solution certainly does not lie in going back to the old supply and demand theory of economics, so persuasively advocated by Milton Friedman, recent Nobel Prize winner. This would merely intensify the movements of the business cycle, as was found many times since the beginning of the Industrial Revolution. In any event, business controls, such as in oil, today are monopolistic. In many large areas of enterprise we no longer have genuine competition.

The best hope lies in governmental programs such as Hoover advocated but did not implement; in those put into effect by the New Deal; and by more realistic and resolute control over prices and incomes. Also we should get busy in conquering the energy problem. We need leadership that can inspire the American people to conserve energy, to develop rapidly through governmental stimulation and action alternative sources of energy, and through effective governmental action manage the importation of oil rather than relying on the big oil companies to do so.

The business cycle—cycles of high and low business activity—is an inherent aspect of the free enterprise economy. I am not yet ready to give up on free enterprise because the alternative, government bureaucracy, does not seem promising. But as society becomes ever more complex, and the interdependence of nations grows, the role of government enlarges.

Matthew, the thing that the people who suffered through the Great Depression learned is the value of money. Their ideas about how to save money, how to avoid debt, and what is worth having and not having, are different from those who have not had this traumatic experience. They also know better how to govern their own lives, including how to take care of themselves and survive through a period of adversity. These are important things to learn. Do you agree?

GRANDFATHER

April 21, 1975

Dear Sabrina,

Now that you are 16 I suppose you spend most of your time thinking about boys. When I was your age I certainly had my eye on a girl—she was the most gorgeous thing that you can imagine. You will probably marry an oil man, and not only have enough gas for your car, while the rest of us are going back to the horse-and-buggy, but you will also have all that money to spend. You lucky stick.

Money, money, money, who wants money? Did you know that I was a millionaire once? Really. And the money lasted only a week. Some big spender, eh? You see, Philip, a friend of his, Alan Hartell, your Grandmother Anne and I were in Greece, and we rented a car, with driver, to take us around to the classical sites. This was arranged through the American School of Classical Studies in Athens. But of course we had to pay for it. Well, the bill was in drachmas. It came to 1,400,000 drachmas. That was because the exchange rate was 14,000 drachmas to $1. This illustrates how the value of money can fluctuate when inflation runs rampant. So, for one week I was a millionaire. Somehow I didn't feel especially wealthy. Money comes and goes, and one day I had lots of it. So much I had difficulty in stuffing it all in my pockets.

I was rich on another occasion too. Rich because I cornered the money market. It was my first year in college, 1914-15, at Kansas Wesleyan. In an accounting course, using play money. Part of the course was a game in which we pretended that we were running business enterprises of various kinds—retail stores, wholesale houses, factories, and others. We would buy and sell chips of, say, 100 pounds of flour, or a carload of lumber, or a ranch in Western Kansas. Each enterprise was a corporation, which we had to run in order to get the experience. Well I noticed that some fellows were dropping out, so I conceived the idea of getting from each of them all of the paper money they had left. Then I slyly bought stock in various corporations until I owned 51% of each of several of them.

When a meeting of the stockholders was called, there I sat with controlling interest in these companies. When I insisted on naming all the directors and laying down the policies, the other students yelled like stuck pigs. They appealed to the professor, C. W. Page, who looked as though he had never been confronted before by such a situation; but he had to rule that I had the legal right to do what I was doing. Under corporate law, to heck with all the other stockholders. That was an interesting experience. I can still feel how clever I was, and smarter than the other students. I can also understand the anguish felt by innocent owners of stock when they find they are powerless when an in-group seizes control. However, I was rich. And powerful.

Don't get me wrong. I grew up on a farm where the concern of our lives was food, clothing, horse feed, and getting our ploughshares sharpened. We had a good sustenance because we had all the eggs, milk, vegetables, chickens, and hogs that we could eat. We also hunted rabbits and went fishing—all in a day when one could do these things. The rabbits were not yet infected with tularemia, and the streams, though muddy after the rains, were not polluted and so contained lots of edible fish. I think I still have a bone from the first fish I caught. A big carp.

So we didn't need much money. Of course, some for clothing—although Mom did a lot of sewing, we boys had to be fitted out at the stores in Salina. And this took cash. But we had corn and wheat crops, mostly sold for cash. We also had excess eggs and butter which we would take to Solomon and trade at H. Bannon's or another store, for canned salmon, sugar, spice, coffee. Bannon had a huge, hand-operated coffee grinder, so we always had him give us freshly ground coffee.

I remember two things vividly about the Bannon store. One was the odor of coffee that permeated the store. The other was the personal service that Mr. Bannon gave. My father got big laughs out of a story he told more than once. He said when a woman entered the store and asked for a length of yard goods, Bannon would turn, start up the aisle, and over his shoulder say: "Walk up this way, madam." The point was—you would have to see Bannon to get the full impact—he was very bowlegged. Probably didn't have vitamins when he was a boy. We traded with him because he would give us 2¢ a dozen above the market price for our eggs. No money needed to trade at the store.

During the Depression of the 1930s I helped to start a barter business in Yellow Springs. The idea was that since people didn't have much money coming in, they could get necessities by bringing things they could spare to our store and trade them for things they needed. We got a stock of paint, staple groceries, and household items. But the project never really became successful. People by 1930 had become habituated to the use of money as the only thing they could exchange for something else, so a flea market exchange just didn't appeal to them. They forgot that their ancestors lived largely by trade.

There is another dimension to this subject. Sabrina, I wonder if you know a good tomato from a poor one. The tomatoes one buys in the chain stores are so godawful tasteless. You know what happens? The big agricorporations, with their machines, have taken over the harvesting of tomatoes and other vegetables. To make more money they now harvest the fields of tomatoes only 3 times. This means that each of these times they pick tomatoes by size regardless of their ripeness. Then by treating them with ethylene gas the tomatoes turn red, or sort of red. Red enough to fool the people that come by with their market baskets. So we really are eating tomatoes that are green.

Fruit gets its sweet taste, and its juicyness, in the ripening process while on the tree or vine. Farmers used to pick tomatoes twelve times during the season taking only the ripe ones. Maybe you have been conditioned to think that a green tomato is ripe if it has a reddish skin. Too bad. For you and all others of the younger generation.

The same thing has happened to the taste of beef and chickens. Both are now kept penned up, without exercise, and fed stuff that hastens the date when they weigh right for the market. Can you add sugar to tea and not taste it? OK, you taste these hormones, or whatever, in the meat. And when the poor chicken grows up standing on wire netting, how can the muscles get the natural development they need. Do you know the difference in taste between a chicken and a pheasant? Why does wild meat taste so different? Carol had two pheasants sent to us as a Christmas present, a gorgeous gift. But when we tried to eat them they tasted awful—from the preservatives. Perhaps most customers don't know how a wild bird should taste; they don't know that they are "relishing" additives rather than pheasant.

Well, in the corporate search for maximum profits we are doing something terrible to the flavors and quality of our foods. Also try to find a restaurant that doesn't serve frozen foods.

It is the overriding hunger for profits that is causing our corporations to adulterate our foods. And build obsolescence into our appliances so that we will have need for lots of repairs—much greater profits are made from repair parts. And we have to trade in more often. To boost sales. And profits.

Dollars, not flowers

I sometimes think that I could have been a successful business man. I did start, and supervised the management of some companies in Yellow Springs. Three of them have been highly successful. When I was at the Harvard Business School, I made a case analysis of a problem of the Virginia-Carolina Chemical Company. A copy of my report was sent to the company, and thereupon they asked me if I would consider a position with the company. Just think how the chemical industry has grown, and how much money I might have made.

Then after I had been at Antioch for a few months, Fred Lazarus of the Lazarus Department Store in Columbus, Ohio, invited me to see him. When I arrived at his office there was present also his brother Simon. They said they were looking for a man to head up their research collecting information from similar stores, analyzing it in relation to their own data, and using the results to help determine policies for the store. On the spot they offered me the job, at a salary more than twice my salary at Antioch. I thought a moment and then said: "Thanks, no thanks." I guess I made a big mistake. Do you know what happened later? The Lazarus Brothers bought up some other stores and started the Federated Department Stores, with Fred as president. I suppose I could have been his principal assistant. I could have owned 3 Cadillacs, and a yacht, and a tax shelter in Mazatlan.

The trouble is that I was raised in a Populist environment. My parents were not really Populists, although they talked a lot about how Wall Street ran the country. And controlled the price for which they sold their wheat. But the environment in Kansas was Populist at the time. If you don't know what Populism is, listen to your neighbor, Senator Fred Harris of Oklahoma, who talks the lingo. Incidentally his wife, Ladonna, is a full-blooded Indian and is a great lady. Agents who were trying to organize the farmers into a union used to come to try to talk my father into joining. One man would talk by the hour. I am sure that what he said influenced my thinking; but all I remember is that he would begin nearly every sentence with "I says, says I . . ."

When I was in high school, my buddy's grandfather, the local butcher, was a Socialist. He had lots of literature on the subject and let us borrow and read it. His name was Butcher, so probably his family had been butchers for many generations. My mother didn't like him because when she would ask for hamburger he would always put more meat on the scale than she had requested, then ask: "Would a pound and a half be a little bit too much?" I was also influenced by my favorite college professor, John Ise, an authority on economics. Ise at times sounded like a revolutionary, although he was really a critic of abuses of power. It was he who first called attention to the ripoff of the Teapot Dome during the Harding administration.

I must stop telling you all these things; what if you do marry that oil heir and he gets the notion that your grandfather was a Socialist when he was young? Well, I am merely trying to describe to you why I grew up as sort of a Populist. I not only thought that meat and potatoes were more important than how much money you had, but I held strong views about the inheritance of wealth. I didn't like the inheritance of privilege of any kind. I thought having Lords and Ladies in Britain was all nonsense; and also a burden on the people.

I held this feeling about Lords a long time. I recall on one occasion when Lord Bertram Russell and Lady Russell were guests in our home, I asked Russell, standing before the fireplace and contentedly smoking his pipe, what he wanted us to call him. He responded that I could call him anything, that the title of "Lord" was something he had inherited and there was nothing he could do about it. It was just there. I thought to myself, you could renounce it. But I said: "OK, I'll call you Mr. Russell in the American way." The next day I really got in Dutch with his wife. I introduced her as Lady Russell—which revealed my timidity in the face of women—whereupon she whirled on me and said we should treat them the same. If I called her "Lady" I should call him "Lord." Oh Lord! This Mrs. Russell was the fourth wife and I suppose on the make. But women are testy, aren't they? I once introduced Pearl Buck as Mrs. Buck, whereupon *she* lit into me—"It's *Miss* Buck"; but I knew perfectly well that Buck was really the name of her first husband from whom she had been divorced.

I think it is proper to permit inheritances of heirlooms, relics, and even a modest portion of money; but the inheritance of large sums of money, or of aristocratic privileges really means the inheritance of power over other people. Every person should attain power and special privilege in accordance with his or her individual merit, and not because Richard the Lionhearted killed his enemies, or John D. the First siphoned off a lot of oil that nature had left to all of us and left the proceeds to successive generations of Rockefellers.

American hunger for money! We are going to pursue money to the point where the disparity between the affluent and the poor will be so great that the poor will rise up and slit some throats.

Money, money, money, money.... Oh well, you do have to have

some money—to buy milk, cereal, and chickens, a dress now and then, and to go to college. Where I hope you will learn about other values for living the good life.

GRANDFATHER

October 31, 1979

Dear Matthew,

So this is Halloween! Granny and I will have to start thinking about what to hand out tonight as the kids come to the door. It's a bit of a problem because they all seem to want candy, and we think kids eat too much candy. Peanuts? Well that favors Jimmy Carter and I don't favor reelecting him if there is any reasonable alternative. We have lots of apples from our trees, but kids stick up their noses at apples. So what will it be? Apples.

When we stopped in New York 3 weeks ago on the way home from France and Spain, I spent a couple of days in downtown New York. On one of them I went to see the World Trade Center. Here are these two great skyscrapers that outshine all the old ones—the Woolworth, Empire State, and Chrysler buildings at which I used to crane my neck. But that's all they were, just skyscrapers. I like the Apparel Mart, designed by your father's firm in Dallas much better. Not only is it a graceful shape, harmonizing nicely with its environment, but when inside one can see all the teeming life there. You can visualize people as well as steel and glass.

Because the World Trade Center is near Wall Street I got the inspiration to walk over there and take a peek at the financial capital of America and also at the building, 61 Broadway, where I worked for a while. On the way I walked through the old cemetary that surrounds the church at the head of Wall Street. Many famous people are buried there. They did great things, then made way for others, their power disappearing like the sound from a snap of the fingers. But I like to meditate on their experiences and their achievements. And pay tribute to them.

I worked at 61 Broadway during the summer of 1925. I was already committed to go to Antioch College in the fall, but I wanted a summer job. A professor at the Harvard Business School recommended me to the Associated Gas and Electric Company. He was a consultant to it and the job sounded good.

So Anne and I rented an efficiency apartment near Columbia University. Anne was able to take some courses at Columbia. I had to commute by subway to the Wall Street exit, at the height of traffic, so I got pushed around a lot in the crowded cars, and someone was always stepping on my shoes, ruining my shine. When cattle are shoved into a railroad car they get lots of fresh air through the slats. hence the stench is bearable. People in a New York subway have to gasp for air while holding their noses. I decided then and there that I would never live in New York City unless I was paid a very high salary that would enable me to get away frequently, or live in some place like Connecticut. At a later time I was offered 5 very nice jobs in New York, but I turned them down. I guess I am a country boy.

The middle 20s was the period in which the electricity producing and gas distributing companies were consolidating in a big way. The Associated Gas and Electric Company was doing this. Before that time the companies had been small, originated locally in accordance with the needs of the community. Solomon, for instance, built its plant when I was in high school. Thus electric power displaced the kerosene lamps and the hand operated machines and appliances. One could even buy one of the new fashioned refrigerators to keep milk, eggs, and meat, instead of lowering the milk into a deep well and salt curing the meat. What a change this made in the way people lived and worked. On the farm in 1920, Dad installed a diesel power unit in the basement of our house, and thereafter we had electricity. It wasn't until the 1930s when rural electrification brought power lines into the country areas, that the farmers could have 60 cycle, alternating current.

I guess I must have seemed to the company officials to be well qualified because I was already a Certified Public Accountant and a lawyer, as well as having been at the Harvard Graduate School of Business. In any event they handed me some jobs that were beyond my experience; I wondered how to cope with them. Almost immediately I was sent to Plattsburg, New York, to audit the books of a company they had just purchased. This little company had been built up by a local man who knew everybody in town. His books were in a mess. When a customer paid a bill, he would make a brief note and stick it into a drawer expecting to enter it on the books later, but often forgot. When a customer didn't have cash, he would take in a cow, some hens, or a few bushels of corn. However, it took me only about three days to straighten out his books and prepare a financial statement for the New York firm. This paying utility bills with cows was before the invention of computers.

Upon my return I was sent to the Harlem Valley where AG&E had bought 13 companies, including 1 holding company that in turn owned 3 operating companies. Several men were sent with me, so there I was with a bunch of men to do a big audit, and I hardly knew how to begin or what to do. Fortunately some of the men were much more experienced than I and helped me to plan how to proceed. In the course of these conversations I learned that the staff had a motto—"bring something back." By this they meant always bring back to the office a stack of papers even though much of the content was merely copied out of the ledgers. This used up time and made an impression on the superiors, who apparently never bothered to check up on what was being brought back.

While there, beginning the audit, I was visited by a man who said he was from an engineering firm that made appraisals for the AG&E. He instructed me that the company wanted to keep two sets of books, one reflected the property at the greatly increased appraisal values, the other the actual cost of the plants and machinery. The purpose was as follows: The company needed to report to the Public Utilities Commission of the State of New York on the basis of the costs of things; whereas when the company sold debentures and stock they would use the marked up values. I was so concerned with getting the job done that the real import of this neat plan didn't sink in on me at the time.

My next job was to audit a brokerage company in the Wall Street area. This company surprisingly was in a tiny cubbyhole office with only 1 employee. Its only function was to trade in the stocks and bonds of the Associated Gas and Electric Company. Here again the man didn't keep his books in order. At times he was so involved in so many transactions on the stock exchange that he would simply stick pieces of paper on which he had scrawled each transaction in a big drawer. What a mess. I never did know whether I had found them all, or got the books in proper order. When AG&E wanted to issue some more stock or debentures, they would have this brokerage office start putting a lot of orders into the market—to show that the securities of the company were very popular, but also to shoot up the price.

I learned that the Associated Gas and Electric Company was really 4 partners, 2 of them the operating heads. The other 2 probably were financial backers, but never revealed themselves. The President, H. C. Hopson, and the principal vice president had been employees of the State Public Utilities Commission in Albany. There they had learned how to manipulate companies in the utility business. In having 2 sets of books, for example, they knew they could get by with that. In manipulating the stock market they were not subject to any supervision, such as came later in the Securities and Exchange Commission. So these 2 birds, without any money themselves, proceeded to capture a large utility business. Their technique was simple.

They set up a structure of 5 layers of superimposed companies, holding companies on top of the operating companies. Each successive company as the pyramid ascends owned a controlling, 51% interest in the next lower company. The top company was quite small, and with these 4 men owning 51% of its stock they were able to control the entire empire.

Then they got money by selling securities, mostly debenture bonds, based on the fictitious values, to a gullible public. They were not the only ones doing this in the heyday of consolidations; for example, the Samuel Insull Company of Chicago was discovered to be doing the same kind of thing. And the general public was sold the idea that by buying the securities they were getting in on a big new development that would make them rich. Of course the birds at the top were getting rich hand over fist. As easy as stripping the feathers off a turkey. Matthew, if you want to get rich, it is easy to rip other people off by taking advantage of their innocence and lack of judgment.

Well, in some cases, and notably in that of AG&E, the greed and dishonesty of these men finally caught up with them. The Federal Trade Commission investigated the affairs of the company, issued a voluminous report, and the bottom fell out of the securities that had been sold. A lot of people lost money. Hopson, my boss, was reprimanded, although I think not severely. Isn't it strange that a black kid who is hungry and who steals $10, can be sent to the pen for 5 years, whereas a business manipulator can rob people of millions and get a slap on the wrist.

The room at the office was quite large and had about 39 people in it. Later, through the Federal Trade Commission report, I learned that in addition to the accounting firm, the brokerage firm, and the engineering firm (which was either controlled by or in cahoots with the partners), there were about 2 dozen other little companies operating from that room or nearby quarters. In the case of my accounting firm, the partners—the same 2 top guys—had a real thing going for them. When we did a job they got paid twice for the same thing. The little accounting firm charged for the work that I and others did on a per-diem-plus-expenses basis, but also made another charge as a percentage of the revenues of the operating company, thus filling the pockets of these 2 men.

And to my amazement, I learned that the financial statements prepared by me and other staff of this controlled accounting firm, were accepted without checking the authenticity of the reports by an outside accounting firm which certified the balance sheets of AG&E. Obviously this helped in the betrayal of the buyers of the securities of AG&E.

All of these little companies were parasites, sucking the blood of the operating companies. And filling the pockets of the crooks at the top of the pyramid. An interesting question: Was the Harvard professor, who was consultant to the company, as naïve as I, or was he unconcerned about the ethics?

This experience has left me with considerable loss of faith in big business, and more expecially mergers that result in conglomerates. Most of these moves seem to me to be aimed at ripping off very fine companies that were slowly and at times painfully built up over many years, and which became fine assets to the communities of which they were a part. Along comes a super company and gobbles up the smaller one. Often this is for such purposes as capturing a substantial cash balance, which in turn helps them to buy the other company—the one being gobbled up unwittingly supplies part of the resources used in the gobbling; or to extend the power of the officers of the conglomerate so they can dominate the market; or, sometimes, diversify the line, often into fields with which the management is unfamiliar; or to reap tax advantages permitted by our tax evasion laws.

I am also concerned by the manner in which executives are able to control their corporations, even though their personal investment is very small. They are able to do this because management under our system is almost supreme in authority. Note the large blocks of stock that are always voted in favor of anythng the management proposes. The owners—banks, institutions, insurance companies—are interested in profits and vote with management as long as dividends roll in. The directors know little of what is really going on. What would directors of AG&E, those not "in" on the deal, know about how the profits were being made?

Now it seems that business men and certain politicians are making a drive to tie the hands of such regulatory agencies as the Federal Trade Commission and the Securities and Exchange commission. "The market place will do the regulating." Ha!

Sorry I don't have space left to vent some feelings about the oil monopoly. Just today I noticed that my stock in Mobil has gone up more than 100% in value since I bought it only 4 years ago. Why should I complain?

Matthew, when you graduate from Harvard, that is if you go to Harvard, I hope you do not take a job on Wall Street. Shuffling paper and reading corporate balance sheets. And making money by gambling in stocks and bonds. There are more productive ways of making a living.

GRANDFATHER

VIII

Since I have written so many letters in a serious vein, I have devoted a few to fun and fantasy. Ilya, I wrote the poem because you seem so skeptical about the utility of chamber pots. After sending the captured monster to Matthew, he complained that "it seems to be paralyzed" and asked: "What should I feed the monster, he won't eat anything not even peanut butter." Matthew, try bubble gum.

September 20, 1978

Dear Peter and Matthew,

I have just been to Nevada and had the most terrifying experience. Oh dear, I can't even think about it. I am disgraced. Utterly disgraced. Oh me! Oh my! I can't even tell you what happened, it was so awful.

If you knew what happened you would think me a very bad man. But I'm not really bad, now am I? So if I don't tell you what happened, you will never know whether I was bad.

Oh dear, how will I ever recover from this experience?

You see, I was out hunting, and this sheriff suddenly came galloping up . . . but I really can't bear to describe it. Maybe I'll send you the newspaper with its huge headline. That's the worst part of it, the newspaper learned about it and put the story right on the front page. Everybody in Nevada read it. But if I send you the paper, be sure and not show it to anyone. Not even to your father and mother. And especially not to Ilya. She might tell Alex, and Alex tell her mother, and her mother tell James, and oh dear how could I ever face them?

Well, you see I had hunted all around San Francisco for a horsefeather because I wanted to send one to Matthew. He doesn't believe there is such a thing as horsefeathers, so I had to prove it to him. But I couldn't find one anywhere. Not even on the streets. There just aren't any horses left in San Francisco. Early pictures of the City always show lots of horses pulling wagons, buggies, and street cars. What ever happened to them? Didn't they have any colts?

So I decided to go to Nevada where they have huge ranches and lots of horses. To hunt for a horsefeather.

Well, I had just found one when this terrible thing happened. This

VIRGINIA CITY MIRROR

ALGO HENDERON CAUGHT AS A HORSE THIEF

sheriff came galloping up with a sixshooter in each hand pointed right at me. But I hid the horsefeather and will send it to Matthew. And maybe I'll send to Peter the clipping from the *Virginia City Mirror* with its enormous headline, right on the front page.

What would my father have thought? In his day, a man caught like this would have been strung up by the neck.

GRANDFATHER

ODE TO A CHAMBER POT

dedicated to Ilya – 1978

Wow, what a beauty!
What graceful form,
The silky hair
And flashing eyes adorn.

This beach
Did you ever see the like?
I lie on the sand
And enjoy it with delight.

Hey, I am in Bali
Without a single care,
Isle of romance,
Just sniff that ocean air.

Look! High on top that bluff
Rising straight above the bay,
Silhouetted against the sky,
See that beauteous maiden gay.

She's about to dive!
From that great height!
There she goes————
Cutting the water with all her might.

Water, water, everywhere,
Splashing, surging water,
I rouse myself, and feel
An urgent pressure in my bladder.

From under the covers
A hand I steal,
And beneath the bed
I feel, and feel, and feel.

WHAT!
No pot!
Again I search without abate,
I badly need to urinate.

Then half asleep and half awake
I become aware
That I must get up and walk
To the new-fangled plumbing ware.

So, with half-closed eyes,
Out of bed I crawl,
And begin the midnight journey
Down the dark, dark hall.

OUCH!
My toe,
On some shoes
I stub it as I go.

I subdue my wrath
And rush ahead not far,
When I smash my nose
On a door left ajar.

Curse that door!
I give it a savage push
And again it smacks my head
With a vigorous back rush.

Lest I lost control
I now must race,
So in the bathroom
The toilet I can embrace.

OwWwWw—down I go
On the newly waxed floor,
Hitting my butt a mighty blow,
Where the rug had been before.

I rise, and limping now
Stagger down the hall,
When with a loud crack
I collide with the end wall.

Back three steps must be the door,
So backward I spin,
To find the door shut—
Maybe there's someone within.

Hey you, are you there?
I push the door below;
It yields; I bound within
And desperately let go.

Splatter, splatter—something's wrong.
Damn, the toilet lid is down.
How did I goof?
Makes me look like a clown.

I grab some tissue
And wipe the floor,
And both seat and lid.
Then with water wash some more.

Now with seat uplifted
I let go with a howl,
Flush, and wash.
But where is that towel?

I feel around in vain,
No towel is on the wall.
Aha, now I have it—
Hanging from the shower stall.

Back to bed I go
Limping all the way;
Climb in, shut my eyes
Expecting to make hay.

Alas, I am wide awake,
My mind going round and round;
I turn, and shift, and shake,
And worry all the problems that abound.

Those terrible fuchsia-eating flies,
My eggplant cropped by deer,
Those neighbor's trucks in the drive,
The house painting—why so dear?

What's that? Running water?
A sprinkler? We fixed it.
It can't be the creek.
Gracious, it's that damnable toilet!

Do I go, or don't I go?
I must get some sleep or bust,
But water wasting—it's precious,
So turn it off I must.

I jiggle the toilet handle,
And wait, and wait a lot
To see if the float
Settles squarely in its slot.

Then back to bed again.
My goodness! My pillow is soggy;
What on earth can that be?
Why it's blood, from my banged up body.

Furiously I fling the pillow off.
Now, where to put my head?
Hmmm, well there's the mattress;
I must use it instead.

So there I was in Bali
With joy unbounded,
And now I can't go back,
Or even sleep, confound it!

Poor, deluded granddaughter,
Who thinks she knows it all,
She scorns the chamber pot
And goes traipsing down the hall.

Well, let her do her thing,
And stub her toes,
Bang her fanny,
And smash her nose.

> How does she know how convenient
> To have a chamber pot
> Where one sweep of the hand
> Brings it to the spot.
>
> You do your thing,
> Lay down your head,
> Off to Bali fly
> And never leave your bed.
>
> GRANDFATHER

November 13, 1975

Dear Alex,

Last week while in the dentist's chair, here was the hygienist, a really beautiful young woman, spoiling the effect of her presence by breathing in and out right in front of and close to my face. I didn't mind her breathing in, but at each exhale I was engulfed with carbon dioxide. There was no odor of onions, garlic, or decayed teeth, but still the air was saturated with the waste thrown off by the lungs.

Now when you eat solids, you take in at the mouth and defecate the wastes at the lower end of the body. Likewise the liquids. But oxygen, no; although this would be simpler than for solids or liquids. For example, why not have an exhaust orifice at the *bottom* of the lungs? Or use the belly button? Or even at the back of the neck sort of like a whale? It doesn't seem desirable or even efficient to breathe in and then breathe out through the same nostrils. And when people kiss they expel carbon dioxide all over each other's faces. Automobiles shoot their carbon monoxide out of a tail pipe, don't they? Why can't people be as thoughtful and clean as an auto?

Now you told me that deoxyribonucleic acid controls the inherited traits, but that ribonucleic acid can effect changes. So why not implant a new message in the deoxyribonucleic acid so that you could breathe out of one of your ears? After all, did the duck-billed dinosaur *always* have a duck bill?

When sitting in a dentist's chair it is better to think about something fanciful than "when, oh when will she let me spit out all that blood and grime." So I got to thinking about how efficient the ears of a jackass or a llama are. They are also beautifully shaped as compared with the funny folds of cartilage that stick out from the sides of people's heads. And if you watch a llama listening, you will see him rotate his ears back, sideways, and to the front to catch all the sound. You know, just like we rotate TV antennas. Much more efficient; because if we humans want to catch a sound from the rear, we have to turn our head. Only we can't turn it all the way around. And sometimes we have a stiff neck—OUCH! In any event a person would look strange walking along the street with his nose pointed to the rear.

So why don't people have rabbit ears like llamas or jackasses, or TV? Suppose all people had them except one woman. Do you know what she would do? She would go straight to a plastic surgeon and have her ears made to look like rabbit ears. In order to look pretty. Because looking pretty means looking much like all other people. Wouldn't you feel strange if everyone had rabbit ears but you, and you had only some cauliflowers stuck on the sides of your head?

It should be easy to make this change because all you have to do is to extract the DNA molecule that controls the ears of a llama and use it to replace the one that controls the human ears.

Next time I see you I shall inspect you carefully to learn how you are emitting your carbon dioxide and how you wiggle your ears.

GRANDFATHER

Listening with llama ears

March 7, 1979

Dear Matthew,

I know that Ilya has been gallivanting all around over Mexico, but I think you have not. Have you seen pictures of the temples built by the Mayans, Incas, and Aztecs? Long before Columbus and his soldiers, priests, and horses trampled on them. Isn't it interesting how the people in places as far apart as Yucatan, Sri Lanka, Thailand, and Egypt, in earlier civilizations, all built pyramids, apparently without knowing what each was doing. And that they used serpents and monster-looking monkeys as religious symbols, and to guard the temples. Why did they use serpents? And why did the scribes of the Old Testament say that it was a serpent that tempted Adam and Eve?

Well, I was thinking about all of this one day, not realizing that it would get me into deep trouble. The most terrifying experience I have ever had. You see, it suddenly occurred to me that a Mexican jungle was just the place in which to find and capture a serpent or a monster that could serve as the mascot for The Monster That Lived In A Pie As Big As The Sky Club. In the jungle far away from humans there would be monsters that could shriek, wail, and bellow without danger that the vibrations from their sounds would knock down any skyscrapers. If I could capture one and send it to Matthew, he could train it to guard the secret office of our Club.

We were in San Blas, an ideal spot. I persuaded Granny to go with me so she could grab the Monster's tail while I throttled its throat. She didn't like the idea, but I explained how easy it would be. Just the way cowboys grab the tail of a mad bull. When the tail is twisted it makes the bull bellow, and it forgets to charge the enemy. This way your stomach doesn't get gored. By wearing heavily padded gloves, she could protect against the razor-sharp spikes on the tail of the Monster.

Then we rented a boat, with an old Indian as a guide. He said he wasn't afraid of monsters, excepting when they spout flames from their forked tongues. The thing to do is to grab one around the neck and try to hold it so its eyes, tongue, and feet can be kept away from you. He had tried this once, and had the thing about tamed when it suddenly gave a lunge, plunged back into the water, and shot out of sight so fast you couldn't say Jack Robinson.

Leaving the village, one enters the jungle almost immediately. First you go up a river a little way. This was exciting because we passed several men in diving suits and snorkles, and carrying pike-like rods. They were diving for oysters. Each one had an inflated inner tire tube, with sack suspended from its middle, into which they would toss the oysters before taking them to the bank to crack open and shuck. We got some to eat and they were delicious; also huge in size. After that we discovered a place on the beach at Mazatlan where we could buy oysters from the divers, and so we had several feasts.

Presently we entered the mangrove swamp area. Have you ever been in a mangrove swamp? The mangrove grows in the water with stilt-like limbs, so there is a great mass of roots. It is almost impossible to get through the stuff, since you have to slither around like a snake among the roots. If one got caught, then all the creatures that live among the roots would have a great feast, wouldn't they?

We followed a wild sort of path where the current had kept the way a bit clean, and threaded deeper and deeper into the morass. It got dark as pitch because the sun can't get through the mass of leaves, vines, roots, bird feathers, and all that. It was scary just to sit in the boat, much less think of diving into the water. Poor Granny was having a fit because I kept asking the Indian to go deeper and deeper. Would we ever find our way out? We couldn't see the sun, there were no planes flying overhead pointing to a city, the moss grew on all sides of the trees, we didn't have a compass. All that we had was the Indian's sense of direction, and the little signs he knew. I asked him to show me some, but he said it took years to learn them and only an Indian can do this.

But I thought to myself, if we turn back now how will we ever get a really good mascot for our secret Club? And my instinct told me that it was in the inner recesses of the jungle where we would find the Monsters.

There were all kinds of creepy things dangling from the limbs overhead. All the time we were ducking to avoid hitting our heads, or getting yanked out of the boat, and more than that, getting a bunch of spidery things down our necks. Just imagine being bit by a venomous spider when you don't have a razor blade with you to slice the wound and squeeze the venom out. Call a doctor? Don't be silly, how could a doctor ever find us? No, our life depended upon being very, very careful not to get bit or stung.

But we were being eaten up by things we couldn't see. Little black flies, millions of them, that the natives call "no seeums." They swarm all over you and bite like fury. You should see our necks and ankles.

We look as though we had the measles.

We could see the mosquitoes, though. They were as thick as flies, as vicious as hornets, and looked as big as crows. The proboscis was so sharp and so long that one went right through my wrist, bone and all. Reminds me that when John L. Stephens went through the Yucatan-Chiapas jungles in 1841, he and his men had to sleep part of the time in creeks, their bodies under water, to keep the mosquitoes from eating them alive.

Then we came to an area where there was a lot of splashing in the water. And all these fierce looking creatures poking their heads above water, with wide open jaws, snapping their teeth, staring at you—such teeth and such eyes! We sure were shaking in our boots.

Matthew, I beg you, never go into a jungle where the Monsters live. Where crocodiles lie on top of the water snapping their three-foot long jaws at you. Where alligators slither down the muddy banks diving straight toward you, with 6-inch teeth, gleaming white and sharp as steel. Have you ever faced a Monster with smirky eyes, that focus on *your* eyes and hypnotize you so that you can't either move or cry out? And you expect to be gobbled up instantly, not in one piece as was Jonah by the whale—wasn't he lucky—but in a million ground up bits, bones and all.

So why do people venture into such places, knowing that they may land in an alligator's belly? How foolish can one get? Matthew, never, NEVER let yourself get ground up like hamburger.

The trouble is we need a mascot for our Club, don't we? I said to myself, Matthew will be very disappointed if we turn back now. Furthermore, who's afraid of the Big Bad Monster? Not Grandfather. Who could capture a Monster if not Grandfather? We need the fiercest kind of guard so nobody who doesn't know the password can get in.

Just at that very moment I spied a dark, forbidding looking object gliding toward the boat as if to gobble it and all of us in one gulp. It was a MONSTER! I yelled: "This is IT!" and plunged overboard, shoes and all. It was pitch black in the water. I couldn't see a thing. I grabbed here, there, and everywhere, but found nothing. Oh dear, did I miss him? What a tragedy to come all this way, through all those no seeums and huge mosquitoes and not get my prize. *Where* is the boat? I panicked, pawing the water desperately. This action, fortunately, brought me to the surface.

There, to my horror, was the Monster confronting me, his eyes piercing mine, his jaws as wide as a barn door, his teeth a row of shining daggers, his front paws with nails longer and sharper than those of a fighting cock. I was terrified. He had his evil eye right on me.

Yet I collected my wits as quickly as you can say jack rabbit, extended my bionic left arm 10 feet, and as slick as a python can entwine its body around its victim, I coiled my arm around the critter's neck. Immediately I felt for his jugular artery to shut off his blood supply. Then through a message from my brain to the right spot on my arm, I made a hard knot like a fist in the muscle, and clamped it against the artery as in a vise. Now I thought I sure have him.

He struggled ferociously, whipped his long tail on the water, and tried repeatedly to ram the boat. In a moment, down we went into the murky water again, the Monster's neck still clutched in my arm. I extended the elbow of my bionic arm until it reached the mud, then riled the water so badly neither of us could breathe. We had to come to the surface.

You should have seen this furious battle between two giants. The Monster turned, writhed, wriggled, stuck out its fiery tongue, and whipped its tail up and down making the water look like a plunging cascade. All the while it had those beady eyes fastened on mine, trying to make me doze off and loosen my grip on its neck. I thought to myself, I have braved wild lions and tigers in Africa to get their pictures, but nothing in all my adventures compares with this life-and-death struggle.

It suddenly dawned on me, this really is a life-and-death matter. Either I subdue him or he eats me. The worst part was I had got him so furious that after grinding me to bits, he would have started on Granny, then the Indian, and then the boat. Not even an oar would be left. People everywhere would wonder what had ever become of us. My, what a predicament I had got us in. All because I was determined to get a Monster for our Club.

Down we went again, but this time I knew how to get us up where I could breathe. But I must have got a lot of mud in my eyes which caused me to loosen my grip on the neck. He took instant advantage, gave a quick turn, swung his long tail out over the boat, aiming straight for Granny's head. She was so scared she forgot she had on special gloves with which to catch the tail and hold it. Luckily she dodged just in time, because the end of the tail slashed past just over her head. If it had hit her in the neck, her whole head would have bounced off into the water. I watched with horror.

I thought to myself just like Elizabeth I chopping off the head of her half-sister, Mary Queen of Scots, just to keep her from being next in line for the throne. All because Mary was a Catholic. I also thought of this guy in Western Kansas who, riding on a motorcycle, hit a barbed wire some farmer had strung across the road. Off went his head into the ditch. Isn't it odd what strange thoughts flash through your mind when you are in mortal danger.

While my teeth were chattering I must have relaxed my grip on the creature's neck, because the Monster shifted his horny head in my direction, rolled out his foot-long tongue, each fork of which was ablaze with fire, and aimed it straight for my face. I dodged quick as you can say Jack Holligan, but the tongue of fire nevertheless struck my hair. Poof, and a wisp of my hair was gone. Golly, was I lucky. My whole face could have been burned to a crisp. UGH, I hate even to think of it. Imagine going through life without a face!

After these two near fatal events, I realized that I was getting either careless or tired. But I was in a struggle that only one of us could win. How thankful I am for that bionic left arm. I just coiled it tighter, at the same time forcing the belly of the animal away from me so he couldn't rip a big gash in my belly. Unfortunately the Monster has a gash in *his* belly. At one point, the Indian thought I was a goner, and reached over with his hunting knife and ripped into the belly of the Monster. I had it sewed up after stuffing some cotton in the gaping hole.

We went down several more times, but I realized that the critter was getting weaker. At long last it stopped its writhing. With my unusual arm I still had the strength to lift it into the boat.

Matthew, because you are President of our secret Club, I am sending the Monster to you. Take good care of it. Watch out for its razor like teeth, its 3-inch claws that are sharper than tacks, and especially its dragon-like tail. And if you look into its eyes, be sure your gaze is stronger than his. If you are going to keep a Monster, you must have full command over it. Be its Master. And never try to subdue one in the wild until you are old, tough, clever, and wise, like your grandfather.

And of course, teach the Monster our secret password, so it can guard the recesses of our cave, and not let strange, curious people near, especially those who are ignorant of our sign language and don't know the password.

To our Club; may we never let it down.

GRANDFATHER

P.S.: Don't let Peter mislead you. He will probably say "Oh Yaaaah, that's just a story." Well how could I send you the Monster if I hadn't got it somewhere?

August 26, 1981

Dear kids,

At last the end!

The end of what Peter calls "the long stories." Ah! now I can find time to make myself a yi haw whimmididdle and play with it.

Everything I have said in these letters is absolutely true. Everything. That is, almost everything.

I did chase fish in the corn field; sounds fishy, or corny, doesn't it? But Honest Injun, I did it, with my big pitchfork. I scrubbed those filthy spittoons. UGH! I watched my Dad, with his razor, operate on my sister, Beulah.

For some reason the FBI got the jitters over some of my actions, though goodness only knows how much better their time might have been spent. Anne served tea on the terrace of the House of Commons, and I conferred with Harry Truman in the Oval Office.

I did all the things just as I have said.

Well, there were a *few* exceptions. Ilya, I hate to clean a chamber pot. Matthew, Granny and I, accompanied by Molly and Steve Sestanovich, explored that dark and scary jungle near San Blas; but if you ever go there, I can tell you how to get a monster with its belly already sewed up.

As for that 6-shootin' sheriff in Nevada—that's a lot of horsefeathers.

With much love,

Algo D. Henderson

Back to earth